ALL STANDING

The Remarkable Story of
the *Jeanie Johnston*,
the Legendary Irish Famine Ship

KATHRYN MILES

SIMON & SCHUSTER PAPERBACKS

New York   London   Toronto   Sydney   New Delhi

Simon & Schuster Paperbacks
A Division of Simon & Schuster, Inc.
1230 Avenue of the Americas
New York, NY 10020

This Simon & Schuster trade paperback edition January 2014

SIMON & SCHUSTER PAPERBACKS and colophon are registered
trademarks of Simon & Schuster, Inc.

For information about special discounts for bulk purchases,
please contact Simon & Schuster Special Sales at 1-866-506-1949 or
business@simonandschuster.com.

The Simon & Schuster Speakers Bureau can bring authors to your
live event. For more information or to book an event, contact the
Simon & Schuster Speakers Bureau at 1-866-248-3049 or
visit our website at www.simonspeakers.com.

Book design by Ellen R. Sasahara

Manufactured in the United States of America

1 3 5 7 9 10 8 6 4 2

The Library of Congress has catalogued the Free Press
hardcover edition as follows:

Miles, Kathryn
All standing: the true story of hunger, rebellion, and survival
aboard the Jeanie Johnston / Kathryn Miles.
p.   cm.
Includes bibliographical references and index.
1. Ireland—History—Famine, 1845–1852. 2. Ireland—Emigration and
immigration. 3. United States—Emigration and immigration.
4. Jeanie Johnston (Ship). I. Title.
DA950.7 M55 2013
941.5081—dc23   2012034035

ISBN 978-1-4516-1013-0
ISBN 978-1-4516-1015-4 (pbk)
ISBN 978-1-4516-1016-1 (ebook)

For Colin

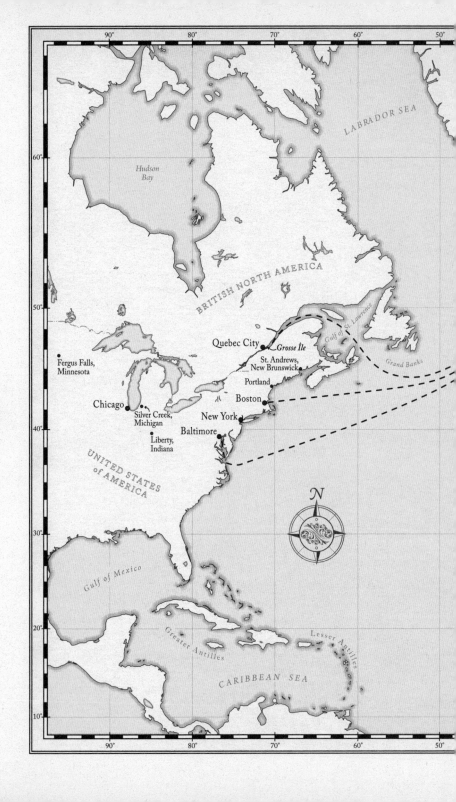

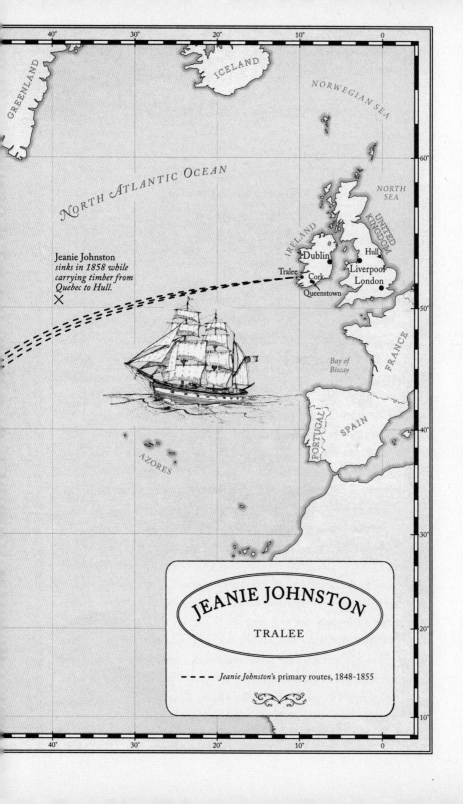

North Atlantic Ocean

Jeanie Johnston
sinks in 1858 while
carrying timber from
Quebec to Hull.
X

Tralee
Dublin
Cork
Queenstown

Hull
Liverpool
London

Bay of
Biscay

Azores

JEANIE JOHNSTON

TRALEE

- - - - *Jeanie Johnston*'s primary routes, 1848-1855

PROLOGUE

Fergus Falls, Minnesota
Friday, August 27, 1883

On most evenings, a steady stream of patrons crossed the Red River footbridge to have a drink at James K. O'Brien's saloon. But not that night.

The Sullivan Troupe's Irish Revue was in town for one night only, and everybody who was anybody already had a ticket. That meant business was slow at O'Brien's Saloon in the Grand Hotel. All evening its lone bartender, Nicholas Reilly, stood at his post between the shelves of spirits and the glistening new bar, watching as residents of Fergus Falls paraded up Lincoln Avenue, dressed for the show in their Sunday best.

Two blocks away, Nicholas's wife, Cecilia, tended to their two young children, William and Helen. Somewhere on a floor above him, Nicholas's younger brother, Eugene, was settling into one of the small rooms O'Brien set aside for boarders. It was a good night to be inside.

A steady and unexpectedly cold rain dotted the saloon windows and puddled in the street, but the townspeople seemed impervious. The Sullivan Troupe's vaudeville act was the biggest event to visit the Red River Valley; no one worth his salt was willing to miss it, even if doing so meant ruining a taffeta dress. All of Fergus Falls, it seemed, had suddenly contracted a whopping case of Irish fever.

Twenty-five years had passed since the Great Hunger had claimed the lives of a million Irish people and forced a million more onto North America's shores, forever marking the famine as one of the greatest human rights atrocities in recorded history. Since that time the United States had formed a complicated relationship with its new Irish brethren,

CONTENTS

Contents

Cast of Characters

James Attridge: captain of the *Jeanie Johnston*

Henry Blennerhassett: longtime physician around Tralee, Ireland, and medical supervisor for famine relief there

Richard Blennerhassett: Henry's son and ship's doctor for the *Jeanie Johnston*

Thomas Campion: Attridge's first mate

Sir Edward Denny: member of the landed gentry who controls much of the town of Tralee

Nicholas Donovan: Tralee's leading importer/exporter and owner of the *Jeanie Johnston*. His wife is Katherine Murphy Donovan.

George Mellis Douglas: physician and medical superintendent at the Grosse Île quarantine station in Quebec

Henry Grey, Third Earl Grey: British colonial secretary from 1846 to 1852

John Munn: shipwright and builder of the *Jeanie Johnston*

James K. O'Brien: bar owner and gamester. Brother-in-law of Nicholas Reilly and husband of Harriet Bunberry O'Brien

Daniel and Margaret Reilly: farming couple aboard the *Jeanie*'s first voyage. Nicholas's parents

Nicholas Reilly: born aboard the *Jeanie Johnston*, eventually marries Cecilia Bunberry Reilly

John Russell: prime minister of England from 1846 to 1852 and then again from 1865 to 1866

Charles Trevelyan: assistant secretary to HM Treasury and responsible for administering famine relief

Edward Twisleton: chief commissioner of Poor Laws for Ireland from 1845 to 1849

All standing: 1) To be equipped or rigged. 2) To turn in fully clothed; at the ready. 3) To be brought to anchor, at a full stop. (*The Sailor's Word Book: An Alphabetical Digest of Nautical Terms*)

PROLOGUE

Fergus Falls, Minnesota
Friday, August 27, 1883

*On most evenings, a steady stream of patrons crossed the Red River
footbridge to have a drink at James K. O'Brien's saloon. But not that night.*

*The Sullivan Troupe's Irish Revue was in town for one night only,
and everybody who was anybody already had a ticket. That meant business was slow at O'Brien's Saloon in the Grand Hotel. All evening its lone
bartender, Nicholas Reilly, stood at his post between the shelves of spirits
and the glistening new bar, watching as residents of Fergus Falls paraded
up Lincoln Avenue, dressed for the show in their Sunday best.*

*Two blocks away, Nicholas's wife, Cecilia, tended to their two young
children, William and Helen. Somewhere on a floor above him, Nicholas's
younger brother, Eugene, was settling into one of the small rooms O'Brien
set aside for borders. It was a good night to be inside.*

*A steady and unexpectedly cold rain dotted the saloon windows and
puddled in the street, but the townspeople seemed impervious. The Sullivan Troupe's vaudeville act was the biggest event to visit the Red River
Valley; no one worth his salt was willing to miss it, even if doing so meant
ruining a taffeta dress. All of Fergus Falls, it seemed, had suddenly contracted a whopping case of Irish fever.*

*Twenty-five years had passed since the Great Hunger had claimed
the lives of a million Irish people and forced a million more onto North
America's shores, forever marking the famine as one of the greatest
human rights atrocities in recorded history. Since that time the United
States had formed a complicated relationship with its new Irish brethren,*

based alternately on pity, curiosity, contempt, and, most often, a thorny combination of all three. The Sullivan Revue capitalized on that complexity, promising an evening of historic lectures, romantic ballads, and side-splitting satire.

Everyone was on their way to the show that night, and yet, oddly, Jim O'Brien—the saloon's owner and Fergus Falls' most prominent Irish resident—was nowhere to be found. His absence was inexplicable to most people in town, but not to the saloon's young bartender. Nicholas was growing accustomed to O'Brien's mysterious disappearances, although that didn't make him overly comfortable with them. Truth be told, Nicholas wasn't comfortable with much about his brother-in-law.

Since opening that summer, O'Brien's Saloon had become the unofficial epicenter of town activity; on most nights, a never-ending chorus of shouted drink orders added to the din already created by well-used billiard tables and one of the only full-size pianos in town. Nicholas liked the frenetic pace required to keep up with all the activity, and the bar was doing well—that much was obvious every night when he emptied the cash register before crossing the street to join Cecilia in the cramped apartment they shared with Jim and his family. But even with the overflowing till, Nicholas was hard-pressed to account for the purchase of this massive brick hotel. And then there was the inexplicably large stack of money and whiskey bonds in the saloon's brand-new safe, which was almost as enormous as Jim O'Brien himself.

Nicholas knew he would have to get to the bottom of these puzzles— and that the future of his family would no doubt be better without Jim O'Brien in it. But tonight his thoughts, like those of his fellow townspeople, were all about Ireland. As he watched people hurrying toward the theater, he cast his mind back to a place he never really knew.

Hardly any of the passersby bothered to look inside the saloon's rain-smeared windows. Even fewer paused for a pint before heading to the show. That was really too bad. Had anyone stopped long enough to chat with the young man standing behind the bar, they would have been treated to a story worth far more than the admission being paid at Gray's Hall.

Nicholas, after all, was more Irish than the Sullivans and O'Briens put together. However, as he was always quick to explain, he wasn't really *from there. Nicholas Reilly was born at sea, and he made a point of stating that fact on every document, governmental or otherwise, that asked for his place of birth. He also listed his legal name as Nicholas Johnston Reilly on such papers, but that was really just for convenience's sake. His full name, he liked to say, was Nicholas Richard James Thomas William John Gabriel Carls Michael John Alexander Trabaret Archibald Cornelius Hugh Arthur Edward Johnston Reilly, so named for the owner, doctor, and crew of the* Jeanie Johnston, *the legendary famine ship on which Nicholas was born thirty years earlier.*

That he was born on Easter Sunday, the very day the vessel was scheduled to embark from County Kerry on her first refugee voyage, was noteworthy enough. That he and his family survived the arduous journey that followed was nothing short of astounding. Mortality rates on the aptly named coffin ships could be as high as 70 percent.

Not so on the Jeanie Johnston. *Beginning with the much publicized announcement of Nicholas's birth, this little square-rigged barque was known far and wide as a charmed ship—the only coffin ship, in fact, to keep all of her passengers alive. And with each of her eleven successful trips to North America, the reputation of this vessel continued to grow. Soon it was said around the world that to sail aboard the* Jeanie Johnston *was to survive despite crushing odds.*

Aboard the Jeanie Johnston, *these odds would spur people like the Reillys and their crew to travel thousands of miles from home in search of a new beginning. These odds would demand that they risk their lives at every turn. More than once it would force them to flout naval law and invite arrest—or worse. And yet the sterling record of the barque and her occupants would stand, their mythology building with each subsequent year, eventually making them luminary figures in one of the most calamitous moments in history.*

The epic story of survival on the Jeanie, *and how Nicholas Richard James Thomas William John Gabriel Carls Michael John Alexander Trabaret Archibald Cornelius Hugh Arthur Edward Johnston Reilly came to be born on it, was a story so fantastic that not even the world-renowned Sullivan Troupe Irish Review dared tackle it. It would take over a century of study and discussion prompted by marine architects, naval historians, and the leaders of nations to tease out the story of Nicholas and his namesake vessel. In the intervening years, many refugees who sailed aboard would call the* Jeanie *miraculous and her builder, owner, and crew saviors. Historians would puzzle over why this ship—and this ship alone—managed to keep all of her passengers alive. Medical and nautical officials would study and eventually revolutionize sailing procedures as a result of her accomplishment. Critics would accuse the men most closely associated with the ship of capitalizing on misery, of exploiting those desperate to travel by charging astronomical passage fees, of being no better than human traffickers. They would speculate about the demons and guilt driving the vessel's historic course. And yet, for all that, they would all agree on one crucial truth: the story of the* Jeanie Johnston *is indisputably the stuff of legend.*

1

The Gathering Storm

IT BEGAN in an instant. Across North America and Europe that spring, farmers went to sleep one evening, content that all was well in their fields, then awoke the next morning to find their entire crop ruined. The stories they told were as apocalyptic as they were consistent: a strange cloud of mist hanging over their fields, the overpowering stench of something rotten, beds of healthy potatoes turned into rivers of putrefied slime.

The summer of 1845 had been a foreboding season from the start, filled with uncharacteristic thunderstorms and heat waves, followed by pervasive and unrelenting fog. Under the cover of that ominous cloud, farmers in Pennsylvania and Maine first reported the destruction of their potato fields. They were soon joined by farmers in Belgium, then France, Germany, and Switzerland. Not long afterward, testimonials surfaced from the Channel Islands and England. Finally, the report everyone in Ireland feared: a worker in Dublin's prestigious Botanical Gardens confirmed the telltale signs of blight there.[1] In less than a month, the disease would sweep across all of Ireland. In its wake, acre upon acre of potatoes, all in full bloom, suddenly withered and fell, scorched black as if they had been burned.

Farmers said it was the stench that first gave away the blight's arrival. Over and over again, they described the smell of death, of tons of potatoes rotting just below the surface of the earth, a smell so potent it was said to have mass and to hang more heavily than the cloud of fog that threatened to suffocate the region. It was intolerable, enough to make even a passerby weep. Families, desperate to save any remaining potatoes, took to the fields with cloths tied around their mouths and noses but were forced to surrender their salvage projects after the reek became too noxious. Others hung their hopes on those potatoes already dug and stored in dry pits. But these too fell prey to the blight, leaving behind them oily puddles of decaying vegetable matter. With nothing left to do, an entire island of families sat on fencerows and stood beside their fields, wringing their hands and lamenting the great hunger that would soon be upon them all.

Why and how this blight appeared remained a maddening mystery. Botanists hired by the British government to investigate returned to London defeated and without a clue; there was no reasonable explanation for the scourge and no solution. Some people claimed it was witchcraft. Others swore they had seen bands of warring fairies flying overhead and cursing the crop. What else, after all, could so dramatically and instantaneously destroy more than two million acres of healthy tubers? Still other people called it the canker, a treacherous and immoral disease. Pathologists in the United States contended that the putrefaction must have been caused by a gross atmospheric disturbance.[2] More than one leading botanist of the day argued that this plague must have been sent by God and thus was beyond the scope of human correction.[3]

Using the lens of modern biology, it's easy to see why any of these explanations seemed plausible. *Phytophthora infestans*, the fungus-like microorganism responsible for the destruction of the potato, is a tricky being. The pathogen releases millions of tiny spores that are easily carried in the wind for several miles, thus blanketing an entire region. There they remain all but dormant, just waiting for the right amount of temperate moisture. When those conditions appear in the form of cool rain and humidity, both of which were in great abundance in 1845, the spores spring to life, migrating across plant surfaces, leeching water, and leaving cyst-like lesions in their wake. These lesions and the rot they create take hold of potato plants, compromising their systems and leaving them susceptible to secondary infection. Meanwhile the spores begin to germinate, sending forth veins of fungus that quickly erupt and force the collapse of the plant's cellulose. A seriously infected plant often dies within a day or two.

Present-day botanists agree that there are few pathogens quite as destructive as *Phytophthora infestans*. In fact one hundred years after the Irish Potato Famine, the blight's continued virulence prompted a series of nations, including the United States and the Soviet Union, to consider utilizing it as a biological weapon. The United States, at least, would have pursued that course, had the country not suspended its biological weapons program in 1969.

These facts might have resonated with Daniel Reilly, who in 1845 was a young famer working his fields in the west of Ireland. That autumn, he watched, awestruck, as many of the fields surrounding his house fell into ruin. But even had he known the full extent of the organism he was battling, Daniel would surely not have taken much comfort in that knowledge. Nor would he have appreciated the irony in scientists' later theory that *Phytophthora infestans* followed the same course as the potato itself, coming to Ireland first by way of the eastern United States and, before that, the hills of Central and South America.

It certainly wouldn't have mattered to Daniel that those same scientists now hypothesize that the hills in Central and South America contained blight-infected bat and seabird guano, which was shipped to places like Philadelphia as fertilizer to ensure healthy crops. Or that the same cargo ships that carried the guano to the United States then brought timber, grain, and tiny, insidious, potato-loving spores to Europe. In his twenty-six years, Daniel had never seen a bat and didn't have many opportunities to observe seabirds or timber ships in his native Ballybeggan, a small farming community just outside the city of Tralee and nearly seven miles from the ocean. Seven miles might very well be seven hundred for a nineteenth-century Irish farmer, particularly one who had just become a husband and father-to-be and thus found the bulk of his energy focused on maintaining his small cottage and ten acres of land.

Remaining focused, however, was becoming increasingly difficult for Daniel. All around him, people were beginning to go hungry. And if continental Europe was any indication, conditions were about to get much worse. In France, poor farmers resorted to eating cats and dogs. In the Netherlands, mothers fed their wailing children bread made out of straw and sawdust, hoping to fill their aching bellies and ease their suffering.

By the spring of 1846, it was clear that Ireland was in the midst of a catastrophic famine that eclipsed even the suffering of continental Europe—and no place was harder hit than Daniel's native County Kerry. He watched helplessly as people began bleeding their livestock to make black porridge. When the animals became too weak, they were killed and eaten. Families pawned all of their household goods, followed by their hair and then the shirts off their backs. Soon the pawn offices were overflowing with clothes, utensils, and tools, none of which the impoverished residents could afford to buy.

When the local magistrate was summoned to a widow's house upon the accusation that she had taken a few half-rotten potatoes from a nearby field, he discovered that they had been added to a stew composed primarily of the remains of the family dog. Horrified, he delivered both the widow and her stewpot to the judge. Once in the courtroom, she broke down and admitted that she and her children had gone without food for two days before she made the decision to kill and cook the pet. The judge was so moved by her tale that he gave her money from his own pocket.[4]

Not everyone was so lucky.

Two boys found gleaning discarded seed potatoes were seized by a bailiff and marched back to his home, where he chained them both to a cow stake outside his barn. Their mother learned of her children's fate and rushed to the bailiff's house, where she pleaded with the bailiff's wife. Fearing for her own well-being, his wife refused to help. The widow returned home and summoned all her remaining strength into an incantation and curse. Those close to him say that the bailiff was immediately stricken with a pain so agonizing it forced him to the ground, where he writhed in torture for a few hours and then died.[5] Not far from him, another local man met his end not with a curse but with a spade used to bludgeon him to death after he was discovered stealing a turnip from another man's field.

Like other residents in and around Tralee, Daniel Reilly received these reports with growing concern. He too had lost his potato crop, and he walked his remaining acres daily, looking for signs that the disease was spreading. A multigenerational farmer, Daniel had been born in this lowland; since childhood he had worked the same dense soil cultivated by his father and grandfather. Now he had his own family—and it was growing.

Despite the ribbing they would endure for their choice of days, Daniel Reilly and Margaret Foran were married on April Fool's Day 1845. His brother, Eugene, stood as best man. Margaret, just seventeen at the time, came with her friend Joanna O'Sullivan and her brother John. The daughter of a steward in a nearby town, Margaret brought with her a modest dowry.

Although he was ten years Margaret's senior, Daniel nevertheless had little experience with women. They were both no doubt surprised to discover that Margaret was pregnant less than two months after their wedding. She took it with the same good-natured humor with which she embraced most things. Daniel wanted to do the same, but he couldn't help but feel troubled by the ominous signs that Ireland was about to undergo a massive agricultural crisis.

There had been lean times before—even entire crop failures—but none as dire as this one. It was as if the entire island, usually flush with delicate purple blossoms and dense green foliage, had been poisoned. What was left was as barren as the depth of any winter. Daniel may not have known any more than the botanists about why this was happening, but he surely knew it was dire. And without seed potatoes, the following year would no doubt be even worse.

Such was the sentiment at every family dinner and local gathering, where conversation was filled with little other than the failed potato crop. The collective worry was present everywhere, perhaps best exemplified by a letter Daniel's cousin James Prendergast wrote to relatives in America:

> Unless some such measures be taken to provide against next year greater fears are entertained for the coming than the present season. The Potatoe crop is much worse than the last. The disease that was

not perceived until September, and even December in other places last year is now complained of throughout the Country. It is felt more severely as we have not the fourth part of last years produc [*sic*] even diseased. We expect good measures from the British parliament this year but we mus [*sic*] wait to know the issue.[6]

James Prendergast and Daniel Reilly were not waiting alone. Mindful that Ireland was on the brink of disaster, even the English press demanded action. The *London Times* called on Parliament to intervene immediately in order to "prevent, as much as possible, the horrors, the high prices, and extortion of a famine."[7] Petitions from local governments throughout Ireland's west foretold indescribable suffering and destruction. Given the reports of violence and the befuddled botanists still without a solution, the implications of these petitions and the suffering they predicted now seemed all too imminent.

And so those in power took action, but it was far from what people like Daniel had hoped. Britain's Queen Victoria, just twenty-six years old and still adjusting to her new life as a monarch, canceled her first scheduled visit to Ireland, citing concerns for her own safety as justification; her Conservative Parliament, led by Robert Peel, was also in no hurry to visit its beleaguered neighbor. However, a series of relief depots was established in the hopes of averting mass starvation; and in an effort to make grain more accessible, Parliament threatened to ban brewing on the island entirely. Concerned that these measures might not be enough to keep mortality figures in check, Prime Minister Peel also arranged to secretly import cornmeal from America, a decision that would soon cost him his political career, as those in Britain were already critical of any attempt to assist the Irish at state expense. Meanwhile resident Quakers convened at a coffee shop in Dublin, where they spearheaded what would become some of the most heroic attempts to keep the Irish people alive. They soon dispersed about the country, arriving in places like Daniel Reilly's town of Tralee to establish soup kitchens to feed the destitute. With their somber black suits and foreign-sounding speech, the Friends seemed as alien as the queen herself might have, had she made her scheduled visit.

The contrast between Victoria's and Daniel's experience of the blight is too telling to be ignored. Like the monarch, Daniel was also twenty-six, and he too had a young family. But unlike his new queen, Daniel also had a front-row seat to the misery that was about to irrevocably change the destiny of a people. He saw his neighbors, hat in hand, begging for the opportunity to break stone in exchange for bread. He stood helpless as the land turned into poison. But he arrived at the very same conclusion drawn by Victoria—a conclusion as simple as it was true, and perhaps all the more so given the disparate people who arrived at it: this was no time to be in Ireland.

To avoid the blight and its fate, to ensure the safety of his own family, Daniel knew he had but one choice: to get them aboard one of the very same cargo ships that had delivered this scourge to his island, reversing the course of both the potato and the blight back across the Atlantic, where the Reillys could escape the suffering and the authority of Britain's crown and forge a new life deep in America's heartland. All that remained was to figure out how.

2

A Great Hunger

THE IRELAND Daniel Reilly sought to escape was marked by dramatic transition. Once a densely wooded island populated by the Celts and Vikings, it had since been converted into a hinterland colony by its neighbor, England. Under the reign of Elizabeth I, Ireland, still a heavily forested island, had served as a timber nursery for a growing Imperial Navy. Once its innumerable trees were exhausted, the newly pastoral landscape was designated the breadbasket for a growing empire. Oatmeal, wheat, and flax were grown on arable acreage. Pigs, cows, and sheep grazed patchy grassland. They, along with the grain, were raised by a few small-scale farmers almost exclusively for English consumption. What was left—the rocky soil of the north, the boggy lowlands of the south, the inhospitable cliffs of the west—was frocked with potatoes. Collectively these potato fields dominated the face of Irish agriculture and diet.

First introduced as an inexpensive ground cover, potatoes soon proved an effective means of feeding people. Prior to the blight's arrival, they were everywhere. Frustrated by the tuber's abundance, peasant farmers would stack potatoes like firewood at the edge of their fields. They would fill ditches with the excess crop and light it on fire. And, of course, they would eat them. On the eve of the famine, the average Irish adult was eating about fourteen pounds of potatoes a day, approximately thirty contemporary baking potatoes. But unlike our modern-day supermarket spuds, these potatoes were remarkably nutrient rich, lacking only protein and vitamin D, both of which could be ably sourced with a glass of buttermilk a day. Though undoubtedly monotonous, this diet was also remarkably healthy, so much so, in fact, that at the time of the famine, Irish people were taller than many of their European contemporaries and had a longer lifespan and lower infant mortality.

As far as the British government was concerned, these were not heartening statistics. By the time the potato failed in 1845, Ireland was home to more than eight million people. Census officials predicted that the population would top nine million by 1851. Most of the Irish lived as cottiers, poor subsistence farmers who cultivated a fraction of an acre in exchange for the opportunity to grow the potatoes that would feed their families. Theirs was a life based not on money and commerce but rather on self-sufficiency and trade in kind. Many had lived like this for generations, paying a pittance or trading produce to their largely absentee landlords in exchange for the roof over their head. It was a hardscrabble life without luxury or reprieve. But, like their diet, it also kept an entire class of people alive—and multiplying.

For decades Ireland's Protestant gentry, joined by many in Britain's Parliament, worried aloud about the inefficiencies of the cottiers' agricultural system and the growing number of people who depended on it. In a world increasingly dominated by capitalism and a free market economy, self-sufficient subsistence farmers were not just archaic; they were a liability, incapable of contributing to the gross national product.

This belief only intensified with the arrival of the Industrial Revolution. Along with advancements in transportation and manufacturing, the new era brought a wholly altered relationship with the landscape. In England, families moved by the thousands from the country to cities like London and Manchester, where they went to work in cotton mills or coal mines. No longer farmers, these new laborers looked outward for their food. And with a population of 15 million—nearly twice that of Ireland and rapidly climbing—England's grocery bill was substantial.

Ireland had yet to make the shift to an industrial-based economy. That meant its intended role as breadbasket for the empire was falling short, making it more of a liability than an asset. Furthermore the island's singular reliance on the potato as the diet of an entire class of people created a food system contemporary theorists call "vulnerable," which is to say that it was, by its very nature, predisposed to disaster.[1] It would take only one bad frost or drought or disease to wipe out an entire crop, leaving the cottiers with nothing and the rest of Ireland with nothing to eat. That's the kind of liability that made British authorities more than just a little nervous.

As early as 1845, cultural observers saw how this vulnerability could destroy much of Ireland. "The Irish peasant starves," wrote the editor of the London Times, "because his whole subsistence depends on the produce of his own patch of ground, and in that failing he has nothing to offer in exchange for the necessaries of life elsewhere. In England, on the contrary, the laws of commerce operating fairly will preserve us from this horrible affliction."[2] Though no doubt insensitive in its tone, this assessment was nevertheless true for much of Ireland, and in no place more so than in Daniel Reilly's native Tralee.

Like much of Ireland's west coast, the landscape surrounding Tralee is a place often hostile to human activity of any kind, thanks to its relentless southwesterly winds and rocky geography. Just to the south of town rest the imposing Slieve Mish Mountains, a series of sprawling peaks rising over eight hundred meters (about half a mile) and blocking the rest of the horizon from view. They take their name from a mythic Irish princess known for her cruelty, an apt allusion on many days, when clouds pushed to shore by Atlantic winds are sliced open by the mountain summits, spilling rain over the region on a day even twenty-first-century meteorologists swear will be perfectly sunny.

For centuries, locals in the west of Kerry have joked that they have far more weather than they do climate. Winters are particularly blustery, with epic storms marked by unrelenting wind. Gales are not uncommon, even in the spring and summer. Because of these conditions, the region's coastline shifts almost daily, reconfiguring itself according to the brutal tides and winds. The local flora—not to mention many of the human inhabitants—stand at a sharp angle, braced and pitched against the strong westerly winds. In fact the trees there—mostly hazel and a few hearty conifers—are so wizened by this constant battering that they escaped the notice of British foresters in the sixteenth century altogether.

Instead of loggers, a royal family by the name of Denny was granted occupancy of the region, encouraged by the crown to settle this landscape with peasant farmers, preferably of the Protestant variety. Under the vigilant eye of the Denny family, Tralee grew into a vibrant outpost in a region often believed to be populated exclusively by savages and otherworldly banshees. It also became a place of profound social contrast. At the end of the eighteenth century, the region was home to communities of spinners and weavers who made their living creating goods made of wool and flax. With the advent of mechanization, however, this work had been exported to enormous mills and factories throughout England and Ireland's north. What remained were entire families with no means of supporting themselves. They, like the cottiers, composed County Kerry's largest—and poorest—class. A census report completed by the British government in 1841 deemed three-fourths of the population of Kerry "destitute." It also found there Ireland's highest illiteracy rate—over 60 percent—and its lowest household incomes. The area surrounding Tralee claimed the greatest concentration of Ireland's lowest class of homes: one-room hovels with mud floors and no windows. Surveyors of the poorer parishes in the region failed to find a single glass window, manufactured shoe, comb, clock, bonnet, or pair of scissors.[3]

Daniel and Margaret Reilly were two of the more fortunate in Kerry's agricultural class; they owned their farm and produced enough food to keep themselves fed: an egg now and again for breakfast, bread and cold meat at tea, a platter of cabbage and potatoes for dinner. There was whiskey punch made in a copper kettle on special occasions and a feather bed on which to sleep and nurse their newborn son, Robert. Unlike the majority of cottiers in the region, Daniel grew not just potatoes but also grain for sale—some of the 285,000 tons exported to England each year.

If the growing catastrophe of the famine had a silver lining, it came in the fall of 1846, when grain prices reached historic highs and farmers like Daniel found themselves in great demand. That harvest season he worked relentlessly to cut his grain fields, sometimes not resting until he had cut an entire acre with the scythe carved to fit his calloused hand, stopping only to sharpen the blade dulled by the toughness of a late-season crop. He was buoyed through it all, no doubt, by the promise of high prices and cash in his pocket—cash he would need, in the absence of the potato, to feed his family.

The grain trade was also Daniel's introduction to the opulence that constituted Tralee's other world. Each year at harvest time, he and his crop made the five-mile trek from his farm to the bustling center of Tralee, where horse races, agricultural fairs, and grain auctions dominated the social landscape, along with Tralee's most formidable trader and the man who would soon hold the fate of the Reillys in his hand: Nicholas Donovan.

Like Daniel, Nicholas Donovan was particularly busy that harvest season. The failure of the potato crop had only intensified England's desire for grain, and Donovan could not fill his leased packet ships fast enough. Each week they made their way into Tralee Bay and up the narrow canal into the city—a canal, he liked to remind his fellow businessmen, he himself had been responsible for engineering. In the fall of 1846, that canal was littered with boats waiting to export food from the starving region.

Ensconced in his grand Edwardian offices on Denny Street, the very heart of Kerry commerce, Donovan was able to keep a polite distance from much of the suffering overtaking the region. With their vaulted ceilings and a view of the town's rose gardens, the offices of John Donovan & Sons Ltd. were a far cry from the cottier cabins that dotted much of the area's landscape. There Donovan could keep a close eye on the ledgers that recorded deliveries from people like Daniel Reilly. That was reason enough for concern: even with the flush harvest, there wasn't enough grain to supply English demand. Even more troubling were the insinuations from London that merchants like Donovan would soon be required to keep the year's harvest in Ireland as relief for the poor. That was bad for business. Worst of all were the rumors that Parliament would soon close Irish ports altogether in an attempt to keep food on the starving island. It was within the government's power to do so, and it would surely ruin an importer like Donovan.

Speed, then, was a greater concern than ever for a man eager to get his shipments out on the open water, where they could move unrestricted. From his desk, Donovan kept close tabs on the stockyard next to John Donovan & Sons, where he could count the imported barrels, metal hoops, and thick timber staves for sale there. His grain dealings, on the other hand, required him to call for his carriage and make his way through town, past the growing number of beggars who lined the streets and the watchful eye of Sir Edward Denny.

When he set off on these jaunts, Donovan was sure to be noticed. With large, prominently set eyes, a high brow, and broad lips, his sheer physiology alone was likely to command attention. But he wasn't content with that; to present himself as a leader and social force, he carefully styled his hair with pomade and trained it in a severe part, favored high collars and long coats, and wore an elaborate mustache in the style of Archduke Franz Josef, heir apparent to the Austrian Empire. Like the young nobleman, Donovan carried himself with a certain degree of entitlement. His preferred pose for portraits was one in which he stood angled away from the camera, arms crossed, daring the photographer with a sideways glance and casual jut of his hip. The effect suggested he was skeptical—even outright dismissive—of both the cameraman and any subsequent viewers.

A similar attitude marked his dealings with the town. As a successful Catholic merchant, Donovan was a member of the newest and arguably most powerful class in Ireland. For centuries, his ancestors had been hemmed in by penal acts restricting their rights to own property, hold public office, or even vote. A series of reform bills culminating in 1832 had changed all of that, allowing Donovan and other Catholics of his generation to exert the kind of influence he coveted. At least, they did in theory. The truth of the matter was that Nicholas Donovan was still very much under the thumb of Sir Edward Denny and his aristocratic perception of the town. Even Donovan's offices, built out of stone from the Denny castle and still owned by Sir Edward, remained out of Donovan's complete control. No amount of posturing or grooming was going to change that, and that made the importer more than a little bitter.

Donovan was nevertheless relentless in his attempts to make a mark on the town, and in so doing left a trail of resentment in his wake. First, there was the canal he muscled through, despite questions concerning its

13

management. Then there was his push to locate the markets and grain depots not in the town square but on the edge of Tralee and away from the influence of Denny. The nobleman and his followers were not impressed. Nor were they thrilled with the way Donovan managed to insinuate himself onto every town committee and even the Grand Jury, a move the Protestant-leaning newspaper in the region bemoaned as evidence that the once patrician town was now being run by "shopkeepers."

Even the most critical among the leaders in Tralee knew there was little they could deny Donovan. Everyone in the town depended, to some degree, on his ability to participate in global trade—the seeming ease with which he could bring in goods ranging from wood to wine or export the produce of Tralee's farmers to the larger marketplace. And so they quietly stewed as they admitted him onto the town's planning board and boroughs commission, the relief committee and local chamber. Donovan, it seemed, was a necessary force in the town's quest to enter the Industrial Revolution.

Certainly he was one of the town's most dedicated residents. That harvest season, as the blight continued to decimate the potato fields surrounding town, he focused on Tralee's grain crop with nothing short of single-mindedness. Each night, the gas lamps at 11 Denny Street shone well after dark. Those who lingered on the wide dirt thoroughfare below the grandly paned windows would have seen a thirty-one-year-old man, assiduous in his dress and comportment despite the late hour, toiling over ledgers until the wee hours of the morning, when he retired not to his seaside estate but to the small apartment on the third floor above his office. The new Whig government had promised an end to preferential subsidies on everything from rum to hoop skirts. That was good news for an importer with access to the global market. So too was the speculation throughout the empire that a railway boom would soon usher in a new phase of the Industrial Revolution. Donovan intended to capitalize on both, and he stayed up each night strategizing how to do just that. It was only at the week's end that he made his way out of town to the seaside resort of Fenit Spa, where his wife, Katherine, sister of the Murphy Brewing scion, waited piously in their Italianate mansion surrounded by lavish gardens and grounds.

As he made the three-mile trek home, Donovan had no choice but to observe the rapidly deteriorating conditions among Tralee's poorest set. The noxious odor of the blight was now mixed with an equally acrid stench of burning thatch and down, the smoldering remains of cottages once occupied by cottiers who were now unable to pay their rent. Donovan saw the constabulary serving eviction notices, followed by the torches that would set many a hovel ablaze. He saw the bruises and blackened eyes on those who resisted. He saw the barefoot children, now homeless, begging outside churchyards, and the enfeebled old men shuffling to the town center hoping for bread.

There was much to pity about the scene. But there was also much to be gained—of that Donovan was convinced. And though he wasn't yet sure how, he was nevertheless certain that he could find in the famine tremendous opportunity not just to make a pretty profit but also to finally make his mark upon the town.

3

Ships, Colonies, and Commerce

London, 1846

O N THE OTHER SIDE of the Irish Sea, Henry Grey was also kept awake by the growing crisis and the opportunities it presented. As colonial secretary, Earl Grey was responsible for overseeing the British Empire's massive global holdings. This was no small task, particularly for a resource-poor island like Great Britain. From the sugar plantations of the Caribbean to the opium fields in Bengal, Britain needed productive colonies if it were to remain a world leader. "Ships, Colonies, and Commerce" had been the rallying cry for well over a century, and the empire had ensured its primacy in all three by insisting on extensive protective tariffs that privileged colonial ships and goods, thereby ensuring a ready and closed trade capable of providing England with every possible commodity she needed—and more—all without the niggling difficulties associated with political alliance and global diplomacy. The advent of free trade, however, was changing all of that. A truly global marketplace meant an end to the protective tariffs that kept the empire's goods competitive. It also threatened to make Britain's colonies—along with their colonial officer—obsolete.

If Grey needed evidence of this fact, he had only to look as far as his crumbling office on 14 Downing Street, a dilapidated structure built over a sewer on a dead-end street. So decrepit was the building that housed the colonial offices that reams of old files were now being used as impromptu support beams in the basement, from which seeping water had to be pumped twice a day.[1] Grey's staff, already meager by bureaucratic standards, had dwindled further in recent years, with undersecretaries reporting for duty a few hours each afternoon and long after they had had their first glass of claret.

Grey was not the kind of man to take this state of affairs lightly. At forty-five, he already had a reputation as a cranky malcontent. When he didn't like a member of a committee or agency, he refused to join; when he disagreed with a decision made by his peers in the House of Lords, he threatened to resign. Colleagues called his petulant behavior perverse and his disposition tetchy. The reputation stuck, no doubt strengthened by Grey's severe underbite, which gave him a countenance marked by what appeared to be a perpetual grimace.

Whenever he considered the matter of Ireland, that grimace became all the more apparent. Colonies were supposed to support their motherland, not the other way around. The blight had become an untenable departure from this plan. Each day, Grey received reports from throughout Ireland about the growing distress among its poorest class. The most dire reports came from the area surrounding Tralee, a place he had never visited and never intended to. Stories of the growing suffering there made him uncomfortable. Worst of all, though, was the economic liability places like County Kerry were now thrusting on the empire. As far as he was concerned, the calamity in Ireland was entirely of the colony's own making. "The evils of that unhappy country," he told Parliament,

are not accidental, not temporary, but chronic and habitual. The state of Ireland is one which is notorious. We know the ordinary condition of that country to be one both of lawlessness and wretchedness. It is so described by every competent authority. There is not an intelligent foreigner coming to our shores, who turns his attention to the state of Ireland, but who bears back with him such a description. Ireland is the one weak place in the solid fabric of British power—Ireland is the one deep (I had almost said ineffaceable) blot upon the brightness of British honour. Ireland is

17

our disgrace. It is the reproach, the standing disgrace, of this country, that Ireland remains in the condition she is.[2]

Grey wasn't about to let that condition stand. And he was joined in this commitment by his new prime minister, John Russell, along with Charles Trevelyan, a civil servant and rising star who had just been appointed assistant to the Treasury. Together these three men represented the central nervous system of famine relief and the administration of Ireland. While they were distinguished by social class and position, they were nonetheless united by the fervent belief that the suffering now befalling Ireland was part of God's plan. Collectively this triumvirate—and many of their followers—were motivated by Providentialism, the idea that God rewarded and punished as needed, that the virtuous would be provided for, while the depraved and iniquitous perished. As far as they were concerned, the growing crisis in Ireland was a result of the grossly primitive nature of the Irish people, who had grown slothful and indolent. The famine, though clearly unfortunate, was an opportunity to correct that once and for all. Those unwilling to work would perish; those capable of industry and self-reliance would find their way—and without the help of the government.

The new Whig government sought to undo the meager aid policies established by the previous administration, beginning with the practice of importing cornmeal from America, which they saw as unduly influencing the British grain market. Better, they insisted, to let private market forces dictate price and availability. That was good news for Nicholas Donovan, who no doubt read with great relief the reports from London assuring merchants that the government planned to reduce its aid and announcing its refusal to close Irish ports.[3]

Also good news was the new government's insistence that the famine presented an opportunity to correct the gross inefficiencies in the Irish agricultural system. What Ireland needed—what all of the British Empire needed—was fewer farms and more acreage on each, along with the new machinery needed to make work efficient on them. That also meant fewer farmers—and fewer Irish people, which would surely be a blessing for everyone. At least, that was the firm conviction of Charles Trevelyan. "A population," he insisted,

whose ordinary food is wheat and beef, and whose ordinary drink is
porter and ale, can retrench in periods of scarcity. But those who are
habitually and entirely fed on potatoes live upon the extreme verge
of human subsistence, and when they are deprived of their accustomed food, there is nothing cheaper to which they can resort. They
have already reached the lowest point in the descending scale, and
there is nothing beyond but starvation and beggary.[4]

Grey and Russell agreed, so they charged Trevelyan with the task of determining how to limit both. His decisions were immediate and, by many
accounts, draconian. In place of Peel's food depots, Trevelyan erected
soup kitchens resembling those established by the Quakers. But unlike
the Society of Friends, Trevelyan's relief centers offered no bread or soup.
Instead his menus consisted entirely of stirabout, a cooked porridge of
corn. Not only was this grain the cheapest on the market, but it also had
the appealing attribute of going bad quickly. "Stirabout," Trevelyan later
wrote in his history of the famine, "becomes sour by keeping, has no value
in the market, and persons were therefore not likely to apply for it who
did not want it for their own consumption."[5]

To further restrict application for aid, he established a byzantine system of forms and prerequisites along with the mountains of paperwork
both required: tens of thousands of applications and ledgers, along with
an estimated three million ration tickets, all of which had to be catalogued
and tracked not by government bureaucrats but by new local poor com-
missions made up of resident gentry and rate payers—in other words,
people like Sir Edward Denny and Nicholas Donovan.[6]

Meanwhile Henry Grey launched an audacious project of his own,
one that sought to gut all vestiges of preindustrial Ireland. Doing so, he
insisted, was not only his God-given right; it was also his duty to the rest
of the planet. "There is not," he told Parliament,

a foreigner—no matter whence he comes, be it from France, Russia, Germany, or America . . . who visits Ireland, and who on his
return does not congratulate himself that he sees nothing compara-
ble with the condition of that country at home. If such be the state

of things, how then does it arise, and what is its cause? My Lords, it is only by misgovernment that such evils could have been produced: the mere fact that Ireland is in so deplorable and wretched a condition saves whole volumes of argument, and is of itself a complete and irrefutable proof of the misgovernment to which she has been subjected.[7]

Best to liquidate the island and begin again, Grey concluded. There were no doubt thousands of famine sufferers clamoring to leave. Why not help them by paying for their passage out of Ireland?

That doing so flew in the face of the laissez-faire politics Grey himself promoted was of little consequence to him. He saw in this proposal a ready solution to myriad problems: the shortage of labor in British North America's timber region, the overpopulation of Ireland, the vast unprotected border with the United States. And so he continued to work the floor of Parliament, now hoping to garner support for an assisted immigration policy that would conduct famine sufferers to interior Canada, where they could harvest much-needed timber and grow food, all the while keeping an eye on the Americans looking for their own piece of virgin forest.

Grey found support in unlikely channels, including the same erstwhile editors of the *London Times* who had beseeched Parliament to provide the Irish with relief support. "Ireland's difficulty," they wrote in a front-page editorial, "is England's opportunity."[8] The majority of Grey's fellow Parliamentarians agreed.[9] But they fell short of an all-out approval of state-assisted immigration to make good on this opportunity. Such an endeavor had been tried in the years leading up to the famine. Not only had it been expensive, but many of the Scottish and Irish families who had sailed to Canada on government-subsidized trips suffered terribly under the brutal conditions of the timber camps. They fled for the United States, where they were under no obligation to fell timber or grow food for the crown or reimburse the British people for their passage. In little time, the program had proven an embarrassing failure.

Grey's opposition in Parliament was quick to remind him as much, eventually forcing the colonial secretary to withdraw his proposal, lest he experience embarrassing political defeat. But Grey was far from done with his scheme. Trevelyan, no doubt instructed by his colonial secretary, adopted a nom de plume under which he wrote a series of editorials in favor of Irish immigration to North America. Meanwhile British shipping agents in New York and Boston began bribing the captains of immigrant vessels to leave the United States and sail north to the St. Lawrence River, depositing passengers there, where they could be of use to the crown. Not to be outdone, the British consul in New York began plying local ship pilots and the emigrants themselves to continue on to Canada. Colonial officials also created guidebooks that sung lyrically about the opportunities for farmers just like Daniel Reilly in the fertile land of Canada. They posted warnings about the "aguish swamps of Illinois or Missouri, or other distant regions of the Western States."[10] British North America, they insisted, was about to become the new city on a hill.

More than a few of Ireland's landlords, eager to remove cottiers from their property, leaped at the chance to send out their tenants—even at their own expense. And they found vessels aplenty on which to do just that. British ship owners and landlords didn't really care if Canada was Shangri-La, El Dorado, or anything else. All that mattered to them was that there were Irish peasants eager to get there. Hundreds of ship owners saw in Grey's proposal their own opportunity. For decades, they had been bemoaning inefficient triangle trades. There was Canadian timber to ship to England and the Caribbean, not to mention the tons of sugar and rum to feed the empire's growing vices. Britain, however, had precious little to ship back across the Atlantic. An empty vessel is an unstable vessel, and that meant sailors had to spend valuable time and resources loading the enormous cargo vessels with sand and stone as ballast. *What would happen,* they wondered, *if they replaced that stone and sand with ballast that could load itself? And what if that ballast was willing to pay for the privilege to do so?*

It was an audacious plan, but it worked, perhaps better than anyone had hoped or feared.

4

Dominion

1846

A LREADY THE CENTER of British shipping and a thoroughly
cosmopolitan city, Quebec City seemed immune from Irish
distress. The city played temporary home to thousands of
sailors hailing from locales as far-flung as India, the South Pacific, and the
Caribbean. They mixed—to varying degrees of success—with Quebecois
timber drivers, escaped slaves from America, and the continuing influx of
British immigrants. It was a cacophony of cultures, with all the sounds,
smells, and sights that accompanied them.[1]

Added to this dynamism were the vestiges of the city's frontier ori-
gins still worn proudly by Quebecois. Amid the coffeehouses, brokerage
offices, and fine restaurants were plenty of reminders that this was a city
on the edge of civilization: sleds pulled by wolf-dogs skirted the narrow
streets, Abenaki tipis dotted the river's edge, otherwise respectable businessmen wielded hatchets to slice off sections of animal carcasses they
had cached in snowbanks. Then there were the trees, millions of tons of
them, all harvested in the wilds of the Ottawa Timber Valley—a region
populated by outlaws and rowdies that made Quebec seem demure by
comparison—then floated down Canada's massive rivers to the dozens
of timber coves lining the St. Lawrence. There they were either ushered
onto vessels destined for places like Nicholas Donovan's import yard or

rendered into the massive tall ships that would carry future loads of wood staves and boards.

It was this industry Grey hoped the Irish would soon enter, and at least one Canadian official had assured him that Quebec could easily absorb the influx of immigrants. That the reality was proving otherwise was of no matter to these men of high ideals. So they kept sending boatloads of famine refugees. The lucky ones—those who already had families and friends waiting for them—loaded their stained mattresses and beaten trunks onto steamers and trains bound for the Ottawa timber camps or the American border. The plucky ones strode into pubs with names like St. Michael's Immigrant Tavern and the Dublin Inn, where they hoped their accent might afford them a drink. The most resourceful made their way to the shipyard of John Munn, a boatbuilder who was known far and wide for his philanthropy and great love of an immigrant story.

They arrived by the tens of thousands. Most were young cottiers made all but destitute by the blight's return that season. Their clothing, already coarse and worn, was reduced to rags during the fifty days at sea. Their hands and faces were filthy; with only a few pints of water allotted a passenger each day, using it to wash was a luxury few could afford. Their bodies were rail-thin. All showed signs of hardship. Some were visibly marred by grief: a son crushed by a lifeboat or drowned; a wife lost to childbirth unassisted by a doctor or midwife; a father consigned to the sea after succumbing to fever. To the residents of Quebec City, the arriving refugees were the nameless throngs of Irish threatening to overtake a city already perched on the cusp between order and bedlam. To the waiting families in places like Boston, Toronto, and the Great Plains, they were the hope of reunification and new beginnings. To British colonial officials, they were wards—liabilities, really—with no means of support.

Still, they kept coming.

The last day of the 1846 shipping season was October 30, and although the arrival of new vessels had slackened considerably, it was still a busy afternoon on the docks of Quebec City. As a gale swept along the coast threatening to soak everyone and everything, more than four hundred immigrants were disembarking from two large cargo ships. Dozens of others were arriving from the Grosse Île quarantine station by steamer, including seventy-three emaciated refugees from Tralee, all of whom had almost perished aboard a ship aptly named the *British Empire*. The vessel's owner, perhaps hoping to cut costs, had replaced the mandatory one pound of oatmeal or sea biscuit ration required for each passenger with moldy cornmeal he ordered from New Orleans. The results were disastrous.

Few of the *British Empire*'s passengers had the means to provide their own food for the voyage, and many soon fell ill from the contaminated rations. Even had the meal been in good condition, it was far from sufficient to nourish a healthy individual; when given to a famine victim, it was a death sentence. Three passengers perished of starvation over the course of the fifty-day passage to Quebec. Those who survived presented what colonial officials soon identified as the classic symptoms of severe malnourishment: low-grade fevers, diarrhea, ashen skin, pronounced lethargy. Even after weeks in the quarantine hospital, their bodies were skeletal, save for their distended abdomens and protruding eyes.

That the refugees from Tralee managed to blend in with the other immigrants landing that Friday afternoon says much about the collective condition of those fleeing the famine. So too did their willingness to be treated like chattel as they disembarked onto the bustling cargo docks in Quebec's lower harbor. They picked their way hesitantly around enormous piles of deerskins, boxes of goose wings, heaps of pig iron, and casks of porpoise oil. They threaded around the towers of timber and barrels of sugar; they fought the overpowering smell of turpentine and rotting mackerel.

George Mellis Douglas, medical superintendent for the Grosse Île quarantine station, had spent the past several months monitoring the Tralee refugees' well-being and looking for any sign of sickness. Disease spread rapidly among immigrants, he knew, and it was his responsibility to ensure that the approximately thirty-two thousand Irish who passed through his station before arriving on the mainland of North America that year did not bring with them an epidemic. On this, the last day of the season, he should have been relieved. Instead he was visibly concerned.

Douglas had taken great care in writing a letter to colonial officials warning them that, while a crisis had been averted that year, they would no doubt be far less lucky the next. The passengers who crossed his hospital's threshold were already showing demonstrable signs of malnourishment and desperation. Another winter would only worsen that, along with their susceptibility to disease. Although it was still months away, Douglas eyed the next shipping season with worry. There were rumors of epidemics in continental Europe. It wouldn't take long for disease to reach Ireland, and when it did, the starving people there would be helpless to combat it. Douglas also sent a requisition for an additional two hundred hospital beds and eight hundred cots to accommodate those healthy passengers required to land as part of the quarantine. He requested £3,000 (about $300,000 today) for structural expansion during the off season and urged officials to take precautions to secure the city proper as well. [2] He was given £300 along with a polite note thanking him for his concern.[3]

5

Phoenix Rising

A CONFIRMED BACHELOR who lived the ascetic life of a monk,
John Munn was nothing short of an oddity in Quebec's high
society. His only known companion was Elizabeth Allen,
his matronly cousin who kept his house. He rarely ventured out for
the regattas and festivals that infused life into the city's port. He never
attended dances or parties, nor did he spend money on gay carriages and
pianofortes. Instead he pledged his money—nearly every cent of it—to
orphanages and hospitals, immigrant relief funds, and schools and homes
for the destitute.

Munn was also known far and wide as the laborer's friend. He regularly employed Irish workers, despite the fact that, for most of them, the
only vessel they had seen before arriving at his yard was the one that
ferried them across the ocean. He took in Native Americans and freed
slaves with the same equanimity and happily fostered a reputation as an
employer who insisted on a fair wage. (In fact the British Navy used his
labor rates as their own gold standard when considering compensation
for their seamen.) The newspaper *Le Fantasque* deemed him "the father
and supporter of the working class."[1] Crimpers—brokers who lured sailors out of their contracts only to force them into indentured work at
shipyards—bragged that they could exploit this cheap labor at any yard
except Munn's.[2]

In short, John Munn's shipyard was the golden ticket for anyone seeking an honest day's wage. Men of every stripe went to his yard in search of salvation. But in the fall of 1846, they found something that looked a whole lot more like Armageddon. Half-finished buildings and piles of ash stood where Canada's most prolific shipyard had once stood; Munn's was one of the hardest-hit properties in a massive fire that had killed hundreds and left thousands homeless just a year before. Damages to St. Roch, a suburb to the west of Quebec City and already the locus for Britain's greatest shipbuilders, were estimated at £1.5 million—well over $40 million today. On St. Dominique Street, not a single house remained. King, Queen, and Prince Edward Streets fared only slightly better. Munn's yard was burned to the ground. Throughout North America, people speculated about whether this disaster would be the end of Munn, if he would leave the shipbuilding business altogether, perhaps to return to his native Scotland. But Quebec had become home to him, and more than ever he felt a responsibility to stay.

Since the fire, Munn had dedicated himself to the process of rebuilding—not just his own compound but also the larger neighborhood. He petitioned officials to increase the width of the streets to allow the fire brigade easier access. He contributed part of his insurance settlement to resupplying that brigade. Still, the reconstruction of the yard had been frustratingly slow. The stone for his new steam building had not yet arrived; his low-slung sawmills were still missing half their roofs; and the narrow spire that housed his shipyard bell, which announced the beginning and end of each work day, lay unceremoniously in the midst of charred rubble. Other than the slow tempo of working roofers and masons, the yard was uncharacteristically silent.

When the late-season Irish refugees arrived at the Munn yard, he was, for the first time in his career, forced to turn them away. As it was, Munn still had no work for his two hundred regular employees, most of whom were highly specialized tradesmen—sail makers, block men, and hull caulkers—whose hands and skills were at home only on a ship. As yet another biting winter set in, many faced the prospect of homelessness, or even starvation, themselves. Next door, Munn's competitor—and hundreds of employees—were busy at work on the *Wilson Kennedy*, said to be the most impressive vessel to be launched in Quebec the following year. By comparison, the Munn yard seemed positively desolate.

Something about this grim state of affairs must have stirred Munn. Despite the unfinished state of his yard, he spent the remainder of the season obtaining contracts to build three vessels: the *England*, the *Cromwell*, and the *Blake*. He also signed on 180 of his regular employees to construct them. That still left about forty men without a paycheck. He consulted his finances. Insurance had covered a good part of the rebuilding; the rest had been taken from his residual profits. There was still enough, he decided, to finance the construction of a fourth ship on his own.

This was a risky venture. Like most wrights, Munn preferred to construct two ships a year—one in the fall, one in the spring. Three was a risk. Four seemed absurd and would certainly mean a confusing overlap of space and supplies. Then there was the problem of a buyer. Rumors of an economic depression prompted sales of cargo ships to collapse that year, and already many vessels awaited purchase in Liverpool and other ports. Munn decided he would worry about that later. In the meantime, he hatched plans for a ship he would call the *Jeanie Johnston*.

The weather had turned bitterly cold—so cold, in fact, that the woodstoves in the new yard did little to alleviate the chill. Most of the workers wore layer upon layer of clothing, covering their heads and hands with fur if they could afford it and wool if they could not. Munn would have liked to have worn thick mittens as well, but he needed his hands free to carve the *Jeanie*'s half-model, a two-foot approximation of the ship's hull he would eventually build. Normally a wright would consult a number of half-models he had used on previous vessels when conceiving of a new ship; all of Munn's, however, had been lost in the inferno. He could have used the one he created for the *England* and the *Cromwell*, but those two vessels were much larger—over seven hundred tons—and Munn didn't have enough capital to finance a ship of that size himself. No, the *Jeanie Johnston* would need to be a much humbler sort of ship, the kind he had first learned to craft while working as an apprentice for his father.

As he sat watching the construction on his new yard, Munn took his knife to a hunk of pine, just as he had been taught forty years earlier.

He imagined the straight lines of the *Jeanie*'s stern, the thick rounded hull that would carry tons of timber from his coves to ports around the world. Like most timber vessels, the *Jeanie* would have a deep, square hold. Somewhat unusually, Munn also chose to create a particularly spacious area between decks with clearance high enough for a grown man to walk about. Did he know that this decision would someday make passage across the Atlantic far more bearable for the thousands of people who would travel there? Perhaps. Like many town leaders, Munn believed the reports predicting that the flood of immigrants would only get worse. Whether that prediction dictated the dimensions of his new ship, we will never know, but we do know he committed to build an unusually spacious and sound vessel.

After Munn completed this boxy half-model, he moved to his molding loft, the three-hundred-yard-long shed that would give birth to the vessel. The wooden floor still bore the patterns of that season's larger vessels, so he ordered his carpenters to sand down the floor until it was once again bare. For days he paced the blank floor, imagining the true dimensions of his new project. When he felt confident he knew the *Jeanie*'s contours, he bent down and, using paint and a yardstick, drew a large grid that covered the entire loft floor. Then, on his hands and knees and in painstaking detail, he sketched the barque that would soon make history.

6

Ship's Fever

1847

A S THE CALENDAR ushered in the New Year, construction on all four of Munn's vessels was well under way. Workers vied for space in the sawmill and the rigging shed. The sail loft overflowed with canvas, including the fourteen sails that would soon be set on the *Jeanie*. At 734 tons, the *England* required the lion's share of Munn's men and his attention, but he had a soft spot for the boxy little vessel he himself would finance, and he instructed his workers to take extra care when planking and caulking her hull.

As construction neared completion, Munn chose to paint the *Jeanie* a subdued black. For her figurehead, he selected a simple scroll of parchment rather than the garish female bust gracing most merchant ships. Both cosmetic choices captured the mood of a city that should have been animated by a stream of ships, cargo, seamen, and immigrants. Instead 1847 was proving nothing short of a failure. Prime Minister Russell's government had succeeded in repealing corn and sugar duties, but instead of prompting a run on the market, this decision had panicked both growers and buyers into a spending freeze. To make matters worse, the promised railway boom failed to materialize, leaving speculators on the edge of bankruptcy and yards filled with unused ties and half-constructed ships. The British economy was now in free fall, with commercial failures in

England topping £15 million and rumors of a full depression sending panic-stricken mobs to make runs on banks.

Meanwhile the U.S. national debt was skyrocketing, at least in part because of the country's war with Mexico. On the front page of every American newspaper, headlines about the war vied for space with the most sensational story of the year: the brutal winter had forced members of the Donner party into cannibalism after being trapped in the Sierra Nevada's notorious snow and cold. It seemed an apt metaphor for the new economy.

The weather that killed the Donner party was making headlines in Quebec as well. As late as April, the lingering winter also prevented the normal influx of market goods and gaiety into lower Canada. Flooding had become rampant in the region, after a series of surprise storms met with ground still frozen and unwilling to absorb moisture. An unprecedented amount of ice delayed ship traffic in the St. Lawrence.[1]

At least one man was frankly glad for the delay. Dr. George Douglas's warnings from the previous year had gone largely unheeded, and as the start of a new shipping season approached, he was left mostly to his own devices. On May 3 of that year, he and his family made the steamship ride from their home in Quebec City to the Grosse Île quarantine station, some thirty miles down the St. Lawrence River. It was a difficult day for Douglas's wife, Charlotte, a bright and vivacious socialite who would spend the next six months sequestered on their tiny farm at the base of the island. Four months pregnant, she was beginning to show and was already fatigued from caring for their three young children. Douglas knew the season would be a trying one for her. He also knew it would be exhausting for the staff who joined them. Colonial officials had been miserly in their outlay for his expenditures, granting an additional orderly and nurse as supplemental staff along with the two hundred beds he had requested. He was nervous—nervous enough to requisition another fifty beds and an additional fever shed just before stepping aboard the river transport. Hopefully they would arrive before July, the peak of the immigrant season and undoubtedly the island's most vulnerable time for an epidemic.[2]

But death and disease had no intention of waiting that long.

By the middle of May, the ice had kept all but a meager twenty-six vessels out of the Quebec port, well below the 150 or so that usually had made landfall by that point in the shipping season. Then, without warning, the weather reversed itself. An epic heat wave struck the region, and with it oppressive humidity, unpredictable storms, and temperatures soaring well into the 90s. The air took on a sickly quality, ripe with the odors that came from months of stagnating waste and unwashed bodies. Not long after, scores of people both in the city and in the timber camps began falling ill at an alarming rate, victims of what had come to be known as "swamp ague."

The ague—probably a virulent strain of northern malaria—was marked by fever and chills, sweating, and tremors. For some, it quickly proved fatal. Even those who survived were often bedridden for months. But as dire a condition as that illness caused, it paled in comparison to the mysterious disease that descended upon North America's port cities along with the arrival of the first immigrant ships.

Overnight, it seemed, otherwise healthy individuals of all ages were contracting a dangerously high fever, coupled with a severe rash that made them look as if they had been beaten. They convulsed for hours in agonizing muscle and joint pain, before finally falling into a stupor or total delirium. Then, as suddenly as they had contracted the disease, they died. And the disease was spreading around the world.

Colonial officials were at a loss to explain this new malady. Members of the British Parliament worried that the plague might be a resurgence of the typhoid that killed more than 100,000 of Napoleon's troops during their assault on Russia, or perhaps a particularly deadly strain of influenza. The disease's prevalence on Irish immigrant transport vessels soon earned it the moniker "ship's fever" among American doctors and reporters. William Guy, dean of medicine at King's College in England, insisted that the disease was caused simply by "the unhappy obstinacy of the nation of Celtic savages."[3] The truth, of course, was far simpler—and more deadly.

We now know that the world was suffering from one of the worst typhus pandemics in history. Spread by the feces of an infected louse, typhus enters the human body either when its victim inhales the dust of louse feces or inadvertently scratches that feces into a wound or cut. Once in the bloodstream, typhus kills its victims by causing blood vessels to erupt. The death rate is one of the highest of all epidemic diseases, about 25 percent on average. For reasons no one quite understands, the disease is particularly fatal in adults, which is why, in 1847, cities like Quebec and New York were playing host to an entire generation of orphaned immigrant children.

Even with these rates of infection and death, typhus is not properly defined as a contagious disease. Instead it is, as the contemporary epidemiologist Anne Hardy describes, a disease of "social dislocation."[4] Whenever large groups of people are assembled in unsanitary confines—in, say, a jail or an army camp, a poorhouse or an immigrant ship—blood from a host is soon passed to others by the growing number of lice taking refuge on unclean bodies. Infection spreads based on the movement and appetite of this tiny parasite rather than any direct contact between people. In Central Europe, where the potato crop had also failed once again, scores of starving farmers and peasants sought refuge in poorhouses. There infected lice quickly moved from one body to another. Before long, thousands were dead in Germany, where many of the victims were either displaced farmers or textile workers.[5] In Austrian Poland, more than 400,000 people would die of typhus-related illness between 1847 and 1849.

Statistics in North America were little better. By the end of May 1847, epidemics had also been reported from Nova Scotia all the way down the eastern seaboard. Boston, Philadelphia, and Baltimore all witnessed massive outbreaks; the city of New Orleans reported over a thousand cases within a month. New York was hit hardest of all. Famine immigration numbers had already doubled in the city from this time the previous year. Staten Island—New York's traditional landing place for immigrant ships—had long since overflowed the temporary buildings erected to house patients. Newspapers reported that "every corner" of the island was filled with Irish refugees, many of them sick and dying. Desperate for more space and unwilling to allow infected individuals to land in the city proper, officials began diverting affected immigrants to the lunatic asylum on Blackwell's Island. But the hospital there was already overcrowded, and its meager staff attempted to find supplemental help by enlisting inmates from the adjoining state penitentiary. Neither option lent itself to effective medical care, and the death rate rose steadily, from 10 to 30 percent. Those immigrants already in Manhattan were faring little better. It was not uncommon for forty or more individuals, penniless and desperate for lodging, to pile into single boardinghouse rooms lined only with dirty straw. At one such place, police discovered thirty-five mortally ill immigrants so incapacitated they were unable to rise off the floor. Those well enough for transport soon filled the city's hospitals, including the already notorious Bellevue. Approximately eighty individuals were admitted to the facility each day, joining the hundreds of infected individuals—most of them recently relocated from the city's almshouses—already languishing in overcrowded rooms and soiled beds.

Bellevue doctors were at a loss to make sense of this growing affliction; aside from the fever, rash, and tremors, there was little to unite the victims of the disease. Autopsies revealed severe inflammation and ulcers of the intestines in some patients, while the digestive tracts of others appeared perfectly healthy. Some patients suffered from intense diarrhea and a disruptive "gurgling" of the bowels, while others did not. Just as mystifying for the medical establishment was any consensus about effective treatment. Doctors soon determined that "brandy and milk and plenty of ice" seemed to work as well as anything else.[6] Perhaps not surprisingly, the hospital's death rate soon topped 40 percent.

Public concern about the epidemic was mitigated until people other than Irish immigrants began to fall ill. In New Orleans, residents became alarmed when the spread of ship's fever became unstoppable in the city's largest charity hospital; this alarm only intensified when it became known that employees of the treatment center were becoming ill and dying alongside their patients.[7] Meanwhile newspapers across the country memorialized Bellevue's assistant physician, Dr. Augustus Van Buren, who died while tending to the hospital's fever patients. Twenty-three years old, engaged to be married, and described by his peers as a "devoted" physician showing "more than ordinary promise," Van Buren represented the shocking new reality: well-educated, morally upright, and otherwise hale individuals in the prime of life were not immune to what had become known as the Irish affliction.[8]

A similar story in Baltimore sent more ripples of concern up and down the coast. The city's noted former mayor, Major James Law, succumbed to ship's fever, despite never having set foot on an immigrant vessel. "Let it be remembered," warned the editor of the *Southern Patriot* of Charleston, South Carolina, that this disease "makes no distinction between the native and the stranger. It is to be remembered too that an ounce of prevention is worth a pound of cure."[9] Such warnings soon pervaded other publications. When a Quaker family in Pennsylvania took in a destitute Irish family and then contracted the fever themselves and perished, fear of Irish immigrants grew to something close to hysteria.[10]

New York City officials responded to this growing concern by trying to quarantine Irish immigrants away from Manhattan. But with Blackwell's and Staten Island still well over capacity, they were hard-pressed to find the space. Officials eventually settled on the Farm on Long Island, an almshouse residence for nine hundred children. These young residents were soon dispatched to nearby Randall's Island, and renovation was begun to convert the Farm into a medical facility.[11] The outcry against this plan among Long Island residents was fierce; they objected in a series of increasingly inflammatory public hearings on the subject. When their objections appeared to go unnoticed by government officials, homeowners took matters into their own hands. Just before the stroke of midnight on May 30, a mob formed outside the Farm and set fire to the buildings, burning them all to the ground.[12]

Within a week, the Long Island mob and resultant arson became the top story of most major newspapers in North America. In many circles, the coverage valorized the participants, encouraging similar violence in other afflicted towns. So effective was this rallying cry, in fact, that the destruction of the Long Island Farm became the very emblem of direct citizen action. In Boston, residents inspired by the Long Island action attempted to summon their own mob after officials announced plans to build additional housing for fever victims on Deer Island. Within twenty-four hours of this declaration, handbills appeared throughout the city rallying people to come together to stop the plan from proceeding.

The creators of these handbills were as detailed as they were driven. Each of the posters included the precise meeting time and place for the mob, thereby assuring it would be disbanded by city police. But while law enforcement officials were able to prevent the angry group from succeeding in their plans for arson, they could do little to quell the growing collective ire. Officials in Baltimore found themselves similarly impotent against public sentiment, and thousands of people streamed into public meetings demanding that no person aboard an infected immigrant vessel be allowed entrance to the city. Clearly something needed to be done. And fast.

7

Discord on Downing Street

HENRY GREY read each report on Americans' hysteria with a detached coolness. It was unfortunate, of course, that the United States was encountering such difficulty, but that had little impact on his Irish relocation plan. If anything, Americans' resistance only abetted his project by making it that much more difficult for immigrants to land anywhere other than the timber camps and farmsteads of Canada. Quiet prudence may have been in short supply across the Atlantic, but in the British Colonial Office it remained the rule. On that its secretary insisted.

From the security of Downing Street, surrounded by the civility of tea and long lunches, anything seemed possible. Grey penned a jaunty letter to Lord Elgin, governor general of Canada, proposing that the colony take a more active role in situating the Irish now pouring into North America. Perhaps, Grey wrote, Elgin could create little settlements capable of accommodating entire Irish parishes. They could even replicate the villages in Ireland, save, of course, for the poverty and subsistence farming. And if clergymen could be induced to join the community, order and respectability would be ensured. Incentives, Grey added, would be quick in coming to those colonial officials and communities willing to take up the charge:

Her Majesty's Government have thought that they might confer much benefit on some portion of the persons who are desirous to emigrate, as well as upon the districts where they are to be settled, if they could devise the means of offering to parties proceeding from the same village or parish in this country, especially if accompanied by their clergyman or priest, the prospect of finding ready for them an opportunity of establishing themselves in a body.

Grey was quick to add that it was not in his power to convey "more than very general instructions upon the subject," but he did suggest that Elgin construct log houses "of the cheapest and simplest kind" for each of the families, along with gardens "sufficient to occupy the tenant's spare time, but insufficient solely to provide for his subsistence, or make it unnecessary that he should also work for wages." A cottage "of a somewhat better description" would be needed for the clergymen, along with a "plain and inexpensive building to serve as a school and a church." The remaining details he was delighted to cede to Elgin.[1]

Colonial officials stationed in Canada met Grey's assessment with little enthusiasm. The last thing North America needed was a torrent of immigration. Did Grey intend to offer assistance to these famine refugees once they arrived on colonial shores? Certainly, replied Grey. The British government, he wrote, would "be able to do much for the emigrant when once landed on the other side. True, they could not find him employment, but they undertook to give him full information as to where employment was to be found, and to put him in the way of getting in the cheapest manner to the market for his labour. Under this system, at a small expense, they would be able to show that emigration had proceeded most satisfactorily."[2]

The reality of Grey's program, however, was failing to inspire satisfaction, let alone confidence, in British North American officials. Continuing past practice, nearly half of the new arrivals snuck illegally into the United States rather than remaining in the Ottawa Valley, where they were supposed to be cutting timber and growing food for their mother country. Many of those who tried a life in the timber belt quickly abandoned it after it proved too brutish, mean, and short. Of these, some attempted to join the border hoppers, risking their lives in rowboats on the Great Lakes or in the deep forests of Vermont; others took up residence in the cellars and alleyways of cities like Quebec.

Not to worry, replied Grey calmly. Canadian officials would surely find solutions to these little problems.

Grey's aplomb quickly evaporated, however, each time he stepped into Westminster. There temperatures were rising as members of Parliament argued with increasing hostility the question of what should be done in Ireland. As predicted, the potato blight had returned for the third year in a row. This time the scourge made its appearance both earlier and with greater vengeance than before. Even skeptics in Parliament were forced to concede that at least three-fourths of Ireland's potato crop would soon be lost. Reports from the constabulary there suggested that even this dire prediction was too conservative; by their estimates, the blight had so insinuated itself that the very same acre once capable of producing ton upon ton of potatoes would, at best, yield one-third of a ton—barely enough to feed an individual for a month, let alone a family for a year.[3]

What should be done about the failure remained to be determined. There were those in Parliament advocating—and advocating strongly—a return to the aid policies of Peel. Others were outwardly critical of the modified system Trevelyan now shepherded, and they took to the floor of Parliament with examples aplenty. In Tralee, James Prendergast, Daniel Reilly's cousin and the man who hung his hopes on governmental intervention, discovered that his daughter-in-law was not eligible for relief since her husband had emigrated to America.[4] Nearby, a man was refused assistance "on account of his respectable appearance." He was found dead not far from the workhouse less than an hour later. His official cause of death? Starvation.

Many in Parliament were now calling for Trevelyan's removal. It didn't help that the assistant of the Treasury was unpopular among his subordinates, who were bitter about his inability to delegate meaningful work for them to do. Grey and Russell had emboldened Trevelyan to act on their behalf, and he had every intention of doing so. Trevelyan, after all, was nothing if not driven. Friends and foes alike repeatedly used words like "fervor" and "zeal" when describing his approach to just about everything. He was known on multiple continents as someone whose moral certitude was rivaled only by his reluctance to acknowledge opposition and offense in others. Arrogant, steadfast, and prone to narcissism, Charles Trevelyan was certain about the order of things in the world.

Trevelyan found ready support for his views in the offices of Earl Grey and Prime Minister Russell, both of whom looked to the young civil servant for guidance in dealing with the Irish crisis. They listened when he told them stories about his own encounter with Ireland—how he had visited the west of Ireland on the eve of the famine, when a sense of familial responsibility to a young cousin in Limerick prompted a tour in search of opportunities for the boy. Trevelyan found few and left the island alarmed by the condition of its residents, most notably the laboring population, whose lack of decency and respect for hierarchy galled him. At no time during his tenure in India did he ever feel as threatened as he did in Ireland. He resented that, deeply. Still, he reserved his greatest ire for the landlords there, whom he saw as fundamentally responsible for the colony's gross inequities.

That year alone, more than three million Irish were receiving government aid, especially in County Kerry, where indolent behavior and Catholic beliefs concerning procreation had produced an excessive population—and not just too many people, but people who, inexplicably, assumed that the potato alone would support them. The situation was unyielding: either the people had to find a way to enter the new world order or they would be destroyed by it. The famine and its blight were a local problem. The solution ought to be as well.

And so Trevelyan was soon summoned to the ramshackle building at the end of Downing Street. Once inside, he was charged with the task that would soon convert the famine from a political crisis to one of the world's most notorious genocides. Trevelyan's mandate was clear: immediately cut 20 percent of all persons receiving aid in Ireland, and phase out the system entirely within the year. In its place, Ireland would be managed not by London but by its own taxpayers. Grey and Trevelyan drew a map dividing the island into unions; each would have a board of town leaders who could raise and disperse aid at their own discretion. If they wanted soup kitchens, that was the board's decision. If they wanted to take other action or even none at all, then so be it.

To ensure that this new system would be administered properly, Grey appointed Edward Twisleton as its chief commissioner. Twisleton would serve under Trevelyan, who immediately charged his new subordinate with the task of creating temporary relief programs until the local poor unions could establish their own footing. The commissioner set to work at once, designing work-for-food schemes that had famine victims breaking stones or draining peat bogs twelve hours a day. Such projects, he wrote to Trevelyan, were designed "to be as repulsive as possible consistent with humanity."[5]

Content that his new subordinate had the Ireland crisis under control, Trevelyan took his family on an extended vacation in France.

While the Trevelyans toured the French countryside, Henry Grey stormed Parliament. The new relief scheme was not received well there, and more than ever, Grey was piqued by his peers. He accused some of trying to exacerbate the crisis; he admonished others for not "taking the trouble" to read his reports on Ireland. Had they bothered, they would have read his patronizing account of the failures of the Irish people to solve their own famine—failures Grey insisted were further evidence of the island's parochialism: "There had been much inexperience and want of knowledge—a failure on the part of all ranks in Ireland to assist and cooperate with the Government, as they ought to have done, in endeavouring to surmount this period of severe affliction." Surely, then, it was not his fault that people continued to die there. Nor, he insisted, was it the British people's responsibility. If Grey knew anything, it was that Ireland

could not remain for any considerable time in a situation dependent upon the assistance of England; that she must help herself; that she must put forth her own strength and energies; and that she must not look constantly to this country; for if she did so, the time would come, and speedily, when public opinion in England would be far too strong for any Ministry, no matter of whom it was composed, and when this system must cease. In many instances, the proprietors of Ireland had nobly done their duty; but he must repeat, what he had before stated, that this was by no means uniformly the case. This was a truth of which he was painfully convinced, and, entertaining such a conviction, he deemed it his duty to avow it.[6]

Although Grey's stance was met with opposition on the floor of Parliament, it was shared by a growing number of English people. The country was beginning to show clear signs of compassion fatigue. Two years had passed since the first failure of the potato crop, and still Ireland's difficulties showed no signs of abating. Newspaper editorials complained loudly about hard-earned English wages being sent across the Irish Sea. Political cartoons depicted the Irish as oafish and incapable of helping themselves. It was all the justification Grey needed.

Besides, the colonial secretary had little interest in dithering over how aid was administered on an island of little value to the empire. His real concern was for establishing the kind of commercial presence that would ensure Britain's place on the world stage. That was proving difficult in an age when slave labor no longer defrayed costs. So far, his best plan had been population redistribution. Each day, thousands of indigent people from the Far East—known as *coolies*—were being shipped to the Caribbean and South America to labor as indentured workers in the sugarcane fields. That the rates of mortality rivaled—and sometimes even surpassed—those of the previous generation's slave ships was of little consequence to him. As far as cheap labor was concerned, the plan was clearly working.

Despite growing insistence to the contrary, he was more convinced than ever that a similar plan could work in Canada. He increased his efforts to encourage Irish immigration there, even after members of the Canadian Colonial Office sent multiple petitions asking for an immediate halt, citing too great a strain on resources. But Grey remained steadfast. He had a feeling the North American staff were being unnecessarily shrill, no doubt influenced by the hysteria gripping their U.S. neighbors. What they needed, he decided, was a bit more time—just enough to gain a proper perspective and the opportunity to rely on their own resource-fulness. So he wrote a tepid response to the complaints, assuring Elgin that he would give the objections "serious consideration" at his first available moment. "I have to direct Your Lordship's attention to the importance of enforcing the strictest economy in affording such assistance to the immigrants as may be absolutely necessary," wrote Grey, "and of not losing sight of the danger that the grant of such assistance, if not strictly guarded, may have the effect of inducing the emigrants to relax their exertions to provide for themselves."[7] When that moment finally arrived several months later, North American officials were more than a little disappointed with the response.

8

Visitations from a Vengeful God

HAD GREY SEEN the devastating misery at Grosse Île, he might have been less tempered in his response. Since the start of the shipping season, conditions on the quarantine island had gone from bad to worse. By mid-May they were cataclysmic. More than twelve thousand immigrants languished on the island, long since filled to capacity. "I have not a bed to lay them on or a place to put them," Douglas wrote to Elgin. Yet the vessels continued to pour into the St. Lawrence and were now anchored in a queue that stretched for over two miles. Conditions on board were almost too ghastly to be believed, continued Douglas. While inspecting a single vessel that day, he found

> that 106 were ill of fever, including nine of the crew, and the large number of 158 had died on the passage, including the first and second officers and seven of the crew, and the master and steward dying, the few that were able to come on deck were ghastly yellow looking spectres, unshaven and hollow cheeked, and, without exception, the worst looking passengers I have ever seen; not more than six or eight were really healthy and able to exert themselves.[1]

This was saying quite a lot for a man who had already witnessed a lifetime of suffering in the short month since Grosse Île had opened. Barely three weeks earlier, the *Syria* had been the first vessel of the season to arrive. Not long after leaving the docks of Liverpool, more than two hundred of her passengers fell ill; nine of these individuals died and were buried at sea. Shortly after arriving at Grosse Île, the vessel brought with it the quarantine station's first fatality of the season: Ellen Keane, the four-year-old daughter of a weaver and his wife from Mayo. In the two weeks following Ellen's death, forty other passengers perished while on the island. As troubling as these figures were, however, they paled in comparison to news arriving with subsequent ships: 213 passengers had died at sea; an additional 776 (25 percent of all on board) were diagnosed as suffering from ship's fever and in grave need of medical attention. By the second week of the shipping season, Douglas's hospital was already well over capacity, with four hundred sick immigrants; another three hundred languished aboard ships while they waited for a bed.

In response to these new figures, Douglas strengthened quarantine policy, requiring all passengers, sick or healthy, to submit to longer stays on the island. Grosse Île may have looked like a pastoral island retreat, but it was as much a military fortification as anything else. For the first time since the great cholera epidemic of 1832, Douglas requested the return of the British military to the island. They soon arrived, arming garrisons to sequester the sick from the healthy and manning a large cannon battery in the middle of the island. Pilots delivered warnings to approaching vessels: any captain who did not observe the mandatory anchorage at the island or who attempted to depart before receiving clearance from George Douglas himself would be fired upon until incapacitated.

Douglas also requested that an additional hospital be built and that healthy passengers be moved to nearby Cliff Island, where they could be properly quarantined from the sick and the dead. Both requests were denied. He had no choice but to require healthy passengers to remain on their beleaguered vessels. He would arrange for their effects to be disinfected there and for a daily visit by one of the hospital staff. It was a breach of quarantine law, he knew, but with more than ten thousand people already on the island, he insisted he had no choice. In response, colonial officials agreed to send over an additional four doctors to assist. They also sent another detachment of troops and military tents, along with the suggestion that Douglas pitch these tents on his own farm. As Douglas wrote his cool response, a violent storm swept through the region, sheering away Grosse Île's decrepit wharf. Conditions, he reported, were about as dire as they could get.

With public attention to Douglas's reports growing, George Mountain, Quebec's Anglican bishop, arranged a visit to Grosse Île. He was shocked by what he found there and wrote his superiors that Douglas's reports were indeed accurate: "Conditions, it seemed, could get little worse. Typhus sufferers languished outside in rain storms, covered in rags so populated with lice and fleas that the fabric seemed to move of its own accord. Beds in the newly erected tents contained three or four filthy children each, some of whom had long since died. Orphans sat on piles of unclaimed luggage. Dysentery and disease was rampant." Mountain concluded, "The impression produced upon my mind was that of the hopelessness of doing anything effectual to stay the consequences of such a visitation from the hand of God. A little abatement, a momentary breathing space, was followed by a thickening influx of squalid misery and fatal disease."

Worst of all, no one was immune, including the medical staff themselves. The first to fall was the quarantine hospital's chaplain, who had worked nonstop for over ten days without even bothering to bathe or change clothes. When doctors attempted to tend to him, they first had to scrape his boots and stockings from his feet.[2] Twenty-two of Douglas's twenty-six staff doctors were also sick. Over a dozen of his nurses had died.[3] Finding replacements was all but out of the question: no one in his right mind would willingly take on a position with such mortality rates. Still Douglas persisted, first asking for, then demanding, then pleading for any kind of assistance the government was willing to offer. In the meantime, resident British soldiers stood in, doing their best to tend to the sick and the dying. Increasingly it was the latter who required their greatest attention. Many of the ships arriving now were so inundated with illness that no one aboard was well enough to help. Each day soldiers and priests ferried out to the vessels to collect the dead.

Overwhelmed by reports such as Bishop Mountain's, Canadian officials arranged to have three large steamers—the *Quebec*, the *Queen*, and the *Rowland Hill*—transport seven thousand immigrants directly to Montreal, where the city's hospitals could provide additional quarantine.[4] Few observers doubted that this was but a stop-gap attempt to avert what was about to become a far greater tide of sick immigrants.

They were right. By the second week in June, it was clear that another year of failed potato harvests in Ireland had exacerbated the already dire famine there. New York City alone had already received nearly twenty thousand immigrants, thousands of whom had succumbed to disease and now lay buried in overfilled cemeteries. In Boston, the "ship's fever" had become so virulent that even the 185-acre Deer Island was overfilled with affected immigrants. Residents of the city, still embittered by their inability to prevent a quarantine station on the island, decided once and for all that they had had enough. Hundreds of them stormed Boston's wharves, forcing the harbormaster to turn away the immigrant schooner *Mary*, claiming that her passengers would become an undue burden on the already strapped city.

A disaster of this magnitude required a scapegoat of similar stature, and as far as Alexander Buchanan, chief emigration agent in Quebec, was concerned, the culprits were obvious. Writing to Earl Grey, he insisted that the crisis plaguing North America was, more than anything, caused by insufficient shipping regulations and an inability to control the unscrupulous behaviors of ship owners. He was supported in his claim by Robert Whyte, a cabin passenger aboard the immigrant vessel *Ajax*. Many of his observations on the ship, Whyte wrote, were "too disgusting to be repeated." What he was willing to report included an illuminating account of the inequities and suffering on board. Sailors were given daily rations of beef or pork, along with biscuits, coffee, sugar, and lime juice. The immigrants, on the other hand, were given a half-pound of oatmeal—most of which, Whyte reported, was "bad." Their only means of hydration was "nauseous ditch water" that was "quite foul, muddy, and bitter."[5]

Initially these conditions were the cause of great consternation on board. Passengers complained about their rations and fought over the two meager cooking fires on deck—the only means of making their oatmeal palatable. By the second week of the voyage, however, this tension had been replaced with a collective terror over the escalating death rate on the ship. Dysentery plagued many; the faces and feet of some passengers were "swollen to double their natural size and covered with black putrid spots." In many cases, victims were so disfigured that their own families were unable to identify them. Other immigrants would appear perfectly well, only to drop to the deck without warning, "screaming violently and writhing in agony." So pervasive was the collective suffering, Whyte said, that "the moaning and raving kept" him awake for days on end. And if that wasn't bad enough, the "effluvium of the hold" was so "shocking" he could think about little else.[6]

Small wonder, then, that illness rates on ships like Whyte's were as high as 75 percent or that mortality rates were increasing in kind, surpassing the deaths on both the coolie and slave ships. It was no surprise to anyone that the vessels carrying Irish refugees were now known as "coffin ships." Death, it seemed, followed them everywhere.

While at sea, crew members disposed of the deceased by launching them overboard, consigning the bodies to the anonymous depths of the North Atlantic. Once in the shallows of the St. Lawrence, however, no such invisibility existed. While anchored at Grosse Île, sailors removed the dead from below deck with grappling hooks, and several eyewitness accounts reported that bodies of the "barely dead" were inofficiously cast overboard, often without so much as a shroud or covering.[7] Others described a crude pulley system used by sailors to remove bodies from ships and transport them to the island. It was, wrote one eyewitness, an indisputably ghastly scene:

> On deck a rope was placed around the emaciated form of the Irish peasant, father, mother, wife and husband, sister and brother. The rope was hoisted and with their heads and naked limbs dangling for a moment in mid-air, with the wealth of hair of the Irish maiden, or young Irish matron, or the silvery locks of the poor old grandmother floating in the breeze, they were finally lowered over

the ship's side in the boats, rowed to the island, and left on the rocks until such time as they were coffined.[8]

Commingling with the cadavers were entire families of immigrants, too terrified by the mysterious sickness either to enter the island hospital or to return to their ships. Among them were a disproportionate number of orphans, many naked or nearly so, and without a sense of the direness of their fate. A visiting clergyman wrote in painful detail of one young child who sat for hours playing with the hand of his dead mother.[9]

An Anglican priest wrote to Bishop Mountain that the inadequacies of the island were only intensifying this suffering. "There are a number of cooks and nurses," Father Horan reported, "but never enough. From every side people are asking for food, and when you see how thin most of these poor wretches are, you have no doubt that lack of food is the principal cause of their sickness."[10] Horan and the other priests worked beyond exhaustion, often called in the middle of the night to administer last rites. Each day they traversed the island on foot, calling upon the suffering. Douglas tried to alleviate their hardship and even offered them use of his horse and cart once a day, but any more than that was an impossibility; he too was stretched beyond reason.[11]

Testifying before a special committee, Douglas reported that conditions had deteriorated so badly that the island had become more of a mortuary than a hospital. Six men were employed around the clock to dig graves; by the end of the season, this mass graveyard would encompass over six acres of land. Overwhelmed by the number of bodies awaiting burial, quarantine workers moved cadavers in wheelbarrows to the island's deadhouse, where they were left to wait in piles of wood chips until they could be buried.[12] Those refugees hale enough for hard labor were busy digging long ditches that served as mass graves, covering the layers of bodies with only a few inches of soil. Ship captains and crew members reported that the overwhelming smell of decomposition lingered for over a mile downwind of the site.[13] With so many individuals dying so rapidly, neither the workers nor the geography of the rocky island could keep pace. Eventually officials in Quebec were forced to send barges filled with dirt from the mainland to ensure that all bodies were interred.[14]

Meanwhile the number of stricken immigrants on the island—now fifteen thousand by Douglas's count—overwhelmed the capacity of the hospital and sheds several times over.[15] Quarantine workers enlisted the assistance of waiting ships' crew members to build a village of crude tents constructed out of salvaged ship masts, spars, and sail canvas. Viewed from the decks of the waiting vessels, the scene had a decidedly spectral quality to it: splintered pikes lodged into the rocky soil, covered with tattered and billowing canvas. Below these shrouds sat dozens of emaciated survivors, their gaunt faces a sober reminder of the suffering in Ireland and out at sea.

Douglas and his staff were showing their own signs of strain. Reports were now surfacing that island priests, nurses, cooks, police officers, and undertakers had fallen victim to the disease. Though he tried to hide it, Douglas too had contracted typhus. His fever soon rose dangerously high, plaguing him with severe chills; his body was wracked with pain, and his head felt as if it might split open. Despite protests from his wife, he continued to work. Each morning, nearly delirious, he stumbled to his horse, draping himself across the animal's neck as he rode from the farm to the hospital. He had no choice. His best doctors were dying; others, overwhelmed by the horror of it all, had fled. He had tried to secure suitable replacements but soon discovered that the only individuals willing to set foot on the island were what he called "profligates of the worst kind, who came to prey upon the helpless."[16] When the *Wadsworth*, one of the few coffin ships to travel with a surgeon on board, landed, their doctor offered to remain on the island. Douglas readily accepted. The ship's doctor was dead within a week.

9

A Course for Disaster

A s ships inundated by illness continued to arrive, the *Quebec Gazette* began devoting a column to the names of immigrants who had unclaimed letters at the post office. By June that list consumed almost the entire front page of the paper. Ads begging for information about loved ones also littered the pages of nearly every paper in Canada and the eastern United States.[1] Their implication was clear: thousands of people had failed to make landfall, their bodies defeated by starvation and disease and now left to drift in the North Atlantic.

Meanwhile what had begun as a steady flow of new immigrants was now an unmanageable torrent for the ill-prepared city of Quebec. With death tolls in the thousands, doctors and undertakers in the city proper found themselves stretched dangerously thin. More than four hundred orphaned immigrant children were languishing in the city's churches, schools, and hospitals, none of which was prepared to house them. Those immigrants still well enough to escape hospitalization lingered in boatyards and public houses, looking for work and food. They mobbed shipping agents, slept in alleys, and wandered the streets, looking for places to bury their dead. To any observer, Quebec appeared a city in the last throes of a particularly grisly war.

The scene was more than John Munn could bear. Many of the ships he built were now employed in the immigration efforts, carrying Irish refugees not only to North America but now also to Sydney, Calcutta, and other far-flung places. Munn's barque the *John Bolton* lost 141 immigrants during its summer crossing. Several others had arrived in New York, Norfolk, and New Orleans and were awaiting clearance. Miraculously two of his favorites, the *Fame* and the *Lord Canterbury*, had just passed quarantine in his own city of Quebec with only one immigrant death between them. Others, like the *Douce Davie* and the *Highland Mary*, were not so lucky. Like the dozens of other famine ships, they were forced to lay at anchor off the island quarantine station of Grosse Île, where their casualties quickly mounted. Munn tried to stave off the crisis as best he could. He agreed to take over guardianship of six of the famine ships held up in quarantine; he managed to employ a dozen or so Irish immigrants looking for work; he again led the entire city in money donated for the Irish relief fund. But he knew it wasn't enough to mitigate the extent of a tragedy just beginning.

Construction continued at his shipyard. His workers completed the *Cromwell* first, followed soon after by the *Blake*. Desperate for good news, the press covered their launch with grand treatment, offering subscribers detailed accounts of the event, including descriptions of the cannon fire and visits to the flag-bedecked vessels by local dignitaries. Somehow, as long as John Munn was launching one of his vessels, a tiny vestige remained of life as people once knew it.

A month later, Munn prepared for what promised to be an even more dramatic event: the double launching of the *England* and the *Jeanie Johnston*. Both were vessels of exceptional quality; a surveyor from Lloyd's Register, the leading surveyor and ship classification society, gave the two ships first-rate designations. For their maiden voyages, Munn chose two accomplished naval men as masters: George Rocke would skipper the *England*, and Matthew Armstrong, a decorated veteran of the Patriots' War, would captain the *Jeanie*. Perhaps as a way of showing her owner's preference, the crew would launch the 123-foot *Jeanie* first, allowing the unremarkable barque to lead the much grander *England*, first to the Customs House for registration and then to Liverpool, where she would await a buyer. The event symbolized not only the return of the great wright but what promised to be his domination of the North American shipbuilding industry.

News of this auspicious launch should have made the front page of every newspaper in Quebec, not to mention the shipping reports in London and beyond. And yet not a single paper mentioned the story. In fact for the first time ever, reports on British ship construction had ceased altogether. No ship, no matter how grand, could compete with the worsening crisis plaguing Ireland and now the rest of the world.

Munn hardly noticed the omission. As he stood on the edge of his shipyard, watching the *England* and his stout little *Jeanie* departing for the docks of Liverpool, he looked visibly concerned. Given her overall size and dimensions, the *Jeanie* would probably join the growing roll call of coffin ships plying the Atlantic with famine refugees. The larger *England* might escape that fate and become a Pacific hauler. Still, she too would have to land in Liverpool before being recommissioned. This did not sit well with the shipwright, who knew he was tempting fate with the voyages. By sending these two ships to Liverpool, he was also dispatching their crews right into the heart of one of the century's biggest catastrophes. Worst of all, he knew, those on board would be helpless to combat it.

From the moment the *Jeanie Johnston* left her dock at the Munn yard, the ship and her crew had a front-row seat to much of the drama unfolding on both sides of the Atlantic. The port of Quebec was quiet on June 18, 1847, an unexpectedly sultry day, with little wind and temperatures in the upper 90s. But as still as the harbor may have been, there was plenty of drama to be had farther out in the Gulf.

As Armstrong guided the *Jeanie Johnston* through the Gulf of the St. Lawrence, he passed the *Wadsworth*, the *Scotland*, and the *George*. Later Armstrong would learn that each of these three vessels lost well over a hundred passengers to typhus and starvation.

Even without knowing the precise death toll, Armstrong and his men could tell that many of the immigrant ships were in trouble. The surface of the St. Lawrence was cluttered with obstacles: mattresses and fiddles, teapots and trunks, aprons and trousers—all personal effects of fever victims that had been cast off by crew or fellow passengers thinking that doing so might stave off contagion.[2] Passing Grosse Île, Armstrong and his crew observed no fewer than eighty-four coffin ships anchored around the island. The mob of stricken vessels made navigating the *Jeanie* difficult, even with the mandatory addition of a Quebec pilot to oversee her course.

During the early days of the *Jeanie*'s maiden voyage, Armstrong was kept abreast of the growing crisis through regular contact with incoming ships, many of which were flying their distress flags or laying anchor until the crew was well enough to continue. Their conversations were necessarily terse. Although Morse code had been invented in 1838 and the telegraph in 1846, neither was available to captains like Armstrong, who relied on centuries-old technology at sea, particularly where communication was concerned. By tacking up close to another vessel, he and other captains communicated with one another through brass trumpets, a kind of narrow megaphone about two feet in length used to broadcast news from ship to ship. What Armstrong heard bellowing from the decks of these distressed ships only confirmed what he and Munn had already assumed: that the scene awaiting the *Jeanie* in Liverpool was, inconceivably, even more dire than the one he was leaving in North America.

Once the *Jeanie* and her crew made their way into the Atlantic proper, communication between ships diminished considerably. The chief task now became the assessment of the barque's seaworthiness. The open waters of the North Atlantic challenged the design and craftsmanship of any vessel. That was particularly true for a new wooden ship whose planks would swell and sometimes warp or whose caulking was all that prevented water from flooding the hold. Armstrong's men kept hourly track of the hull and bilge, looking for any sign that the *Jeanie* might be taking on water. They watched the keelson and ribs for signs of strain or splintering; they found none. They worked the hundreds of lines connecting sails to the thick wooden yards and the yards to the *Jeanie*'s enormous masts. Each watch was instructed to look for chafing and wear; a mislaid line or carelessly set rigging could tear through a sail or even an entire mast. None was apparent.

The directions in which a sailboat can travel are known as points of sail. Thanks to the placement and angle of its sails, a contemporary cruising sloop or even a traditional schooner has a fairly wide radius, or broad points of sail. A square-rigged vessel like the *Jeanie Johnston*, on the other hand, could not sail closer than 75 degrees to the true wind. As a result, Captain Armstrong had considerably fewer choices about where he could point his vessel. In the North Atlantic, more often than not, that meant pointing her directly into oncoming weather, requiring continuous heavy work for the crew, with little rest. At every wind shift, Armstrong would call all hands on deck to tack the *Jeanie* or turn her about. A constant team of men worked below, pumping out the bilge as the barque's new seams gapped against the bounding surf.

Aiding the men in their bid to cross these tumultuous waters were the most minimal of tools. They relied heavily on the vessel's weather-glass, a precursor to the barometer in the shape of a teardrop. Filled with colored water, the glass and its accompanying tulle allowed the crew to predict the series of storms that would batter their vessel on this voyage.[3] Equally as important was the ship's "log," a triangular piece of wood invested with lead and tied to a knotted rope. When launched from the stern, the log would immediately sink in the water, pulling out knotted line as it did. A crewman would then count the number of knots that passed by over a thirty-second period, thereby determining the speed of the vessel as measured in "knots," which were then carefully pegged on the vessel's traverse board.[4] This information, coupled with the painstaking navigational records maintained by Armstrong, gave the crew of the *Jeanie Johnston* their most crucial piece of knowledge for the safety of all those on board: knowing where they were.

Armstrong's two most important tools, however, were his compass and sextant, which he used to direct the vessel in a northeasterly arc that would send them to Liverpool. The weather was in his favor throughout the voyage, with breezes from the west that held steady from day to day. With this guaranteed wind from astern, the *Jeanie* maintained an easy speed of 6 knots across the Atlantic. Munn had been generous in his provisioning of the vessel, and the ease of the passage, coupled with these stores, allowed the men to maintain a comfort and regularity not often seen on the North Atlantic. It was a welcome relief, particularly after the scene that witnessed their departure.

As the *Jeanie* neared the Celtic Sea, however, traffic began to increase. The men stood longer watches at the bowsprit and high up in the topmasts, where they had a nearly limitless view of the growing number of ships heading westward. The possibility of collision was significant, and Armstrong relied on his watch to keep him abreast of any other vessel in the area.

Congestion continued to build as the *Jeanie* neared her destination, passing dozens of ships each day—all headed outbound, and most carrying hordes of Irish people. By the time Armstrong rounded Ireland and set his sights on the port of Liverpool, that flow had become a nautical traffic jam.

The one-time locus of the global slave trade, Liverpool had long since established a notorious reputation as a place where everything—and everyone—could be rendered into a commodity. Herman Melville, who visited about the same time that the *Jeanie* was making her arrival, had much to say about the port city and its new Irish population:

> It seemed hard to believe that such an array of misery could be furnished by any town in the world. Old women, rather mummies, drying up with slow and starving age; young girls, incurably sick, who ought to have been in the hospital; sturdy men with the gallows in their eyes, and whining lie in their mouths; young boys, hollow-eyed and decrepit; and puny mothers, holding up puny babes in the glare of the sun, formed the main features of the season.[5]

His friend and contemporary, Nathaniel Hawthorne, agreed. Immediately upon arriving, Hawthorne insisted that famine-era Liverpool was the "most detestable place a residence that ever my lot was cast in—smoky, noisy, dirty, pestilential." Hawthorne was appalled by the number of Irish paupers and their struggle to get by. Their lives, he wrote, appeared marked by filth and resignation: "At every two or three steps, a gin-shop; also filthy in clothes and persons, ragged, pale, often afflicted with humors, women, nursing their babies on dirty bosoms; men haggard, drunken, care-worn, hopeless, but with a kind of patience, as if all this were the rule of their life."[6]

Like it or not, it was to this vista that Armstrong and his men had arrived and where, for the rest of the shipping season, the *Jeanie Johnston* would remain. While waiting for a buyer, Munn had secured a berth for the *Jeanie* at Liverpool's new Brunswick docks, specifically designed to accommodate the growing North American timber trade. The quayside there, engineered with just enough slope to facilitate the unloading of timber, now held millions of cubic feet of pine, stretching from nearby railways all the way to the water's edge. On the river proper, flood gates and concrete walls protected the *Jeanie* and other North American timber ships from the harsh tides and even harsher weather that battered western England. Still, it was not a commodious location. The economic depression ensured that the Brunswick dock was packed to capacity with empty vessels, some similar to the *Jeanie*'s modest dimensions, others fully rigged ships that towered over her masts, still others smoke-spewing examples of the new steamers that would soon dominate the world's oceans. And, like the *Jeanie*, nearly all of these vessels were for sale.

It was common for nineteenth-century ship owners to advertise their vessels in one of the multiple Liverpool newspapers. Indeed publications like the *Liverpool Mercury* included dozens of such ads during the fall of 1847. But Munn chose not to advertise the *Jeanie* here, perhaps assuming that his reputation and the quality of his ship would speak for themselves. By now his reputation preceded him in all of the right ways. He was known throughout Liverpool as a wright who insisted on—and consistently delivered—meticulously high standards. He was also known as a man of unquestionable character. Like Munn's other vessels, the *Jeanie* was registered solely in his name and was listed by his Liverpool agent.[7] Each of his ships would eventually secure a buyer keen to capitalize on the wright's reputation.

The barque's temporary crew did not have this luxury of time. After stepping off the *Jeanie*, they occupied themselves with the task of finding their next ship on which to sail. For most of them, that meant a return to Quebec as crew members aboard one of any number of immigrant ships described by the *London Times* as so heinous that they made the Black Hole of Calcutta seem "a mercy."[8]

It didn't take long for Captain Armstrong to see why the Liverpool docks had become so notorious. From his vantage near the barque's wheelhouse, he watched the dozens of packet steamers and ships vying for position in the overcrowded port. Each was filled with some of the 100,000 Irish immigrants who would arrive in Liverpool that season alone. Many of these refugees were already showing signs of infection. Nevertheless new arrivals were herded into sheds or onto the city wharf, where they would remain packed together until they could be transported out to the waiting ships.

Suspended in this geographic and cultural limbo, few Irish immigrants had the means to make themselves safe and comfortable while awaiting their passage across the Atlantic. From the moment they stepped off the transport ships, immigrants were surrounded by runners and crimps—con artists who made their living by selling forged ship tickets, leasing nonexistent boardinghouse rooms, or stealing luggage. Those immigrants who actually found—and could afford—lodging in Liverpool were packed by the dozens into single rooms, where they were instructed to utilize the limited floor space by sleeping in shifts. By some estimates, more than thirty-five thousand Irish lived in Liverpool under these conditions for much of the summer.[9] Theirs was a largely hidden existence, tucked into cellars and alleys and away from the brightly lit world of commerce and trade.

Infection spread rapidly in such conditions; by the time the *Jeanie Johnston* arrived, more than eighteen hundred Irish people had died in these refuges. In the ensuing months, an additional sixty thousand people in the city would contract typhus; the majority of them would not survive. More than 2,300 would be interred in a single crypt at St. Anthony's Catholic Church, where bodies were stacked from the floor to the ceiling. Countless others were laid to rest in Liverpool's other burial grounds.

Even Henry Grey's most ardent supporters began to admit alarm about this situation. Indeed by the time the *Jeanie Johnston* arrived in Liverpool that August, few doubted the cataclysmic extent of the epidemic now molesting the city. Leading the opposition were the newly installed Irish members of Parliament, who demanded that Irish emigrants be treated with at least as much consideration as convicts aboard transport ships. For years Parliament had required that these prisoner vessels not carry cargo and humans simultaneously and that they provide the convicts with both a shipboard doctor and provisions that included weekly allotments of meat. The captains and owners of famine ships were under no such obligation. Why?

Earl Grey was forced to concede. Speaking before Parliament, he "grieved to say that it was too true that the Government had received accounts of most deplorable sufferings endured by the emigrants. He had anticipated that this would be the case, and his anticipation had unfortunately turned out to be too correct." The reason, he suggested, must be the "mere change of life" inherent in leaving one's homeland, coupled with the "weakened state" of famine victims, rather than any deleterious conditions aboard the ships. Yes, he had heard about the number of deaths and the overrun quarantine stations throughout North America. He insisted, though, that the "scale of immigration" he envisioned could not only still be enacted but could be successful without any official governmental support for the immigrants.[10] Surely the Colonial Office could rectify these problems with some added precautions at key medical outposts.

But precisely which precautions remained anyone's guess. The leading practice of the time found doctors prescribing typhus victims a toxic tincture of nitrous acid gas that they were to inhale through a pipe. Other physicians preferred the repeated inducement of vomiting, along with doses of opium, Epsom salts, lead, arsenic, or turpentine. If that didn't work, patients would also endure blistering, a shaved head, the application of leeches, or baths of vinegar and mustard—all vigorously applied to instill confidence in patients until they (no doubt mercifully) died.

City officials took their own steps to stem the disease, largely by seeking to sequester it from legal residents. One such precaution was the construction of a series of lazarettos in the Mersey River, where it was thought that this addition could keep the sickness from penetrating the city itself. Floating islands of pine and oak, these barges measured nearly an acre in size and were said to have a carrying capacity of forty thousand individuals. Provisional nods to safety had also been granted to this new landing stage: a lighthouse was fashioned at one end to prevent collisions, and a fortified iron bridge connected the platform to the main Liverpool pier.[11]

What wasn't considered, however, was the fact that, at full capacity, each person on this barge would be allotted just over one square foot of standing space: perfect conditions for infected lice to hop from one immigrant to another. Nor were officials—or anyone else—aware that typhus has a gestation period of fourteen days, during which time a sufferer shows no apparent symptoms. Thus those individuals given a clean bill of health by one of the immigration officials would immediately be granted permission to board a waiting immigrant ship, often carrying infected lice or the disease themselves. That vessel—and the typhus-infected lice—would be well under way before anyone realized they were in trouble.

Henry Grey didn't know this, of course. Nor did he know that his laissez-faire policies had turned this already deplorable situation into a tinderbox. Blinded by his own moral rectitude, he continued to urge the vessels on. Once he was content that the trade was moving apace, he picked up his pen and wrote to Lord Elgin, who had been eagerly awaiting a response to his earlier plea for help. Surely Grey would write and assure him that the crisis was coming to an end.

That's not the letter Elgin received, however.

In his long-awaited dispatch, Grey insisted that the suffering endured by the immigrants was not the responsibility of the British government. Any death or damage, he explained, "did not appear to have been produced, or aggravated by our measures, or by our having neglected any precautions that it was in our power to adopt." Despite the protestations to the contrary made by people like Father Horan and others toiling at Grosse Île, Grey insisted that, if anything, the casualties were probably caused by an excess of free food given to people long accustomed to starvation.[12]

With this in mind, he urged Lord Elgin to take no more state action than was absolutely necessary, assuring him that the unaided immigrants would find their own way on the new continent. "I have to direct Your

Lordship's attention to the importance of enforcing the strictest economy in affording such assistance to the immigrants as may be absolutely necessary," Grey wrote, "and of not losing sight of the danger that the grant of such assistance, if not strictly guarded, may have the effect of inducing the emigrants to relax their exertions to provide for themselves." Meanwhile Britain would do all that it could to keep the tide of immigrants coming. North America, he insisted, would find a way to rise to the occasion.[13]

George Douglas did not respond to Grey's dispatch, which was sent to all colonial employees. Instead he quietly tended to the sixteen thousand people still on the island. As the shipping season came to an end in September, Douglas prepared to close the quarantine station for the winter. Those still living had been transported to Montreal and Quebec City, where their fate was left to someone other than the exhausted doctor. Once the island was empty of its patients, Douglas and his remaining staff fumigated the sheds and tents. They stacked bed frames and burned mattresses. They celebrated the birth of his new son, George—the first new life to visit the island after so many months of death and despair. Then, in late October, as the first snow swirled around the island, they made a somber processional to the hummocked rows of mass graves at the island's west end. The eighteen men brought with them a small stone pillar marking the sacrifice of so many: the four quarantine doctors who died of typhus that summer; the attendants and nurses and priests and cooks who succumbed along with them; the thousands of immigrants who now lay in their quiet graves. It was a private ceremony, without fanfare or political agenda. And for that, it was all the more poignant.

10

Pestilence and Plague

A S THE START of yet another winter bore down on Ireland's west, Daniel Reilly struggled to make sense of the scene around him. Life was now marked by the kind of pestilence and plague suffered in the Old Testament. An unrelenting rain that summer had encouraged the blight to blanket all of western Ireland, taking with it the last of the remaining potatoes. That was bad enough, but now the grain crop was suffering as well. Just before harvest time, Daniel and the other farmers around Tralee battled a cloud of locusts miles long and more numerable than any army of insects on record. Once the insect cloud lifted, the farmers found much of their grain had been destroyed by the assault. Not long afterward, Tralee's civic leaders made a discovery as inexplicable as it was troubling: the town lost all of its potable water. Somehow the entire supply had become poisoned with salt.[1]

But the most apocalyptic stories were those of the continuing famine and subsequent epidemic. Landlords were hiring armies of local men to guard their meager patches of turnips and cabbage. The houses of fever victims were being pulled down on top of the victims inside; for most neighbors, the risk of going in to retrieve the bodies was just too great. Their fear was fed by newspaper reports and doomsday scenarios. "A pestilent fever, more mortal and destructive than cholera or plague," wrote the editor of the *Tralee Chronicle*, "is carrying off the poor. The dead are barely pushed outside the thresholds, and there suffered to dissolve in an advanced state of putrefaction."[2] Throughout the region, every cemetery was overcrowded with uncoffined dead. Graves were shallow and often redug to accommodate additional victims. Some cottages were said to be surrounded by "ramparts of human bones," often rising in a ring several feet high and encircling a dwelling; their surviving occupants were too weak to dispose of the bodies any other way.[3] There were accounts of dogs and other animals tearing apart the dead.[4] Those on the scene of such scavenging claimed that what remained of the bodies was better suited for a small sack than a coffin. And that was just the beginning. In one particularly horrible case, the *Chronicle* reported that a father and son were found lying dead in the doorway of their cottage, three of the father's fingers still half chewed in the mouth of the son.[5]

Meanwhile the death count kept climbing. Each morning, as Daniel walked the road connecting Ballybeggan and Tralee, the rising sun revealed additional casualties: three, four, five, sometimes even more famine victims who collapsed of hunger or fever while trying to make their way to the city workhouse. Their mouths and chins were stained green from a last meal of grass and nettles. He passed women with dead children slung over their shoulders, hoping to make their way to a cemetery—any cemetery— where their sons and daughters could at least receive a proper burial. Once there, they often had to dig the graves themselves; undertakers were just too stretched with their gruesome task of burying the mounting dead. In at least one case, grave workers were no longer even bothering to distinguish between the dead and the nearly so: both were piled into wheelbarrows and placed into the filling trenches, in which survivors crawled around in search of anything edible, their arms and legs discolored and bloated; others, barely alive, knelt or lay supine, begging for food.

It wouldn't take long before Daniel Reilly would have no choice but to join them. What remained of his crop that hadn't been ravaged by the locusts had been all but wiped out by the pervasive rains that had deluged Ireland that summer. For the first time in his life, he was nearly penniless, and he was forced to harvest his grain weeks before it was ready. This early harvest would barely cover expenses; too much of it had to be dedicated to food for his family and his animals. Once his grain was sold, Daniel would be hard-pressed to find money for simple comforts like clothes and blankets. Margaret was doing her best to stretch what they had. She spent her days trying to patch Daniel's work clothes and make new trousers for Robert. Nearly two years old now, the boy was growing rapidly. Thanks to Margaret's care, he was largely oblivious to the catastrophe surrounding him. The meager profits from that year's grain harvest were all but spent at the Tralee market, where food was at a premium and selections were abysmal. With the economic depression created by the famine, few shopkeepers even bothered to replenish their stores. Somehow Margaret found ways to make meals out of more than they had. For now, at least, no one in the Reilly house was going hungry.

But that didn't necessarily make them safe. The government's decision to localize aid was proving ruinous, and residents were growing restless. The Quakers, having long since exhausted their own resources, shut down their soup kitchens after local governments assured them that similar stations would be established by the taxpayers. Certain that the government would succeed where they were failing, the Friends instead dedicated their remaining funds to establishing long-term relief programs. The local boards of guardians, however, soon discovered just how difficult the task of feeding the hungry was. They lacked the infrastructure needed to manage their food supplies, which soon ran out. Workhouses, poorhouses, and hospitals began to fill. Hungry people clamored for the opportunity to try Edward Twisleton's repulsive work-for-food schemes; the lucky few selected soon found they were too weak to complete the work.

Not surprisingly, desperation soon turned into violence. Throngs of famine sufferers stormed docklands, seizing bacon and bread from overwhelmed sailors. Not long afterward, a mob appeared at the Tralee workhouse gates, brandishing a black flag and shovels and shouting that if they were not given work they would starve. The workhouse overseer escaped to the nearby military barracks, insisting that his life—and those of Tralee's residents—were in danger.[6] Parliament agreed and quickly dispatched military troops to "repress any outbreak among the people," as merchants like Donovan continued to move Daniel's grain from Ireland to the markets in England. The dragoons, it was said in Parliament, were expected to be stationed in Tralee "for some time."

This was no place to keep a family or raise a child. Robert was now walking. Margaret was pregnant again. In a matter of months, they would have two children to shepherd into this uncertain world. It was time to leave, and Daniel knew just where they had to go: Indiana, a little state on the edge of the American West.

It might have seemed a curious choice, this state Daniel had never visited and knew about only from letters. Still, it was the closest thing to home he would find in North America. No one remembered who had first settled there, but for two decades the people of Tralee had slowly been making their way to the heartland of the United States. Their successive journeys were part of the same chain of migration happening throughout Ireland: one family or group of families safely made their way across the Atlantic, found work, and set up homes. The next season, they sent money back to Ireland. A few months later, a father or brother or friend would join them, followed by another. It was comforting to know that people you loved were waiting for you—that they had a place for you to stay, that they knew how and where to find work.

Daniel had ties to Indiana: a man named Michael Reilly, age twenty-six, was listed as head of his household on the Indiana census. Living with him was Cornelius, age twenty-four; probably one of the men was Daniel's brother. Certainly they were at least cousins, as were John, Patrick, and Honora, three teenagers who also resided in Michael's home. Perhaps their parents—an older sister or brother of Michael's—died on their voyage over. Maybe Michael and Cornelius agreed to become the teenagers' guardians while the parents remained in Ireland, hoping to earn enough money for their own passage. Probably they sent money back to Ireland to assist people like Daniel in his own voyage. There were other people from Tralee living nearby as well. Together they offered the promise of community in a town with the reassuring name of Liberty.

Indiana had big plans for the coming decade: hundreds of miles of railroad lines, canals, and roads, along with new schools and hospitals. There was plenty of railroad work already in Liberty, along with schools for Robert and shops filled with food. That was all Daniel needed to hear. When the next season's coffin ships began departing Ireland, the Reillys would be on one. Whether they were among the fortunate ones who made it to the other side would be up to fate to decide.

11

An Audacious Plan

FATE WOULD no doubt play a part in the Reillys' future. But as it turned out, Nicholas Donovan played an even greater one. The Whigs' decision to locate famine relief in Irish unions had been a boon for the ambitious importer, and although he would never admit to as much publicly, the famine was proving more profitable than he had imagined.

His wife, Katherine, was a natural at public relations and a darling of the local press. She was decorous and pious without seeming sanctimonious; she wore her hair in elaborate coils and preferred the latest in French fashion: full-sleeved dresses with copious amounts of ribbon; a bare neck; and a large brooch her only jewelry. She was lovely and moved about society in the easy way of someone who had always been invited to do so. With her grace and pedigree, Katherine was a master of fund-raising, and she led the new Tralee ladies' relief fund in donations garnered. Her efforts had been well rewarded with newspaper commendations. So too had Nicholas's personal contributions to the general relief fund. Now seemed as good a time as any to push through some of his more ambitious plans for the town. And that meant doing what he could to get out from under Sir Edward Denny's controlling thumb.

Just as everyone had expected, Denny had named a group of his lackeys to the Tralee Board of Guardians, and they were wasting no time in doing his bidding. They proposed a new relief market where famine sufferers could buy discounted food; they began sourcing traders in America who could ship cornmeal at cost. But as far as Donovan was concerned, this was his purview, and he began rallying other merchants in opposition. It would be far more beneficial for everyone, he insisted, if the merchants were allowed to operate alone on this venture. The same was true for the importation of Indian meal from America. Why not let the moralists' free market ideology do its work for Tralee? Besides, anyone could see that the new Board of Guardians was clearly in over its head. Already the town had the second largest Poor Union in all of Ireland and was tending to nearly 100,000 sufferers in its charge. Its overseer, Colonel George Stokes, a retired army commander recently returned from India, was proving little more helpful in his paternalism than Trevelyan and Grey. Both the fever hospital and the workhouse were filled well beyond capacity; women managing the soup kitchen complained that they were unable to meet the demand of so many hungry individuals. Meanwhile the poorhouse, which was intended to be a place of refuge for those who would otherwise certainly starve to death, was anything but. With dozens of residents dying each week, inmates braved pouring rain in order to scale the poorhouse walls without leave, desperate enough to try their luck begging in the streets. There they joined the six thousand people already seeking outdoor relief in Tralee.

Donovan approached Denny and Stokes, suggesting that the three form their own importing venture. They agreed on a plan: they would sell the cornmeal to famine sufferers nearly at cost, and all profits would be returned to relief fund contributors.[1] Such a system, they hoped, would sustain the cycle of support and consumption until the potato crop could be restored. It would also, the young merchant hoped, solidify his role at the center of what had heretofore been an exclusively Protestant-driven town.

But Stokes and Denny soon had a change of heart, so Donovan hatched his own plan. If town leaders weren't interested in the project, he alone would bring the first unsubsidized cornmeal to the west of Ireland. He alone would show that one could recoup any financial investment while providing food to people in need.

While such a move raised the ire of Denny and his sense of paternal responsibility, it was precisely what leaders like Trevelyan and Grey were hoping would transpire across Ireland. And Nicholas knew he wasn't alone. Katherine's brothers, perhaps spurred by what was happening in Ireland, soon initiated their own entrée into the grain business. With the market for beer in its own famine spiral, they attempted to convert unutilized space in their brewery into a corn mill. But their insurers, seeing no profit to be made in selling cornmeal to people without the cash to buy it, objected. So instead the Murphys pursued importation, contacting correspondents in London about the grain trade there as well as wholesalers in New York and New Orleans about shipment availability.[2] Financial depression aside, the Murphys decided the market looked good. Nicholas Donovan wholeheartedly agreed.

He began bringing corn into town at his own cost and expanded his exportation of wheat and oats from the blight-stricken region to the Liverpool markets. All three decisions prompted local papers to accuse him of acting out of self-interest and neglecting civic process.[3] The *Kerry Examiner* chastised him for refusing Denny's offer of support; even the Catholic-leaning *Tralee Chronicle* questioned the motives behind his so-called charitable acts.[4]

Still, Donovan held fast to his vision for the town—and his prominence therein. While Stokes railed against the idea of selling grain to the destitute, Donovan remained certain that a profit could be made. Even more, he sorely needed that to be true. The stockyards of John Donovan & Sons were filled with piles of slate, iron hoops, and coal awaiting buyers. Inventory was flush—too flush for his taste. For the first time since taking control of the business, Donovan found himself in the uncomfortable position of importing more goods than he could sell. It was undeniable: the famine and subsequent economic depression had stymied his import business. Newspapers reported that the commercial crisis was creating "frightful agitation" in the Liverpool markets. There were rumors of bank stoppages as well.[5] In fact it seemed the only profitable venture was the exchange of natural resources for famine sufferers; throughout England and Ireland, merchants continued to find hefty profits in the new trade of Irish immigrants for North American timber.

This realization was all the impetus Donovan needed to hatch his plan. Instead of ballast, why not send his corn ships back to North America filled with emigrants? He had seen the growing number of farmers and cottiers arriving at the Tralee Bank with checks from relatives drawn on American banks. He knew as well as anyone that they were eager to spend this money on passage across the Atlantic. Despite the harrowing conditions of the previous season, thousands would soon be clamoring for passage on those same ships.

This was not the first time Donovan's mind had settled on such a plan. He and his father had dabbled in the emigrant trade once before, leasing both the *Maria* and the now infamous *British Queen* to send subsidized emigrants from throughout County Kerry to North America. And unlike the *British Queen*'s current manager, the Donovans had succeeded in avoiding the notoriety that surrounded that vessel. True, they had not been plagued by a famine. True, an epidemic had not been racing across the globe. Yet Donovan was confident he could replicate his previous success.

It would be a risky enterprise. Donovan had read the accounts proffered by people like Robert Whyte, which illustrated the deplorable conditions on board the coffin ships. Just recently, Stephen Edward De Vere, a member of the Irish Parliament from nearby Limerick, had published his own account on the subject. A baron of considerable wealth and advancing age, De Vere nevertheless determined to sail aboard one of the coffin ships to gain a better understanding of what was happening therein. What resulted was a newly published treatise entitled *The Elgin-Grey Papers*, which had brought the abusive practices aboard coffin ships to light. With or without Earl Grey, Parliament was preparing action on the subject. In the meantime, ship owners and captains were enduring increasing scrutiny. To establish himself as a legitimate exporter of people, Donovan would have to distinguish himself from the other coffin ship owners.

As far as he could tell, the problems aboard these vessels stemmed from the conditions in steerage. People were packed so tightly that they couldn't even change their position, let alone walk about. Severe bed sores were common. Food was scarce or nonexistent. Water was insufficient and did not allow for washing—either bodies or soiled beds. The most iniquitous ship owners continued to charge anywhere from £5 to £10 for steerage passage aboard their vile ships. And even those with consistently high mortality rates could not keep up with the demand of famine sufferers yearning to climb aboard. Donovan saw in this a tremendous opportunity as well. If he could convey people from Tralee to North America—and keep them all alive in the process—he could fetch just about any price. Perhaps more important, he would finally become a social force few could ignore.

He began to consider the logistics of such a venture. First and foremost, he would need a vessel large enough to hold over a hundred immigrants and to give them enough space to move. Such a ship—the first he would ever own outright—could also bring back grain or timber, the only commodities assured a profit in famine Ireland. Owning a ship would mean he would need to employ a full-time captain, and for that position, he had in mind his cousin and a Cork native, Captain James Attridge.

12

Signing On

ABOVE ALL ELSE, James Attridge was a man of the sea. Born into a seafaring family, the captain had seen more than his fair share of peril aboard wooden vessels. He first signed on as a ship's apprentice at the age of fifteen. At twenty-three, he had become one of Ireland's youngest masters. Together with his two brothers, he purchased the *Abeona*, making him the first owner-captain in all of Ireland. This was no amateur venture. Their vessel was a two-masted brig that required an experienced captain and a nimble crew to keep her close to the wind. This was particularly true in the tumultuous Irish Sea, a place still known by today's sailors as Ireland's nautical graveyard. Even with this reputation, the Sea was also where Attridge and his complicated little ship regularly ran packet trips between Ireland and England, often under the employ of Donovan & Sons.

That he managed to do so time and time again without incident had already earned Attridge the reputation of being one of Ireland's best sea captains. Now forty-four, he embodied the image of a master and commander: staid, confident, and authoritative. Seamen often sought out his ships, hoping to work under the man who was known for his strict adherence to naval law and the discipline to see any ship to safety. What they found was a captain with a thick Cork brogue and the formal costume— heavy wool trousers and an embellished, double-breasted coat—of a British merchant officer, a man who expected militaristic precision from his crew, who carried himself with the calm bearing of one who had bested storm and sail. When Nicholas Donovan decided to purchase his first transatlantic vessel, he naturally contacted his cousin. Donovan trusted in Attridge's seamanship, along with his reputation for discipline among his sailors. No matter the crisis at hand, this captain always insisted on the kind of calm order needed to dilute any tension or dissension among crew or passengers.

Agreeing to accept the post of commander of an immigrant ship was not a decision Attridge made lightly. Although ten years Donovan's senior, Attridge nevertheless deferred to the classic nautical hierarchy: a captain was master and commander, unless he was dealing with a ship's owner, at which time he was just a hired hand. Surrendering his own claim to ownership would mean that Attridge no longer had the final say on how his ship was run. Still, Donovan assured him that management of the vessel would be left to him alone. That appealed to Attridge. The growing economic depression plaguing Ireland was making the once lucrative *Abeona* an increasingly risky investment; taking command of an Atlantic cargo ship would mean steady income—£10 per voyage—and the opportunity to focus on what Attridge loved most: a life at sea. Then again, that life would be dramatically altered by the addition of two hundred famine-stricken passengers. This was not an area in which Attridge had any experience, and he worried about the added responsibility of all those people. Could a crew really tend to them and a square-rigged vessel at the same time?

From his house on the quay of the River Lee, Attridge had unfettered access to Cork Harbor, the third largest natural harbor in the world and long since a major seat for shipping in Ireland. The neighboring town of Cobh, which shared the harbor, could easily host three hundred vessels at a time. Cobh and Cork had other, less savory distinctions too, including the highest rates of sickness and mortality aboard immigrant vessels.[1] James Attridge had seen the state of dozens, if not hundreds, of coffin ships as they departed and arrived at the port. Like the countryside around Tralee, it was not a scene to be taken lightly. Still, and after no small amount of deliberation, Attridge finally agreed to Donovan's proposition.

As 1847 came to an end, Captain Attridge found himself dispatched to the bustling hive of the Liverpool docks. There he visited dozens of vessels for sale, ranging in size and condition. Immigrants were being shipped out on every type of vessel conceivable, but Donovan wasn't just in the immigrant business; to get grain to the starving people and to continue importing timber and lead, he would need a proper cargo ship, one fat enough to hold his orders and stable enough to stay afloat, even while storms threatened to overturn it. In the mid-nineteenth century, there was only one type of vessel that would do: the barque, that three-masted workhorse to which John Munn had dedicated his career.

It was most certainly a buyer's market that season, and Donovan could have his choice. Perhaps showing his own preferences, Attridge directed him to what he had found on the Brunswick wharf. The noted shipwright John Munn now had two vessels for sale: the *England*, whose original financing had gone awry, and the *Jeanie Johnston*. Would John Donovan & Sons be interested in either?

Donovan was delighted. His own dealings in trade had taken him to Quebec on at least one occasion, so he knew well Munn's reputation for quality construction. He considered the vessels. The *England* was far too big—and expensive—for his needs. The *Jeanie Johnston*, on the other hand, seemed ideal for carrying both immigrants and cargo. Her lack of a buyer these six-odd months had made the price a good one. Yes, Donovan responded, this was the ship he wanted.

By the start of 1848, the *Jeanie Johnston* was the official property of Donovan & Sons. It would be several months, however, before she would arrive in Tralee. First, Attridge needed to finish outfitting her with the long boats, chains, and other accessories she would need in regular service. Donovan had insisted on a full survey of the vessel as well, which necessitated relocating her in dry dock while Lloyd's officials catalogued every inch of the barque. Completing such a study would take weeks, if not months. (So thorough was this survey, in fact, that 150 years later it would be used to re-create the ship in painstaking detail.[2])

Attridge was frankly glad for the delay. The month of January saw an unprecedented number of wrecks along the western coast of Ireland. Early February looked no better after another heavy storm struck the brig *Phoenix* off the coast of Tralee, dashing it to pieces and killing all on board. This was clearly no time to be taking an unfamiliar vessel near that dangerous coast. As he waited for calmer seas, Attridge resumed his packet trips, ferrying Indian meal from Liverpool to the waiting famine sufferers in Cork, who were now dealing with bitter cold and snow in addition to the crises of starvation and disease.

But as the brutal weather continued back in Tralee, Donovan began feeling the urgency of completing work on the *Jeanie*. He had just received the official survey report, and the news was good. The Lloyd's surveyor had reaffirmed the rating given to the *Jeanie* in Quebec: a five-year designation of A1, the highest class a ship built in North America could hope to achieve. It was time to move forward. He again dispatched Attridge to Liverpool, this time to fetch his new ship and bring it to Ireland. Donovan had arranged to fill his new barque with goods before departure from Liverpool, and it was an impressive list of cargo, ranging from rock salt, oil, and soap to turpentine, plaster, and nails. And, of course, ton upon ton of planks, staves, and square-deal timber, all soon to be available for purchase at John Donovan & Sons.

Before the *Jeanie* could make her first voyage to her home port, however, she would need a crew. Choosing the men who sailed was the purview of any ship's captain, and Attridge took the selection seriously. The most important hiring decision he would make was for the position of first mate. A good mate became almost a partner to a captain and shared in many of the managerial duties on board; a bad mate could turn an entire crew against a master and subvert his authority in the process. Attridge demanded a man of the former type, and with the approval of Donovan, he chose Thomas Campion, a thirty-one-year-old from northeastern England. Like Attridge, Campion came from a seafaring family; his father was a registered master, his brother a sailor as well. For the past several years, Campion had sailed as a mate out of Liverpool on vessels similar to the *Jeanie*, and Attridge had enough confidence in his new employee to leave the governance of the ship to him as long as they were anchored. Attridge also brought with him one ordinary seaman, a twenty-four-year-old fellow Cork resident by the name of Cornelius Crowley, who had sailed with Attridge aboard the *Abeona*. Two additional ordinaries hailed from Tralee and were well known to the captain. The rest he would have to get to know as time progressed.

In total, eighteen men would sail aboard the *Jeanie* with Attridge. The majority came from towns throughout England and Ireland. A few did not: Carls Brown, a twenty-six-year-old from Stockholm; Alexander Matthews from New York; and Gabriel Seldon, described as a "mulatto with a distinctive scar on his face," from Halifax, Nova Scotia. At forty-one, Seldon was the oldest member of the crew and just a year younger than the captain. Two teenage boys, Hugh Murphy and Arthur McBretney, signed on as apprentices, completing the roster and creating a span of age over a generation in size. They were a gritty group. Nearly half had been brought to court at one time or another for desertion, a serious offense punishable by thirty days in jail. At least four had been arrested for drunk and disorderly conduct, along with a series of assault charges. One year prior, Gabriel Seldon, who was serving as ship's cook, had been accused of breaking and entering homes in Quebec.[3] Although the accusations had never been substantiated and Seldon testified under oath that he had not even been in Quebec at the time of the incident, they were nevertheless indicative of the checkered reputation accompanying many nineteenth-century sailors. Yet in an industry where crime and violence was so commonplace—even aboard the vessels themselves—the *Jeanie*'s crew was as upstanding an assemblage as Attridge could hope for. That was important to a captain who prided himself on never having been cited for an infraction in his already long career.

For all that differentiated them, these eighteen were clearly identifiable as the *Jeanie*'s crew. Though not required to maintain the exactitude of dress required by the British Navy, merchant sailors nevertheless cut a distinctive figure: pants hung low around the hips and billowing around the calf, checked shirts, black hats, and soft-soled shoes made their uniform as identifiable as any military man; their nimbleness bespoke their years balancing aloft; their rough hands and faces were testament to their working conditions.[4] A nineteenth-century sailor had to know who he was and what he needed to survive, particularly given the uncertainty that marked so much of his existence. Nowhere was that more true than on a new, untested vessel.

It was with no small amount of wariness, then, that the new crew of the *Jeanie Johnston* assembled on the deck of the barque in March 1848. There they met Campion sitting behind a table and holding the ship's articles, contracts stipulating their rights and responsibilities on board. Of particular interest to many of the men was the explanation of provisions. Famine ships were notorious for providing crew members subpar food during the journey. One of the new crewmen, Archibald Campbell, had recently abandoned the *Calcutta* after its captain, Thomas Fraser, refused to hand out limes to the crew. Campbell's decision might have seemed rash to some, but he knew as well as anyone that something as simple as the omission of lime juice could cause debilitating scurvy and even death. That wouldn't happen aboard the *Jeanie Johnston*. Although Campion had yet to meet her owner, he knew Attridge's reputation well enough to know that every nautical law—and then some—would be followed to the letter. To demonstrate as much, he paid each man, save the apprentices, half his salary upon signing; the balance would be received from Donovan back in Tralee. Then they set to work, for Attridge had entrusted his men with the task of preparing the *Jeanie* for her first trip to Ireland.

As they set off for the short voyage from Liverpool to Tralee, Attridge made certain the men understood his commitment to regulation and order. Without adherence to the strictest protocols, these men and their little barque wouldn't stand a chance.

13

The People's Physician

THE GLOBAL MILIEU in which the *Jeanie Johnston* sailed that spring was increasingly tumultuous. As she departed the Liverpool docks, reports of rioting throughout England began to spread. In London, an open-air meeting on the abolition of the income tax became fierce. When police attempted to intercede, the mob responded by lobbing stones and rioting. Police subdued the crowd with truncheons and eventually took more than eighty men into custody.[1] Similar direct action was taken by residents of southern England, where it was a shortage of bread rather than commitment to Libertarian ideals that sent individuals into the streets. Meanwhile, in Attridge's hometown of Cork, rumors of a collapse of public securities forced a run on the Cork Savings Bank and prompted similar scares in Limerick and other cities.[2] Reports of a growing insurrection sent an entire fleet of the British Navy into Cork Harbor, ready to be dispatched anywhere in the west of Ireland.

That, despite all this tremendous distress, news of the *Jeanie*'s first voyage to Tralee filled the local papers was a testament to just how significant the vessel was for the area and its inhabitants. Even the Protestant-leaning *Kerry Evening Post* called her "a fine new barque" and her owner "an enterprising townsman." The paper made repeated mention of the *Jeanie* in the March 25 issue, noting in detail her cargo, her progress, and the fact that, upon arrival, she would "immediately set sail for Quebec with passengers, for which purpose she is peculiarly suited, from the great

height between decks and her general capabilities as a seagoing craft."[3]
Donovan was delighted with the coverage.

The harbor outside Tralee was unusually crowded when the *Jeanie*
arrived, with no fewer than twenty-five vessels vying for space in a deep-
water bay that had never before seen so many ships at one time.[4] Once
the *Jeanie* was divested of her cargo, Donovan instructed Attridge to
begin the necessary retrofitting that would convert the vessel into a passenger ship.

This was no easy task. Even with the unusual spaciousness he had created, Munn had built the *Jeanie* primarily as a cargo ship, which meant
she contained a single interior broad deck intended to shelter stacks of
timber and sawn boards, not hundreds of humans. To accommodate passengers, the crew would have to construct temporary bunks that would
serve as accommodations for the two hundred emigrants Donovan hoped
to pack onto the vessel later that spring. Each of these platforms measured six feet square and, at full capacity, would hold four grown adults. It
would be the only space allotted the passengers, who would use the area
for everything from sleeping to eating to worship. Stacked three high, the
bunks would not allow enough clearance for a full-grown man to sit up.
They would be, Donovan hoped, sufficient.

As the crew finished clearing out the ship's hold, Campion and John
Baylis, the ship's carpenter, oversaw construction of the bunks. Attridge
meanwhile set about provisioning the vessel for its voyage across the
Atlantic. A trip across those waters would require at least one full set of
extra sails, reserved for any canvas so damaged by the ocean's ravages
that they could not be patched. They would also need hundreds of feet
of line, dozens of planks, and other material needed to make emergency
repairs. But the bulk of Attridge's attention was dedicated to the *Jeanie*'s
sundries list, which was impressive by any standard: over 2,500 pounds of
food was allotted to the crew alone, including 630 pounds of dried beef,
110 pounds of butter, and four gallons of the all-important lime juice. An
additional 12,000 pounds of grain would keep the passengers alive.

Once the task of securing provisions was completed, Attridge and
Donovan turned their attention to the selection of the ship's doctor. The
need for a physician was something on which both men had agreed from

the start. Early that year, the *Kerry Evening Post* had reprinted an editorial from the *Liverpool Mercury* insisting on the inclusion of physicians on all immigrant ships. The paper reported that passengers were making the addition of a doctor "a *sine qua non* in choosing vessels in which to emigrate." This, said the *Mercury*, "is how it should be, and many valuable lives will be saved by these means."[5] The editor of the *Evening Post* clearly agreed. Although Parliament still had not passed a law mandating as much, it was clear that the owner and captain of the *Jeanie Johnston* sided with the growing press and public sentiment on the subject.

As an oceangoing captain, Attridge had learned through trial and error the basics of medicine; weeks on end at sea doing dangerous work meant that injuries and illness were common. With land often hundreds or even thousands of miles away, it was up to the captain to stitch lacerations, see to the prevention of scurvy, and in some cases even perform surgery. That might be enough to ensure that most crew members lived to see their home port, but it was utterly insufficient for the daunting task the *Jeanie* now faced.

In truth, the training most physicians received was also woefully insufficient when it came to keeping coffin ship passengers alive—assuming they received any legitimate training at all. Part of the problem was that the medical field still remained in sharp disagreement about what was causing the deaths aboard these ships. In addition to theories such as those propagated by Earl Grey, many circled back to the ancient Roman belief that miasma, or poisonous particulates in the air, spread disease. Thought to be identified by its noxious smell, miasma was most commonly countered by curtailing the flow of air in rooms and hospitals or by requiring doctors and patients to wear garlands of flowers around their mouth and nose. On ships at sea, where flowers were unavailable and noxious air was already in great abundance, captains and undertrained doctors insisted on strict protocols that included restricting emigrants to areas below deck with the hatches closed so that no air could circulate and promote miasmic outbreaks. That these actions did little to prevent the spread of disease left mariners and ship's doctors at a loss.

As word of these conditions and their concomitant death rates continued to spread, a physician by the name of Andrew Combe set out to investigate by contracting to sail aboard one of the immigrant vessels. Like Whyte and De Vere before him, Combe observed the conditions in which his adopted ship's 360 passengers were kept, which included what he described as "vitiated air, filth, and moral depression." He found no attempt whatsoever to stop the spread of disease, nor any attention to hygiene or cleanliness.[6]

But what was most upsetting to Combe was the lack of sustenance provided to the emigrants on the ships—and the fact that no authority seemed to care. The focus of his critique landed squarely on the colonial secretary and his earlier comments on sustenance. "Earl Gray himself seems not to be fully aware of the facts of the case," Combe complained. "His Lordship is reported to have said, that 'those emigrants had gone out in ships as well provided as such vessels usually were, but they had embarked in such a state of health that in some cases the very change to a better diet on board the emigrant ships had caused fever to break out among them.'" That, insisted Combe, was patently false. While there may have been plenty of food aboard any one of these ships, it wasn't being offered to the passengers in steerage, who were required to provide their own, save for the paltry pound per day of flour or oatmeal mandated by Parliament. Consequently many of the passengers had grown so weak they could no longer rise from their bunks, even to relieve themselves. Combe observed dozens of such individuals unable to do anything other than lie in their own waste for days on end. Could anyone really be surprised, asked the doctor, that so many of these emigrants were now dying? Why was no one in England doing anything to stop this?[7]

The answer to that last question was still a long time in coming. Combe, who would die shortly after his return from New York, would not live to hear it. Instead he endured criticism from politicians and fellow physicians alike, many of whom spoke out publicly against his call for disease prevention and nourishment.

Of the few doctors willing to side with Combe, one was of particular interest to Attridge and Donovan. Although just thirty years old, Richard Blennerhassett had already distinguished himself as a talented doctor and a forward thinker. He came from a long line of civic-minded doctors and, as part of the Protestant elite, his family maintained a reputation for philanthropy and a dedication to human rights. His grandfather, who shared his forename, was credited with creating a medical dynasty that would live on for generations. Like his descendants, the elder Richard chose to dedicate his career to serving the poor. By the time Attridge was preparing to set sail, Richard's father, Henry, known throughout Ireland as "the poor man's doctor," had assumed responsibility over the region's fever hospital, and his considered dealings with the conditions there had won him the respect of patients and civic leaders alike. Years later these attentions would be memorialized in an obituary that praised his "large & enlightened views. Unfettered by class distinctions, he was the very antithesis of all that is illiberal in politics or religion."[8]

This sort of distinction appealed to Donovan and Attridge; so too did Henry Blennerhassett's ability to deal with the town leaders of Tralee in all matters related to famine relief. Henry's son Richard promised to be no less praiseworthy. Already he and his brothers had won the affection of townspeople, who relished the boys' exuberance and skills as hunters, athletes, and sailboat racers. Like his father, Richard had received a sterling education, including medical training at the esteemed Edinburgh University, where he graduated with a degree in medicine in 1845.[9] While there, he had attended classes in botany and chemistry, as well as clinical medicine, midwifery, surgery, and pharmacology. He was required to learn dissection and surgery and pass a battery of written exams.[10] This was still an era when textbooks admitted that the cause of ailments such as fever continued to elude the medical establishment, and bleeding was still a recognized treatment; nevertheless the information Richard learned there greatly surpassed the misinformation driving most medical conversations of the time.[11] Since graduating, he had developed his skills even further, completing a residency in Dublin, the seat of administrative power in Ireland. While there he chose to study obstetrics. He also learned enough to rue the policies of Edward Twisleton and his new Central Board of Health, which was also situated in Ireland's capital. Richard Blennerhassett wasn't swayed by theories of noxious smells or that the low morals of the Irish were somehow responsible for their present suffering. Nor did he have much patience for ineffectual policies and political decisions.

But what really interested Donovan and Attridge was the young doctor's subsequent work aboard a coolie ship. Certainly a man of his stature and impressive academic pedigree could have secured a whole host of comfortable positions in Dublin or another metropolitan center, where he would have tended to the minor ailments of the rising merchant class. Blennerhassett instead chose employment aboard the *Bussorah Merchant*, a vessel hired to transport indentured workers from Calcutta to the sugarcane plantations of Demerara, a region of South America in what is now Guyana. His reasons are cause for speculation even today. Some descendants maintain that he fathered an illegitimate child with a young woman who worked as a servant in Tralee; others contend he developed a particular interest in infectious diseases while in medical school; still others cite the family's consistent commitment to public health. Given how little time Blennerhassett spent at his family's home once he entered school and that there was no reason not to acknowledge the child, probably one of the other two reasons, or a combination of them, is the best explanation behind his decision to board this ill-fated ship.

What is clear is that what Blennerhassett saw while on board the *Bussorah Merchant* would haunt him for the rest of his life. Shortly after setting sail for Demerara, many of the 250 coolies on board began showing signs of illness. Within a week, the vessel had witnessed its first casualties. The cause this time was not smallpox or even typhus but cholera, which had again been sweeping through Asia and leaving in its wake thousands of victims.

Hindu law prohibited the coolies from touching their dead, and the crew of the *Bussorah Merchant* had already seen enough sickness to fear contagion themselves. So, with no one to assist him, Blennerhassett found himself in the grisly role of undertaker as well as ship's surgeon. Each evening, under the cloak of darkness, he would drag the bodies of the dead above deck and cast them overboard, a laborious process he repeated fifty-one times before the vessel eventually reached its port. He returned to Ireland with a sadness about him that he would never shake during what remained of his short life and an unwavering commitment to ensure that the fate of those aboard the *Bussorah Merchant* would never be repeated.

During his time in Calcutta and aboard the coolie ship, Blennerhassett learned a great deal about epidemiology, especially the truth behind Combe's theory of vessel management: ships and their passengers must be kept clean and supplied with ample fresh air, water, and food. Just as important was the ability to sequester ailing passengers, lest they infect the healthy. That was just the sort of thinking Nicholas Donovan wanted aboard his new ship.

There was no time to lose if the *Jeanie Johnston* was to sail that season; although spring had not yet taken hold, rumors of yet another failed potato crop were increasing the hysteria throughout the west of Ireland. Death rates continued to mount as cottiers throughout Ireland succumbed to starvation.

It wasn't starvation that was killing many of Blennerhassett's peers, but rather the lingering presence of typhus. In the prior twelve months, two hundred Irish doctors and medical students had perished—a figure three times higher than that of previous years.[12] Once again County Kerry seemed to be hit particularly hard; in the region surrounding Tralee alone, thirty-seven doctors had contracted typhus while tending to the sick, and seventeen had died, leaving nine widows and thirty-five orphans.[13] Staying there, it seemed, was no safer than climbing aboard an immigrant ship.

14

Fare Thee Well

1848

THE PLACARDS started appearing around town on Daniel and Margaret Reilly's anniversary. They hung on gates outside parish churches; they graced the facades of banks and markets. Each offered the same tantalizing promise: emigration to Quebec aboard a brand-new "fine, fast copper-fashioned ship." Fare for a single passenger was £3 10s—nearly a full £2 less than ships of similar size leaving from Limerick and Cork. This ticket was far from cheap—about $300 today and no less than half of Daniel's average annual income. But even if it had been ten times that, Daniel probably would have found a way to pay. He knew the man whose name appeared on these advertisements: when Donovan bragged about the soundness of his vessel, the copious stores of food on board, and the presence of a physician from town, Daniel believed him.

Daniel Reilly was precisely the kind of passenger Nicholas Donovan was hoping to attract: young, healthy, with enough capital to provide for the voyage and his life in North America, and likely to survive an Atlantic passage. Even better, he had people ready to help him on the other side.

In early April, Tralee continued to be plagued by snow, hail, and thunderstorms—often all three on the same day. "No tender bud or leaf or flower," wrote the editor of the *Kerry Evening Post*, "no shrub or plant appears to give promise."[1] It was an apt description of a region still beset by hunger and suffering. At night, thieves would steal into gardens and fields, their shovels and trowels shrouded in burlap or rags to deaden the sound of digging. Mindful of the rise in vegetable thefts, landowners dug giant pits known as "man traps" eight feet deep and filled with water to catch would-be thieves; they also hired armed guards to protect even the most inconsequential vegetables: a few turnips here, leftover cabbage heads there. All had become increasingly valuable as yet another season of famine wracked the countryside.

Daniel wasn't about to allow a similar fate to befall his family. Hat in hand, he arrived at the grand offices of Nicholas Donovan, this time not as someone selling grain but as someone hoping to buy a future with the money he had spent his life accruing. In exchange for nearly all his savings, he was given two adult tickets to sail aboard the *Jeanie Johnston*. They were filled with more legalese than he had ever seen in his life and included the *Jeanie*'s departure date and time. Perhaps more important, they also mandated regulations concerning logistics for the Reillys' time aboard. Each full-fare passenger would be allotted ten cubic feet of luggage space (about the size of today's average kitchen refrigerator) for their personal possessions. They would be given a pound per day of legally mandated oatmeal and rice rations. Everything else, from bedding and utensils to additional food and household items that would get them started in the New World, would be their responsibility—as long as it fit in a medium-size chest.

With the departure date less than a week away, Daniel and Margaret didn't have much time to collect their things. It must have been difficult to leave behind the plows and scythes and other farm tools collected over a decade of hardscrabble farming. Their kitchen table and Robert's crib would have to remain behind as well. What they did take was humble at best: a feather mattress on which they would all sleep, dinner plates, a pipe, sewing scissors, and Margaret's brass thimble. There were goodbyes to be made, knowing that they would never see most of their family and friends again. They visited Margaret's father, who was too old to consider a transatlantic crossing; they promised her brother John they'd send for him as soon as they could. Back home, Daniel packed their trunk. Margaret bundled Robert in as many of his clothes as she could, all the while doing her best to ignore the signs that another baby was on its way.

Beginning on April 18 and amid yet another storm of hail and sleet, the *Jeanie's* ticket holders started to assemble near the large waterfront windmill in the nearby town of Blennerville. The size of the ship's keel was substantial enough that Captain Attridge was unable to sail into the harbor, let alone up Donovan's canal, so smaller sloops and pull boats would be used to ferry the passengers out to the ship. As they began to arrive, Donovan called his crew to the aft of the boat. There, as was customary for such voyages, he addressed the men, explaining the nature of their trip and reminding them of the rules of conduct that would define their time aboard.

Even with this homily from their captain, those crew members sent to assist with the transport of the passengers from the docks were unprepared for the deeply affecting scene awaiting them. Many of the passengers' families had joined them for the short trip to Blennerville, hoping to defer their farewells as long as possible. Some of the bystanders were keening the haunting chant for the dead that marked many wakes in the region. Few tried to hide their tears. Passengers were crying too; not only were they saying good-bye to loved ones, but it appeared that many would have to say good-bye to their livelihoods as well. Unaware of just how restrictive the space requirements aboard the ship were, they brought spinning wheels and cumbersome carpentry tools, thinking this would ease the struggle of finding work in North America. They were disappointed to learn at the docks that there would be no room aboard for such things.

Directing the assembly and dismissal of the passengers was Richard Blennerhassett. He insisted on a thorough examination of each passenger before he or she was allowed to step aboard the waiting boats—or at least as thorough an examination as propriety would allow. He peered into throats, ears, and eyes; he took pulses and checked for fever, making mental notes about which passengers seemed particularly weak or susceptible to disease. It was a sizable task: eighty-seven men, seventy-two women, and thirty-four children would make the trip.

Blennerhassett, though, was relieved. For the most part, the majority of the passengers seemed relatively well-fed and healthy. It would still be a challenge to keep them well, but at least he wasn't beginning with too many severe cases.

There were exceptions, of course. Of particular concern to the young physician was Margaret Reilly. Barely twenty years old, she stood with her young son looking visibly uncomfortable; even with her concealing layers of clothes, Blennerhassett could see that she was not just pregnant but dangerously close to her delivery date. Why Donovan had agreed to allow a woman in this condition on board was a mystery to him. What was clear was that he would soon be forced to assist in the delivery of this baby. He watched her carefully and instructed the crew to do the same. Had he known about the contractions Margaret had already begun experiencing, no doubt he would have delivered more thorough instructions. But for now, it was all Blennerhassett could do to get her safely settled in the bunk she would call home for the next two months.

The short trip on the sloop ferry from Blennerville to the *Jeanie Johnston* was the first time Margaret Reilly had ever been on a boat, and she wasn't sure she liked the experience. As they tacked their way into the bay, she could see the imposing masts of the *Jeanie* rising above all of the other vessels anchored there. At nearly 150 feet, they were the tallest things she had ever seen in her life. And that was just the start of novelty for the young mother. Once on board, she, Daniel, and Robert were met by Thomas Campion, who confirmed their names on the passenger list created by Donovan's clerk and checked their belongings. They also met Gabriel Seldon, the first person of color they had ever seen. Margaret couldn't help but stare. There were accents strange and foreign and the oddities of life on a vessel—hatches and lifeboats and the unfamiliar, pulsing feel of a tide beneath her feet. She and Daniel did their best to settle in.

And then they waited.

By Friday, April 21, all of the passengers had been brought aboard. Attridge was still loading his final delivery of provisions, so Donovan allowed family members as well as interested community members the unprecedented opportunity to visit passengers on board. Doing so was a strategic move that he hoped would result in more positive press. He encouraged visitors to examine the well-built bunks, to tour the decks and even the galley of the ship, taking note of her outstanding design and craftsmanship.

The *Jeanie*'s captain didn't care one way or the other about press coverage, and he would have preferred to avoid the extra inconvenience of so many people coming and going. But Attridge was visibly relieved to see that the boarding and settling of the passengers had gone smoothly. As the last of the visitors made their way back to land, he could tell that his crew was on edge. Below them was the din of two hundred nervous individuals, none of whom had ever been at sea. Sailors prided themselves on their emotional reticence and stoicism. There was little time for anything other than sleep and work aboard, and the only expression of feeling usually came from singing shanties or the occasional fight among frustrated crew members. The scene in the *Jeanie*'s hull was a different matter entirely. Families danced and sang, re-created elaborate prayer services, or continued their laments. There were periods of uproarious laughter followed by sobbing. There was, in short, entirely too much emotion for the comfort of the crewmen.

Later that night, Attridge was summoned by Blennerhassett. Margaret Reilly had gone into full labor and was progressing rapidly. The two men made their way down into the hold of the ship, using a greasy oil lamp and the ship's navigational lantern for illumination. The male passengers had done their best to cloister themselves away from the drama, but the women aboard, most of whom had already witnessed dozens of births, stayed nearby. Neither the captain nor the doctor minded.

As a ship's surgeon, Blennerhassett carried the standard-issue pocket dressing case, which contained a small assortment of medical equipment, including forceps, scissors, and suturing needles. He would need all three to assist the terrified Margaret in her delivery. Even with the added illumination of the oil lamps, visibility in steerage was dim, and the greasy light cast thick shadows across the straw-filled bunk. Margaret labored throughout the night, pushing against the strange doctor and captain for leverage. Just before dawn came the abrupt cry of a newborn child. Mercifully, the birth came off without complications. Blennerhassett received the baby, checked his health, and introduced him to his young mother, who lay exhausted in her bunk.

It was Easter Sunday. The sunrise was a brilliant red and sent rosy light into the hold of the *Jeanie Johnston*. Daniel and Margaret were reunited. He stared at his new son while she recounted her harrowing experience. Their lives, she insisted, were spared because of the kindness of Nicholas Donovan. Who else would have ensured a ship so clean? And one containing a doctor with the skills of Richard Blennerhassett? Not to mention the kind crew. She wanted to call the baby after the people who had shepherded his fate. And so they settled on a name to end all names. This baby—this miraculous boy—would be named Nicholas Richard James Thomas William John Gabriel Carls Michael John Alexander Trabaret Archibald Cornelius Hugh Arthur Edward Johnston Reilly. And because having seventeen middle names would no doubt prove cumbersome at times, they'd call him Nicholas Johnston Reilly for short.

Later that day, and at Margaret's request, Captain Attridge dispatched several crew members to shore to collect Reverend Moore to baptize the baby. Moore was the rector at Ardfert, a town whose name means "hill of miracles," and which was the birthplace of St. Brendan the Navigator, an apt patron saint for a child about to make a miraculous journey of his own. The men rowed the priest in a dory to the barque; no doubt it was the first time he had performed a baptism in front of a crowd of two hundred in the dark steerage of a ship.

Only after Moore was returned to shore and the Reillys appeared to be resting comfortably did Attridge call for the crew to raise the anchor and set the *Jeanie*'s mainsails. Seventeen men sprang into action, dividing themselves among the ship's three masts. After all of the emotional drama over the past several days, they were eager to have familiar work to do.

Attridge kept a close eye on the men. Seeing them in action would tell him a lot about what the next forty-five days would bring. The last thing he needed was any surprises from his crew. There had already been plenty of those below deck. He also knew that their opportunity for a safe departure was rapidly diminishing. That day, heavy weather put back two immigrant ships attempting to depart from the west of Ireland. A third, the *Omega*, foundered off the west coast. Not far from land, she was soon overtaken by the *Barbara*, whose crew staged a brave rescue, saving the more than three hundred passengers, who were certain that Providence and good luck had shone upon them. But no sooner had they settled into the rescue vessel for their return to Ireland when it too was beset by rough seas and gale-force winds. Less than a day after their lives had been spared, the immigrants faced another wreck. By the time splintered portions of the *Barbara* washed ashore, two hundred of her rescued passengers had drowned.[2]

Stories of their perishing were traded among the crew. Lying in her bunk below, Margaret didn't hear any of this talk, but Daniel heard plenty. As Attridge called all passengers above deck for their final roll call, whispers of the drowned immigrants filled the air. So too did speculation about the true nature of the passengers on board this and other vessels. Just weeks earlier, two young men robbed £1,900 from a bank in Manchester, then made their way to Ireland. Nationwide rumors had it that these two criminals were now boarding an immigrant ship destined for Canada, leading many to wonder if they might be among the passengers now standing on the *Jeanie*'s broad decks.[3]

Attridge was frank with the emigrants. He had little time for such speculation; the well-being of these individuals now rested firmly in his hands, and he would be required to submit his own certified list to immigration officials in North America. He was also required to supervise a second medical inspection for Donovan, who would face stiff fines if any of the emigrants arrived at the quarantine station showing signs of sickness or disease.[4]

Attridge then turned his attention to the mammoth task of readying a four-hundred-ton barque for departure. Even with the beating winds that day, he would need to rely on the departing tide to cast his flat ship away from the shore and the dangers that lay there. As the *Jeanie* cast off, Attridge made the first entry in the ship's logbook, marking their precise position and the point from which all subsequent bearings would be taken.[5]

The winds continued to strengthen from the west, forcing Attridge to beat the ship on a hard course north toward the open Atlantic and away from the deadly rocks off the coast. With night falling around her, the *Jeanie* slipped unceremoniously past the Samphire Islands, two small outcroppings rising out of Tralee Bay. It would be the last land those on board would see for some time.

The *Jeanie Johnston* was one of nine vessels that managed to depart the west of Ireland that day. Each was loaded with hundreds of famine emigrants, though no other ship could claim a newborn baby boy. As the ships entered the open water of the Atlantic, the weekly issue of the *Tralee Chronicle* appeared throughout the town. Included among the news was an enthusiastic account of Nicholas Reilly's birth and the fine ship on which he now journeyed. The story described all aspects of the departure in good detail, noting that "very great satisfaction was expressed by the emigrants" about the conditions on board. "Indeed," the story continued, "the friends of the emigrants who had visited them, ere they sped on their watery course, speak with an affectionate enthusiasm of the paternal care paid by the Messrs. Donovan on board."[6]

It was precisely the kind of story Nicholas Donovan had hoped for. At least for the time being, he was a local hero. But as the *Jeanie Johnston* left for her watery course, her crew, doctor, and passengers knew the real test of this vessel still lay ahead.

Cecilia Bunberry was just twenty-one when she married Nicholas Reilly. It was cold, blistering cold, on that February afternoon. Still there was plenty of warmth in the Reillys' sod house, and Cecilia had laughed when Nicholas printed his middle name as "J.J." on the marriage certificate—a much less cumbersome designation, he explained, than his seventeen middle names. There was something delightfully girlish about Cecilia, almost a decade his junior—the easy way she had about her, her sense of humor.

The two had met nearly nine years earlier, when the Bunberrys moved to Silver Creek. The Reillys were already well settled by then, having established their farmstead in 1854. It had taken Daniel Reilly six years of toiling on the Indiana railroad to save enough money for their land. Since then, he had worked the rich black soil of Michigan's western counties, coaxing from it more grain than he ever could have imagined back in Ireland. The Silver Creek harvests were good to him, and he now owned three large parcels of land—plenty to till and on which to support a family. That family had grown to include seven children. Still, they remained one short. Margaret's beloved brother John, whom they had promised they would send for, had never arrived.

Twenty years had passed since Daniel sent passage money to the Tralee Bank. John had written that he would arrive later that year and would meet them in Silver Creek. As the months bled into one another, Margaret became increasingly apprehensive. Daniel took out missing person ads in East Coast papers, hoping John might find them. Still, they did not receive word. They took out more ads, asking if anyone had any information about the quiet steward from County Kerry. They never received a response.

92

Without her younger brother, Margaret, always a dedicated mother, became even more so. She kept their house immaculate and taught the girls—Mary, Margaret, Julia, and Nellie—how to read, make griddle cakes, and knit wool socks. Mary and Margaret married, settling nearby with families of their own. The eldest Reilly son, Robert, had long since decided that farming was no life for him and had moved to Chicago, where he found work as a carpenter and married a woman named Jane. But Nicholas and his younger brother Eugene had remained on the farm, working its ever-growing acreage each year alongside their father.

Silver Creek was a quiet, rural community with a strong Quaker foundation. Once a stop on the Underground Railroad, it had since become one of the Midwest's largest African American settlements. They were joined by a steady stream of German and Irish immigrants, who arrived each year hoping to cultivate their own plot of land. That was what brought the Bunberrys to Silver Creek, all the way from Pennsylvania. Like the Reillys, they were a large Irish family eager to work.

All of them, that is, except for Cecilia's brother-in-law, James O'Brien. Jim swooped into Cass County full of bravado and mystery and promptly settled on Cecilia's older sister, Harriet, for his bride. Harriet was easily wooed by this man and his larger-than-life tales. He owned a hotel and saloon in Kalamazoo and seemed to hold the whole world in his hands, talking about life in places like Chicago and Michigan's Upper Peninsula, which seemed very much a wild frontier. Jim, it seemed, had lived just about everywhere.

And he was still on the move. He had a new plan—this time, to open a saloon out on the Minnesota prairie. They invited Nicholas and Cecilia to join them.

Nicholas didn't know what to make of his new brother-in-law. Jim bragged that he had served as a decorated colonel in the Civil War, though he was vague about where and how he came by that rank. He was even more mysterious about why he abandoned the bar he owned in Houghton, a tiny copper-mining town on Michigan's Upper Peninsula said to be occupied only by thieves, crooks, murderers, and Indians. None of that sat well with Nicholas. But the promise of a new life in Fergus Falls, Minnesota, did. Truth be told, Nicholas had never fallen in love with farming the way his father had, and the idea of tending bar in a bustling town was exciting. Plus, Cecilia wanted to be near her sister. So the young couple agreed to move.

Cecilia had just given birth to their first son, William, when they made the trip. Margaret must have worried for her, having made more than one long voyage with an infant. Though heading to Fergus Falls was a far cry from weeks below the deck of an immigrant ship, it was plenty taxing as the family made the long trek around Lake Michigan and into Chicago before heading west to Otter Tail County.

Nicholas and his family arrived at a town very much on the rise and that seemed to have been built overnight. That wasn't far from the truth. A Scottish trapper named Joe Whitford had claimed the falls and named them after James Fergus, an enterprising mill owner and politician, in 1856. In 1879 the town was flourishing, growing faster and faster as wooden houses and storefronts appeared on every lot. By the time Nicholas and Cecilia arrived, the town even had a roller-skating rink. But what they saw first as they arrived at their new home was the grand Fergus Falls School, set on a commanding knoll that was visible from the prairie miles before you could see the city itself. With its enormous white edifice and coppiced top, the school really did seem like a city on a hill. Nicholas and Cecilia couldn't help but be impressed by that.

Jim O'Brien's new saloon wasn't nearly so grand, and it was crowded upstairs, where the two families, along with an eighteen-year-old domestic servant named Katie, vied for space in the two-room quarters. Nicholas, Cecilia, and William slept on a mattress in the living room. Katie spent her nights in the cramped kitchen. Jim, Harriet, and their four children crammed into the apartment's single bedroom. Harriet was pregnant yet again. Nicholas couldn't imagine how they'd ever find room for the baby. It was claustrophobic, and tensions between the two families were beginning to grow.

Downstairs, though, Jim had created a place where everyone in town wanted to be. His saloon was a dimly lit place with a large bar that ran the length of the room, with plenty of stools—and taps—for patrons. If they preferred, customers could purchase a bottle of their favorite spirits from the casks behind the bar. Sawdust from the local mill caught the drips and hid indiscretions, and the first billiard table to grace the town kept everyone busy. A newly arrived player piano made it that much more fun to spend evenings at O'Brien's Saloon.

Nicholas rarely saw Jim in those days, but it didn't matter. His brother Eugene had joined them from the farm and was working his own shifts at the bar. Cecilia and William were well, and she had her sister for company while Nicholas ran the till. They would need to get a place of their own soon, but Nicholas was sure that wouldn't be a problem. Jim had promised Nicholas that he would be running the bar soon. Maybe one day he'd buy it outright. After all, in Fergus Falls anything was possible.

15

At Sea

1848

A BARQUE IS BUILT neither for speed nor comfort. The noted contemporary naval writer Alan Villiers describes the vessel as "heavy, sluggish in anything short of half a gale, fat in the buttocks and full of drag but powerful as a 3,000-ton elephant."[1] Sailors describe barques with adjectives like "rolly" and "chunky." Still, for nearly a century they were the dominant workhorses of the sea. Their wide hulls, flat bottoms, nubby bows—the very attributes that make these vessels such brutes for their passengers—made them ideal for hauling impressive loads of cargo in harrowing conditions. Little wonder, then, that builders like John Munn dedicated their lives to churning out these behemoths year after year, or that the docks of Liverpool, Calcutta, and Havana were filled with them.

The characteristic rigging for this vessel—two forward masts set with square sails, a third (mizzen) mast set with a fore-and-aft spanker and topsail—makes it easy to spot. In optimal conditions (which is to say, with the wind blowing from its stern or nearly so) they can maintain speeds of 6 or 7 knots: that's not very much speed compared to a schooner from the same era as the *Jeanie*, which regularly made 10 knots, or one of today's giant cruise ships, which cruises at 20 to 25 knots. What a barque lacks in speed, though, it more than makes up for with what sailors call "stiffness," meaning a hull shape that creates good stability. Whereas a schooner or racing vessel wants to heel—to rise up onto one side of its hull, thereby sailing pitched at an angle—a barque wants to lie flat in the water. When faced with wind, wave, and overpowered sail, a barque will struggle to return to this flat position by shifting from side to side.[2] In other words, it pitches, rocks, and rolls. As Nicole Gardiner, the former first mate of the re-created *Jeanie Johnston* puts it, "She wallows. There's not much else to say."[3]

"Wallowing" is sailor language; to the uninitiated, it's more than a little euphemistic when it comes to describing the sensation of being at sea aboard a barque. A sailing novice would probably be more inclined to describe the experience as one filled with violent dips and corkscrews, bucking bows, and the disorienting sensation of pitching from side to side. Aboard a barque, motion comes from every possible angle, and in a stormy sea, it is as irregular as it is pronounced. That motion is also exacerbated by the vessel's relationship to the wind. Wind from behind or pushing on the side of the vessel can make for fairly calm sailing, but as soon as the vessel encounters a headwind (what sailors call beating to windward), the ship takes on added strain. This strain can shear away masts, ripping holes in the deck floor. It can also create fissures in the seams of the boat, allowing in water. That, in turn, creates additional strain on the crew, who must then pump the water out of the bilge and monitor the open seams. It also tends to create unease if not outright terror in the passengers, who find themselves surrounded by a moaning, shuddering ship. In fact the only sound louder than a wooden hull toiling against wave and wind is the sound of that wind tearing the vessel's heavy canvas sails.

Such conditions wreak havoc below the decks of cargo ships, where even well-stowed items like chests and cookware become missiles as the vessel heaves, rocks, and crashes from swell to swell. Privy slop pails overturn; pots of half-eaten porridge and rice tumble to the floor. In addition to the resulting muck, the planked subdeck poses dangers as well, most notably, writes Edward Laxton, author of *The Famine Ships*, from the deck itself. There a sea of constantly shifting boards creates slits and crevices capable of snaring a foot or clothes and trapping a person for hours, or at least until another passenger can free him or her.[4] That kind of peril and vigilant care required of fellow passengers is the sort of thing that turns total strangers into kin. Quickly.

Such was Margaret Reilly's reality for the forty days it took the *Jeanie Johnston* to travel from Tralee to Quebec. From her bunk below deck, Margaret could hear the reverberating workings of the *Jeanie* as she entered the open ocean. Still weak from Nicholas's delivery, she had not ventured far from the wooden platform she and Daniel shared with at least one other couple. From there, the sound of the shrieking wind and the violent convulsions of the hull must have been unimaginable. With no opportunity for air or exercise, her seasickness would have been more difficult to recover from than it would be for other passengers.

She and the other passengers were visited daily by Richard Blennerhassett, who kept a close eye on the young mother and her newborn son. The doctor got to know both well during the journey. That the infant not only survived but appeared to be in good health was nothing short of miraculous. Seeing their continued good health was a rare moment of delight for a man who, in his thirty years, had already witnessed great suffering.

As a member of the landed gentry and an Edinburgh-educated physician, Blennerhassett was distinguished from the crew by his class, even without the indicators of dress and mannerisms. He was considered an equal in station to the captain. The two men divided their governance of the vessel between what happened above deck and below, and they consulted one another regularly. When the weather allowed, the doctor insisted on open hatches and full air circulation in the hold, even though doing so flew in the face of reigning theories on disease transmittal and the prevalence of miasma as an infecting agent. He also mandated daily walks above deck for those well enough to take them and the weekly airing of bedding to avert lice infestations and unhygienic living conditions.

Margaret Reilly wasn't yet well enough to participate in these daily regimens, but Daniel was. Along with the other passengers, he was trying hard to master the unfamiliar protocol of a life at sea. In the short time they had been aboard, the passengers had come to know Captain Attridge as a benevolent force; nevertheless he had made it perfectly clear that he expected everyone on board to maintain strict codes of conduct. He mandated that all well passengers rise at 7 A.M., dress for the day, then roll up their bedding and sweep the deck. Daniel, along with the other male passengers over the age of fourteen, had also been assigned to a cleaning detail on rotation; each day, ten men were responsible for emptying the slop buckets used as privies and dry-scrubbing all floors below deck. This was no small task; with nearly two hundred individuals packed below, many of whom were suffering from severe seasickness, keeping their living quarters bearable could seem a herculean feat and took up the better part of their waking hours. To help maintain order, Attridge also deputized four of the adult male passengers, granting them the power to enforce policies and to serve as liaisons between him and the passengers.

During the day, Daniel and his son Robert ventured above deck for twenty minutes at a time—just long enough to get a sense of the massive ocean surrounding them and watch the toiling crew. It was during these intervals when families could line up to receive their daily water allocation—a mere six pints in total. When twenty or thirty passengers were in the open air at one time, the women took the opportunity to wash clothes in rainwater or use the two cooking stoves.

Few items on the *Jeanie Johnston* engendered as much compulsive attention as these stoves. Each morning, while the emigrants busied themselves with dressing and stowing their bedding, Gabriel Seldon, who was not normally required to stand watch and who had the enviable responsibility of overseeing the pantry and all food, lit a fire in the two small metal boxes lined with bricks that served as stoves for the two hundred passengers. While he turned his attention to making breakfast for the crew, the women made porridge for their family's sole daily meal. That allotment of oats and rice, along with six pints of water, was the standard dietary allocation on board the *Jeanie* and similar famine ships.[5] Each woman had one opportunity at the stove each day to use her allotted oat ration, boil water, and prepare any additional food she could afford to bring on board. All the while, the women were subjected to the conditions of the churning sea and the threat of bad weather. If conditions became too rough, Hugh Murphy and Arthur McBretney, the ship's two young apprentices, would be ordered into the ship's rigging, so that they could douse the fires from above, lest the flames escape their crude brick containers and set the entire vessel ablaze. The same was true for the three small safety lanterns and open hatches that served as the only illumination below deck.

Flame of any sort, though necessary on an oceangoing vessel, was as significant a threat to the safety of those on board as ship's fever or icebergs. Each year, Lloyd's of London reported on tragic fires aboard vessels. With hundreds or even thousands of miles of sea separating them from the safety of land or rescue vessels, the consequences for all those on board were often deadly. The same was no less true for vessels in sight of land. The same season that the *Jeanie* made her inaugural voyage as an immigrant ship, newspapers around the world reported on the fate of the *Ocean Monarch*, a massive 1,300-ton ship carrying approximately four hundred Irish emigrants that caught fire while still in sight of land. The intensity of the heat prompted many on board, including women holding their young children, to jump to their death. Dozens of others perished as the vessel, soon completely engulfed in flames, sank in the cold waters off the coast of Wales. The death toll was over two hundred.

Attridge knew all too well how easy it would be for a similar fate to befall the *Jeanie*. Severe weather, then, would mean an uncomfortable day with no food and next to pitch-black conditions in the berths, where all passengers would be restricted until the seas improved. Even under the best conditions, Attridge insisted on strict boundaries for passengers so that his crew could do their work without impediment or interruption.

The tasks for the crew were also segregated and ordered. Attridge and First Mate Thomas Campion were primarily responsible for management of the vessel and its course. Using a chronometer and sextant, the two determined the vessel's longitude each morning. Then, at noon and with the sun directly above them, they would mark their latitude. Together this would reveal their location. Coupled with celestial navigation, the ability to mark one's position by a fixed astronomical body, such as the North Star, the chronometer gave Attridge the reckoning he needed to locate his vessel on a chart—or at least it did when the clouds broke long enough for him to see either star or sun. Several times each watch, Campion recorded their position in the *Jeanie*'s logbook, which he was required to submit to his captain each day for examination and any necessary corrections. Of all the interactions between a first mate and his captain, this was one of the most important when it came to proving a mate's worth at sea.[6]

Like Attridge, Campion rarely took the wheel when sailing. Under reasonable sailing conditions, that task was left to the ordinary sailors, whom Campion had divided into two watches based on their dispositions and skills. In fact the immigrants rarely saw Attridge, who was most often in his cabin or the chart room, plotting their course and always, always, always double-checking their position and the integrity of his vessel.

The course Attridge set for the *Jeanie* was the same one employed by nearly every other transatlantic vessel sailing that time of year: an arc reaching down from Ireland across the North Atlantic and then sweeping past Newfoundland and toward the more populated latitudes of the North American east coast. This route was known as the "great thoroughfare of commerce" to nineteenth-century sailors. It was also known as the most tempestuous part of the Atlantic Ocean.[7] In his 1851 guide for sailors, M. F. Maury warned captains and their crew that the seas in the Gulf Stream "are terrific during a gale; opposite currents operate to break the direction given them by the wind, when a concussion takes place, causing them to run in all directions."[8]

Even in the best conditions, these waters posed untold dangers for a sailing vessel. Unlike the growing number of steamships sharing the waterway, the *Jeanie Johnston* and her crew were bound by wind and current, which would often force a vessel directly into the path of danger.[9] And, unlike the equally as common schooners, the *Jeanie* was hard-pressed to steer her way out of such peril. Ensuring that she did was the duty of Thomas Campion. Each day he stood on deck overseeing the sailors and insisting that Attridge's orders be executed. It was Campion who would call for the sails to be raised, reefed, or stowed. And it was he who often climbed high up into the rigging to assess the condition of sailcloth and line.[10]

William Patterson, a twenty-six-year-old Scots-Irish sailor from Down, a county in what would later become Northern Ireland, served as the *Jeanie*'s second mate. Patterson oversaw the second of the two watches; however, his supervisory role ended there. He was obliged to keep a foot in two camps without the benefit of belonging to either: Attridge expected him to behave with the decorum and distance of an officer, yet he was still required to toil as an ordinary seaman. This included executing commands to change sail position, tarring the side of the boat, and polishing its many brass fixtures. On watch, Patterson and the other sailors rotated through the various tasks required of them: manning the ship's enormous wheel, housed in the aft of the vessel; maintaining Attridge's course with the help of a magnetic compass; and readying the lines for any tack or change in course.[11] Each time Attridge called for either, seven or eight men would have to set a single sail, and nearly all hands worked to tack the vessel. Up in the rigging, they climbed icy foot ropes and then snaked their way out onto equally treacherous spars, balancing nearly a hundred feet over the deck and open ocean, in order to mend or reef sails. Off watch, they spent their time splicing line, changing chaffed rigging, mending sails, and always cleaning.[12] Intermittently they retired to their bunks in the ship's forecastle. Located near the bow of the *Jeanie*, it was the roughest—and wettest—place onboard and made the Reillys' accommodations seem first class. Indeed it took a seasoned sailor to find any rest at all between the bucking of the vessel and the constant leaking spray. Attridge did his best to mitigate their discomfort by maintaining as regular and humane a routine as the seas would allow. He himself presided over mass each Sunday, the one time that crew and passengers assembled on the deck together.[13]

On fair days, Gabriel Seldon began each morning by lighting the passengers' cooking stoves and began preparing breakfast, and the first watch washed and swabbed the decks and made the rigging neat. They had breakfast around eight o'clock, usually porridge or hardtack and bacon, and then began the series of four hours on, four hours off that defined a sailor's existence. They broke twice for meals, which included dried beef on every day except Tuesday and Friday, when they were served cured pork. They ate dried peas and rice on alternating days, always looking forward to Sundays, when Seldon would also serve them biscuits with butter. They contented themselves with lime and vinegar in their water;

despite the common practice of giving sailors up to a half pint of rum a day, Attridge had decreed that no spirits would be allowed on his ship.

There was, he insisted, little time for drinking, or anything other than work. The exception was the dog watch, that time just after dinner when the vessel was truly their own. This was the time each day when the cooking stove fires had been extinguished by Murphy and McBretney and the emigrants had retired to the dim light of an emergency lantern below deck. Up above, all hands had a brief reprieve to smoke, play cards, or tell stories. Attridge could be seen at his place on the quarterdeck, sometimes with Campion nearby. Seldon finished washing dishes in the galley and made the last tea for the night. And then, every evening at eight o'clock, bells were sounded and the first of the two evening watches began, as the *Jeanie* eased her way across the North Atlantic.[14]

16

Dead Reckoning

A s the *Jeanie* continued to push across the Atlantic, she encountered unrelenting squalls. Four weeks into their trip, these conditions only intensified. The already heavy seas became more violent as large, swelling waves pushed from the southwest. Behind the building clouds, the sky took on an ominous copper color. The barque's barometer plummeted, and then the winds began to gather. Somewhere, just over the horizon, a storm many mariners described as a hurricane was building in strength as it skimmed across North Carolina's Outer Banks, sinking over a dozen vessels along the way. Then, without notice, the storm turned northeastward and set a collision course for the *Jeanie Johnston*.[1]

James Attridge had been at sea long enough to know the telltale signs of the storm's approach. Without delay, he ordered the fires extinguished and the hatches sealed tight, leaving the Reillys and the ship's other 196 passengers to toss about in pitch darkness. Robert howled in fright while Margaret lay with Nicholas clutched tightly to her breast. Daniel struggled to take care of all three.

Amid the moans and shrieks of the other passengers and the scream of the barque's hull and sails, Daniel could hear other, fainter noises as well: the shouts of Attridge and Campion as they summoned the men, the crew toiling in the midship area to keep the vessel on course and bring in the tattered sails. For those on deck, life became a blur of wake up, work, eat, pump, nap, with nothing to differentiate one day from the next. Personal hygiene was abandoned, and the crew felt painful salt water boils where their oilskins chafed at sensitive skin. Exhausted from lack of sleep and worn down by days in wet, cold clothes, they grumbled and railed against their lot.[2]

As the storm raged on, Attridge was unable to do much more than guess at the ship's location; his chronometer and sextant were useless without the sun to mark noon, and celestial navigation, of course, required the stars. It was days before he could take a clear sighting. When he did, he could see that their troubles were just beginning. Just as he feared, the *Jeanie* was now in a veritable minefield of icebergs.

This stretch of the Atlantic was the same one infamously attempted by the *Titanic* some sixty years later. The *Jeanie Johnston* had neither the ocean liner's technology nor its steel hull to protect it from these massive ice formations, which can travel more than fifteen hundred miles at a rate of one nautical mile per hour. Dodging these obstacles even in calm conditions takes an experienced captain and a nimble crew. In a gale, it also requires luck, if not Divine Providence. Attridge knew he would need both as the *Jeanie* rounded Newfoundland and the Grand Banks, a famous fishing ground just south of Newfoundland's east coast.

When approaching the Banks, Attridge and his crew should have encountered a swarm of Boston schooners. The end of May was the start of their prime fishing season, and these slim fore-and-aft-rigged ships were capable of slicing through wind and wave quickly enough to bring a fresh catch back to Massachusetts. Yet the *Jeanie Johnston* encountered not a one. Attridge knew it took a lot to keep those schooner fishers away.

This sparseness of traffic persisted as the *Jeanie* neared the mouth of the St. Lawrence, where the captain and his crew quickly discovered the reason behind it: the Gulf of the St. Lawrence seemed to be entirely filled with ice.[3] In fact, unbeknown to Attridge, only two cargo vessels had made it to port the entire season.[4]

Attridge calculated that it would be weeks before he neared the city. His brief weather reprieve was coming to an end, and he watched as the persistent northwesterly wind that had followed the hurricane suddenly swung and became easterly. It screamed through the rigging, threatening to tear his sails to tatters. As it did, the seas became formidable swells moving into shore and sending icy spray across the *Jeanie*'s deck.

Conditions such as these could easily knock down or dismast a vessel, so, once again, Attridge was forced to call all hands on deck, this time to help brace the sails and yards. Meanwhile he took the wheel and struggled to turn the vessel so that the wind was pushing aft. This kept the *Jeanie* from sinking, but it made it more difficult to keep her on course. It also worsened conditions on board, as the waves struck against the bow of the vessel, sending it—and all those below—rolling precipitously from side to side. Richard Blennerhassett could only imagine the misery his charges were experiencing below deck. It was up to Attridge to keep them all alive. This new gale was driving the ship directly into the St. Lawrence and the river's jagged mouth of ice. To avoid this, he would have to keep the headsails up and intact and his crew alert.

Below deck, even the hardiest passengers were worried. The *Jeanie Johnston* had been at sea for five weeks, and although Donovan had insisted on regulations to preserve the cleanliness of his vessel, conditions in steerage were deteriorating. Quickly. The hatches remained sealed, and Blennerhassett's strict hygiene protocols had been aborted. Even in ideal conditions, the hold of a sailing ship reeks of moldy bilge water. But these were far from ideal times, and the cumulative effect of weeks of sick passengers had made the stench nearly unbearable. Most of the passengers still wore the same clothes they had on when they came aboard, which were now stained with soot and grime and evidence of seasickness. The strain of a limited diet was also showing; even had the conditions not been so precarious, few would have had the energy for anything other than the necessary chores to keep their quarters habitable. Most simply stayed in their bunks, hoping to wait out the voyage.

Attridge was visibly nervous. He paced the oak deck and scrutinized the unsettled water in the Gulf of the St. Lawrence. The collision of currents from the powerful river and the equally vigorous North Atlantic broke and smashed before him, hurling up plumes of foam spiked with errant logs and other forest debris. Enormous chunks of green river ice—some almost as large as his ship—surged through these same waves, threatening to smash even the sturdiest hull. In all his sailing days,

Attridge had never experienced conditions as dangerous as these. He took a deep breath, finally admitting what he had been trying to deny for days: the *Jeanie Johnston* was in serious trouble.

By the time they neared the mouth of the St. Lawrence, this unexpected ice was everywhere and moving at dangerous speeds. Even the most seasoned sailors agreed that it was an awful time to be on these waters. More than that, Attridge would later admit, it was downright deadly.

Attridge was doing his best to reach their mandatory quarantine stop at Grosse Île, but this final leg of the trip was proving to be the most trying. By the time night fell on the last day of May, the storm had intensified around the ship, threatening to blow a gale. As the ship groaned against the storm, Attridge called on his entire crew, already exhausted from extra watches and diminishing food, to shorten sail. Even Gabriel Seldon was told to remain all standing.

Like Attridge, Seldon and his mates had learned to trust in the *Jeanie* during the arduous North Atlantic crossing, but that didn't make battling this newest storm any easier. Swells from the storm crashed into the beam of the vessel, sending violent eruptions of seawater up and over the deck. Freezing rain stung the sailors' faces. It saturated then froze their clothing, making it difficult to move. Their palms, calloused from years of handling hemp line, tore and bled as they struggled to bring in the royal sails and topgallants. The only canvas left unfurled was reefed against the wind. Attridge ordered those deckhands not hauling sail to climb high up into the topmasts. Others lashed themselves to the barque's long bowsprit to scan for icebergs, rocks, and other ships; their shouts would be the only warning the captain would have in advance of an impending collision. To preserve their night vision and reduce the risk of fire on board Attridge prohibited any illumination on the deck. As the last bit of dull storm light was extinguished by the encroaching night, the men on deck were forced to work wholly by feel, counting the number of lines and memorizing their position on the ship's pinrails. More than a test of the crew's mastery of the rigging that controlled their ship, these inky conditions were crucial for ensuring that the men could spot any encroaching hazards on the horizon.

Reminders of how dangerous these hazards could be were all around them. As the day broke, the crew could see a debris field covering the Gulf: floating deckhouses and empty lifeboats, jagged fragments of hull, even travel chests and dishware. A few days before the *Jeanie* entered the St. Lawrence, a barque called the *Astoria* had foundered in the bay after trying unsuccessfully to navigate the thick weather. With the wind blowing hard out of the southeast, her captain was unable to prevent the vessel from striking rock. Immediately after impact, he cut away both the fore and main masts, hoping to prevent further damage. Her crew managed a harrowing escape after the captain shot a lead line to the cliffs nearby. As the sea washed over the ship, he sent his men one by one in a basket up the line and to safety at the top of the cliff.[5] A few days later, another barque was hit by an enormous cake of ice that smashed into its hull, causing significant damage. At least three additional vessels were still bound up in the ice and unable to free themselves.[6]

From his post on deck, Attridge could see these beleaguered vessels. He could also pick out some of the other cargo ships now sharing the channel. He recognized several from his days in Liverpool, others by reputation. The *Robert Jackson*, a cargo ship that left from Liverpool at the same time as the *Jeanie*, limped along, all but incapacitated by a splintered mast and sails torn to rags by the gale. The *Dispatch* and the *Alert* both carried emigrants from the west of Ireland. There were also two haulers from Bordeaux bringing the season's wine to Quebec, the first the residents there had seen since the deep freeze. At long last, it seemed, the shipping season was beginning in earnest.

That was good news for the supply-starved people of British North America, but considerably less so for Attridge and other ship captains. Getting caught in a jam of other ships would undoubtedly turn this already harrowing trip into a disastrous one. The ship's food and water were running low; his men were exhausted. Any additional vessel in this rapidly moving river was one more obstacle Attridge could only hope to avoid. He needed to beat these other ships up river, and that would take every inch of the *Jeanie*'s square sails.

The captain was having a far easier time maintaining his resolve than were his men, many of whom watched helplessly as several other ships foundered and sank.

Unbeknown to the *Jeanie*'s crew, sailors aboard John Munn's other ships were embattled by the weather as well. The *Ayrshire*, laden with indentured servants on the Calcutta route, was imperiled in a storm of similar strength and now risked capsizing. The crew of the *England*, the *Jeanie*'s companion ship on her maiden voyage, were fighting for their lives as well. They had left the crowded lazarettos of Liverpool overloaded with Irish passengers and destined for New York. The same storm that besieged the *Jeanie* stretched down into the mid-Atlantic, where it collided with the tropical depression working its way up from the Caribbean. Even Munn's careful construction was no match for the resulting gale: the winds sheared off the *England*'s mast, immobilizing the vessel and forcing the crew and passengers to await assistance from a passing vessel.

No one aboard the *Jeanie Johnston* would hear of these struggles until long after they landed. Nor would they learn that the *Growler*, captained by Attridge's brother and also destined for New York, was beset by the same storm and had been forced to retreat to Cork.[7] What they did know was that the gale off the coast of British North America raged on. Night fell; all hands remained on deck, wagering their lives on the skill of their captain and the quality of their ship.

17

Quarantine

O UT ON Grosse Île, George Douglas waited nervously for the
first immigrant ship to arrive. It was anyone's guess whether
the typhus outbreak would continue, and to make matters
worse, there were now rumors of a resurgence in cholera across Europe.
Then again, even the best of conditions would have done little to erase
the feeling of dread that pervaded the island. Last year's catastrophic
death toll had shattered any sense of hope among his surviving staff. In
truth, it had killed much of the light inside Douglas as well. His hair was
now prematurely gray; his face showed decades of aging contracted into
a single season. On both sides of the Atlantic, officials were questioning
his soundness as a doctor and an administrator; they wondered about his
record keeping, his ability to manage staff, his understanding of what
plagued the immigrants. They even questioned the ethics of his decision
to sell vegetables to those with money to buy them.

And then there was his wife, Charlotte. She was haunted by the scene
of bodies corded like firewood awaiting burial and by the workers' insistence that the island was haunted.[1] Perhaps it was. Certainly it had witnessed great suffering, and it did seem like a kind of curse had settled on
the barren land. That winter, a series of nor'easters had pounded their
farmstead, tearing at their house, and bullet-like hail broke windows
and left pockmarks on their doors. The already despondent Charlotte

had grown inconsolable. And she was right: you simply could not escape death on this island.

Had Douglas known that, a century later, the British government would deem the island unfit for anything other than top-secret biological warfare and animal pathology experimentation, he wouldn't have been surprised. The island already seemed irrevocably corrupted by death and disease. He could see it in Charlotte's face, the way she never left the farm, the way she walked about like a condemned prisoner. His salary was by no means grand, but it was enough to allow for savings, particularly since there was so little on which to spend it in a place like Grosse Île. There was no reason to make Charlotte suffer any more than she already had. She needed a place where she could walk freely, where she could eat wild berries without wondering what grisly death had fertilized them. So he signed a mortgage he would never be able to repay, purchasing the nearby island, Île aux Ruaux, and arranging to build a new home there.

Then he turned his attention back to the St. Lawrence, once known, somewhat lyrically, as *mélange des eaux*, the mixing of the waters, or the place where salt and fresh water meet, now known perhaps more appropriately as *Le cimetière du fleuve*, the cemetery river. There the season's first coffin ships were making their last tacks against the impossible tides and toward the waiting island.

The first to arrive at Grosse Île that year was John Munn's *Fame*, making land with her full complement of Irish refugees, despite the miserable conditions on board. A week later the *Orinoco*, which left Ireland the same day as the *Jeanie Johnston*, delivered her human cargo. So began the season of immigrant deliveries.

They were not without casualty. Two vessels destined for Grosse Île, the *Governor* from Limerick and the *St. John* from Galway, were already reporting significant losses during their crossing, with forty-nine and twenty-six emigrants dying on board, respectively. Seven had died aboard the *John Hall*. Four hundred fifty immigrants had passed through quarantine and were now cleared to make the final leg of their journey, from the island to Quebec, aboard a large steamer named the *John Munn* in honor of the philanthropist and shipbuilder. An additional thousand immigrants who had passed Douglas's medical screening were awaiting passage the next day. The rest—many dangerously thin, some showing signs of infection—remained closed off in the island's fever sheds. Once again the death count began to rise, and with it officials again looked for someone to blame.

The season's first dispatch from Henry Grey's office sought to allay fears about another typhus epidemic. People were dying, wrote the earl, but they "were almost exclusively Irish of the lowest class & . . . , like those who proceeded from that country to Canada during the past year, they had been in a state of extreme destitution before they embarked . . . they carried with them on board ship the seeds of the diseases which were subsequently so fatal to them."[2]

Douglas could see that, to at least some degree, officials were right. There was infection among these immigrants, but he knew that while even the halest patient was often helpless in a battle against a disease like typhus or influenza, a weak and undernourished one would stand no chance. Before the season was barely under way, he sat down to write another letter, this time asking that the immigrants be given enough food to survive the ravages of ocean travel and disease.[3] He used what remained in his meager budget to ensure that starvation did not occur on his watch, paying farmers on nearby islands for weekly deliveries of milk. It was a treat not seen in over a month for the immigrants. For those who came from the poorer regions of Ireland, it was an altogether foreign substance.

Douglas's outlay was not enough to stem the number of casualties, however. Nor was it sufficient to keep typhus from sneaking onto the mainland. June brought with it the promise of a glorious summer season, but also brought hundreds of new patients to the city's fever sheds, where crudely made wooden beds were tucked so tightly together that nurses could barely pass between. They were again filled to capacity, sometimes with two people lying head to toe and looking, as one attending nun said, "as if they were in their coffins."[4]

Their condition sent Canadian officials scurrying to reinforce their quarantine standards. Within twenty-four hours, the army was again dispatched to man the cannons flanking the center of Grosse Île. The son of a Methodist minister, George Douglas had never been comfortable with the use of force, militaristic or otherwise. But as the influx of immigrants increased, he had to admit he was relieved to have the armed soldiers encamped on the island. If nothing else, they made a clear delineation of right and wrong in a place that seemed otherwise mired in ambiguity.

News of the soldiers' arrival was the last that would reach either side of the Atlantic that year. Within a week, Canada's executive government forbade the transmission of all news from the island to anywhere other than its own headquarters. Presumably this decision was made to combat the poor press received by the island during the catastrophic shipping season the year before. Whether or not such measures were warranted, the press was outraged, accusing the government—as only Victorian reporters could—of enforcing a restriction "as arbitrary as it is absurd and mischievous."[5]

18

Passing Customs

S EVEN IMMIGRANT vessels arrived at Grosse Île on June 8, 1848.
It was a tumultuous day for everyone: the night before, a stiff
northward wind had swept down into Quebec, bringing with
it an unexpected hard frost. Early potato and corn seedlings were killed;
blossoms froze and dropped from the region's fruit trees.[1] Throughout
the city, people reverted to their winter habits, donning warm hats and
lighting coal fires both inside and out. From downtown, those hearty
enough to brave the elements could see that the surrounding mountains
were capped in snow. Later that day, a "terrific thunderstorm" passed
over Quebec and down the St. Lawrence, bringing hail, torrential rain,
and reports of multiple lightning strikes.

Still sequestered in the hold of the *Jeanie Johnston*, Margaret Reilly
could feel first the bitter cold and then the violent thunder. This was
her first real exposure to the climate of her new continent, and it was far
from the temperate weather they had been promised. Even the blustery
coast back home offered more warmth and regularity than this. What
had already seemed an uncertain future now became an increasingly ill-
omened one.

As the thunderstorm swept out to sea, Daniel Reilly joined some of
the other men on deck. He caught his first glimpse of Grosse Île rising
sharply out of the water, a dramatic combination of dark stone and dense
stands of oak, birch, and maple, all wearing the pale green of early season

foliage. Pine trees rose high above them, blanketing the island in shade. Below the tree line, Daniel could see the chapels, bakery, barracks, and housing for the medical staff. Separated from them by the army barracks were the hospital and twelve fever sheds. Armed guards stood watch on the thin neck of the island separating the sick from the well; only a horse-drawn ambulance and the official medical staff were allowed to move from one side of the island to the other.[2] Out of sight but still very much on everyone's mind were the mass graves containing the five thousand victims of the 1847 season; with their wide hummocked topography and whisper of new vegetation, they looked very much like the potato beds in Ireland, an irony lost on few who passed by.

The *Jeanie*'s arrival at the island was dictated not by its captain but by the pilot who had boarded his vessel several days earlier. Nautical law—not to mention common sense—dictated that Attridge welcome a local navigator delivered by skiff for the express purpose of sailing the large cargo ship around the topographic perils of the river. We don't know the name of this pilot, but we do know quite a lot about his qualifications and expertise. A certified pilot was the one individual to whom a captain would cede control of his ship, and in no place was such a decision more warranted than the St. Lawrence—a river notorious around the world not only for its dramatic tides but also for its deadly shoals and deceptively narrow channels separated by innumerable bony islands. A lifetime in these waters, along with years of apprenticeship, ensured that a pilot knew this topography better than anyone on the planet, as well as how to utilize the tides and currents to the advantage of a vessel that had only wind and sail to power it. Most pilots were French Canadian; many maintained island farms during the off months; all were between thirty and sixty-five years old.

They were also adroit followers of British law, a necessity in a region still marred by the traumatic deaths of the previous year. Regardless of how rigorous Attridge had been in enforcing order on board, no matter how stringent Blennerhassett had been about hygiene, the *Jeanie John-ston* was still a coffin ship. And that made her a potential threat to the well-being of those already living in North America. The pilot brought with him a pamphlet from Dr. Douglas detailing what would happen in quarantine and at the anchorage ground surrounding Grosse Île. The *Jeanie* and her passengers would have one chance to prove their fitness to the quarantine doctor, and Blennerhassett was determined they would all pass inspection.

It wasn't just his and Attridge's reputations at stake. After the disasters of the previous season, Parliament had implemented a new fine of 2 shillings for every three days an immigrant remained on Grosse Île. It would do little to mitigate sickness, but at least the cost of that sickness would be the ship owner's responsibility. On some vessels, paying that fine rested squarely on the shoulders of captains and doctors.

There wasn't much time to prepare. Blennerhassett directed the controlled chaos needed to prepare the vessel for inspection: soiled beds and straw were tossed overboard, privy pails were emptied, and the floor of the immigrants' area was cleaned. He asked the crew to fill buckets with the remaining water on board and then supervised the bathing of each passenger.

Meanwhile the pilot and Attridge worked to angle the *Jeanie* toward Grosse Île's main promontory. There a solitary privy stood directly in front of a large rock outcropping. Marking the shortest line to deep water, it also indicated the eventual docking target for the barque. So dramatic are the tides around Grosse Île that the *Jeanie Johnston*, which drew about fifteen feet, still nearly bottomed out at low tide. Jockeying for position were the six other vessels—and their twelve hundred passengers—hoping to make landfall that day. The largest of them was the *Miltiades*, which arrived from Belfast with 315 passengers on board. A fully rigged ship, the *Miltiades* was also faster than the *Jeanie Johnston*. She made her way to the mandatory anchorage before the *Jeanie* and quickly raised a flag signaling to Douglas that they were ready for inspection. Most of the passengers on board were cottiers sent out by their landlords. Attridge and Blennerhassett could see from their condition that clearing them for landing on the quarantine island would take some time.

To occupy his men, Attridge ordered them to douse the barque's immense sails and ready her deck for inspection. They used a noxious combination of lime, sulfuric acid, and hot tar—the only mixture thought strong enough to kill the odors causing ship's fever. They also prepared the mandatory whitewash that would paint over weeks of suffering in the hold.

Blennerhassett continued to organize the passengers. After forty days at sea, they were enfeebled, weary, and impossibly grimy despite his best efforts. They were all alive, though. Some presented with severe dehydration as a result of dysentery and seasickness; others were marked by bed sores and bruises. Their time in steerage showed; still, the *Jeanie*'s passengers had fewer of these maladies than most. After conferring with Blennerhassett, Attridge raised the white flag, indicating that all on board were healthy. Yet the doctor wondered if some of his charges could stand long enough to be examined by Douglas.

It seemed an eternity before the medical superintendent, flanked by two of his assistants, slowly rowed from the *Miltiades* to the *Jeanie Johnston*. As he neared, the nervous tension aboard increased. Douglas had the power to determine their lives in North America—to decide who could enter and who would be detained, to separate mothers and children, husbands and wives. It was not a role he relished, but he performed it with a curt professionalism that some passengers saw as gruff. The last thing a newly arrived coffin ship needed was an emotional outpouring, and Douglas was determined to keep order as best he could. His assistants strung a long rope across the deck of the *Jeanie Johnston* and ordered the passengers to approach one by one.

Daniel and Margaret Reilly watched nervously as Douglas ordered each person before him to stick out their tongue. Based on this—and this alone—the doctor decided on which side of the rope they would stand. Those nearest the gangway would soon be taken to the fever sheds, where they would spend weeks or even longer. Those deemed healthy were sent to the other side of the rope and would soon be on their way to Quebec City and their new lives in North America.

The anticipation and dread experienced by the Reillys at that moment must have been excruciating. Margaret was still quite weak from Nicholas's birth. Would it show in her mouth? Would she be detained—and if so, would Nicholas be allowed to remain with her? If only Margaret were detained, it would be the last she and Daniel would see of each other for some time; visits to the ill were strictly prohibited. Daniel would be ferried by the *Jeanie* to Quebec City; he would have no way of knowing if and when Margaret was released or when a steamer would deliver her to the bustling city docks. In the minutes that remained until she was called, Daniel surely thought of nothing else.

Whether it was her own fortitude, Blennerhassett's studious care, or the sheer grace of God, George Douglas passed Margaret Reilly and ordered her and Nicholas and the children to stand on the healthy side of the rope. The family would remain together—at least for now. But their ordeal was far from over. Douglas conferred briefly with Attridge and Blennerhassett, then departed the vessel without another word. It was left to the doctor and captain to explain to the passengers what lay in store for them.

While Margaret waited on board with Nicholas, Daniel and Robert disembarked to undergo an elaborate disinfection process. The solidity of dry land felt jarring and unfamiliar as they stepped from the ship's deck to the pier, and they swayed unsteadily as their bodies fought to find new equilibrium without the ocean's endless rocking. Under the watchful eye of one of Douglas's assistants, Daniel unpacked the family chest, scrubbed each dish, pair of trousers, and shoe in muddy river water, then found places on the crowded rocks to dry them. He helped Robert bathe with soap and washed his face with vinegar. It took him the rest of the day to complete these tasks.[3] Then he returned to the ship to collect Margaret and Nicholas.

As the Reillys slowly climbed the forty steps that would lead them to the island proper, Attridge and Donovan looked on. The passengers were thinner and dirtier than when they had embarked. Still, they were alive. Up they rose, ascending the wooden stairs and joining the others congregating on the wharf, from where they would eventually make their way to the island quarantine sheds and into an unknown future.

—⟋ɯ⟍—

Jim O'Brien was playing a shell game—that much seemed clear. Nicholas had seen the evening tills, had stayed up late into the night counting the money. The bar was always crowded, and at the end of each night profits were high. Jim didn't let him touch the bar's ledger, but Nicholas was responsible for filling its safe with cash every night. Where it went after that was a mystery. The man from Pabst had taken to dropping by the saloon every week looking for his payment. Whenever Nicholas opened the safe, he found it empty. In exchange for his weak apology, he was given yet another bill and the promise that the collector would be back. There were other invoices as well— from breweries and distilleries, from the ice man and the glass factory. They all said the same thing: if Jim O'Brien didn't settle up fast, they wouldn't be doing business together for much longer.

It wouldn't be much of a pub if they couldn't sell drinks, and that was beginning to seem like a distinct possibility. Not only were the brewers threatening to stop supplying the saloon, but the temperance movement was gaining in strength across the United States. Just a few years earlier, Kansas had succeeded in outlawing alcohol throughout the state. The movement was also growing in Minnesota, and officials were cracking down on saloon owners. Jim O'Brien was feeling the pressure from them as well.

Jim never bothered with formalities, and he rarely had the patience or money for legalities like taxes and licenses. That had come to a head recently when inspectors discovered that the saloon had been selling alcohol without a license. During Jim's trial, Nicholas sat in the back of the courtroom, flummoxed by reports of unpaid taxes and abandoned debts in Michigan. He didn't dare talk to Jim about it,

119

though. His brother-in-law had always been bellicose, and the stress of whatever funny business was going on had brought out a new rage in him that frankly made Nicholas nervous. At a recent meeting of the fire brigade, another firefighter had questioned Jim's character. He responded by punching the man hard in the face. The police officer on duty seemed downright pleased about arresting Jim for assault.

After that, Jim became more scarce than ever, all but living in Chicago. Despite Harriet's growing distress, he was as vague as ever about what he did there. On those rare occasions when he returned to the Grand Hotel, it was with a stack of whiskey bonds that he cached in the safe before so much as removing his hat or saying hello. Whiskey bonds were as good as gold when it came to loan collateral, and the ones in Jim's safe would have been more than enough to pay the saloon's creditors. But Jim never seemed to give the creditors a second thought. Instead he went to the race track or on another of his mysterious jaunts to Chicago, leaving Harriet, Nicholas, and Cecilia to pick up the pieces.

Jim was a schemer, and more than ever Nicholas didn't want to be a part of that. William was now five; Helen was two. The Reillys needed a little space of their own. But when it came to Nicholas's paycheck, Jim always seemed to come up a little short. That, Nicholas was learning, was pretty much always the way with Jim. There was the court summons for falling delinquent on his mortgage and the unfortunate coincidence of the fire at his brewery, which occurred just before he was forced to resign as brigade chief for the Wide Awake Hose Company. Then there was his equally ill-advised plan to buy and sell debt: foreclosed homes, threatened bankruptcies, insurance liability—it didn't matter what form it took, Jim would wheel and deal it, always staying one step ahead of an angry creditor or a town official who thought to ask questions. That too made Nicholas nervous. They were family, yes, but even family had to draw limits.

When Jim announced that he had entered the real estate business, Nicholas was more than a little skeptical. When Jim explained that he intended to buy the disused grand old schoolhouse on the hill and relocate it behind the saloon, Nicholas thought Jim was crazy. Still, his *brother-in-law had a way of making things happen, and before long, a team of draft horses and burly men arrived as promised. How Jim managed to get the biggest building in all of Fergus Falls down a hill and into town—all in one piece—was a mystery. It barely fit in the lot between Rat Matthews's racehorse training stable and the roller-skating rink turned National Guard armory.*

Jim was beside himself with pride over this newest venture. Every day trains arrived in town overflowing with people looking for work. They all needed a place to stay, and an apartment in the town's best-looking building would no doubt be snatched up in a heartbeat. He didn't have much money for the school's renovations, but that didn't matter. Surely Nicholas would be willing to help out in exchange for a deal on rent. He could even have his pick of the units.

Against his better judgment, Nicholas became Jim's first tenant. With Harriet's help, he and Cecilia moved their belongings into the first-floor flat and settled into the grand building. It didn't take long for them to discover that the school looked a lot more impressive than it was. With no insulation to speak of, it became bone cold in the winter and broiled in the summer. Still, for the first time in their lives, they had their own place. And that too was as good as gold.

19

Adrift

1849

ANOTHER NEW YEAR. While much of the world was celebrating, Captain James Attridge and his crew were making their way to the River Shannon before finally laying anchor in the Bay of Tralee. The barque sat heavily in the water, filled this time not with people but with 360 tons of Indian corn, 1,000 barrels of superfine flour, 1,100 barrels of Indian meal, 30 tons of white wheat for seed, and 21,000 timber staves, all collected from the Coenties Slip on New York City's East River. There, amid the steamers, canal boats, and ocean liners, Attridge had filled the vessel with New England timber and grain brought all the way from the American Midwest, goods that would soon be available for purchase (and for a discounted price, no less) at John Donovan & Sons' brand-new—and fully bonded—warehouse in the heart of Tralee.

The *Jeanie*'s return to Ireland was already being heralded as a triumph, yet Attridge would hardly call the previous year a success. After depositing his passengers in Quebec, the captain had tried to maintain order among his exhausted crew. The stress of storms and ice and ferrying two hundred seasick immigrants showed. Immediately after docking, John Daly was arrested for public drunkenness and impeding traffic on the street.[1] Two days later, John Gordon and Alexander Matthews, two seamen in their late twenties, deserted the vessel. From Quebec's docklands, the United

States appeared tantalizingly close. And so, unnoticed, Gordon and Matthews ducked from the *Jeanie* and away from the docklands. They were bound for Matthews's native New York, carrying all of their belongings in their sea chests. They were apprehended by authorities the next day and promptly arraigned. What followed was a week of court appearances for the men and Attridge, who was summoned to give testimony. Gordon and Matthews both pled not guilty; however, the strength of Attridge's statement was enough to persuade the judge. Both men were sentenced to thirty days in jail, a punishment meant to threaten other would-be deserters as much as to penalize the two seamen.[2] It was an insufficient warning; by the time the *Jeanie Johnston* departed Quebec for her long haul back to Ireland, five additional crew members had abandoned the vessel, leaving just Attridge and eleven sailors to man the timber-laden barque as she once again plied the icy waters of the North Atlantic.

No matter how benevolent or fair, a nineteenth-century captain had to expect desertions in his line of work. But on this most recent trip to New York, the scale of desertions had distressed Attridge greatly. The same day that he filed his paperwork with New York Customs, no fewer than seven crew members, including two sixteen-year-old apprentices, had jumped ship. These men and boys were no doubt lured by promises of an American dream and a Gotham already dazzling in what the writer Lydia Maria Child called a "long string of vituperative alliterations, such as magnificence and mud, finery and filth, diamonds and dirt, bullion and brass-tape, &c., &c."[3] The AWOL sailors slipped easily into the tangled forest of ships and cargo on the docks before making their way the short distance to Five Points, already the world's most notorious Irish slum. From there, they began a life of anonymity, lost forever to official record keeping and reports.

The life in Ireland to which Attridge and his remaining men were returning was no less uncertain. In their absence, Parliament had pushed through the Encumbered Estates Act, which allowed heavily indebted estate owners to auction off their properties in exchange for loan forgiveness. Eager to capitalize on the liquidated real estate, speculators swooped in and bought up the land, then promptly evicted tens of thousands of cottiers still living there. In response, tenant groups were forming across Ireland and threatening agitation. Meanwhile insurrections demanding free rule erupted in force, and guerrillas attacked police with guns and pikes. Scattered across the country and with military force, these bands of rebels had forced a six-month suspension of habeas corpus across Ireland. Initially it seemed as if martial law would end the rebels' momentum, but then there were rumors that a new outbreak of violence would soon begin. Home owners throughout Ireland reported strange robberies in which perpetrators stole lead from roofs and shovels from barns. Many were confused by the strange choices of the thieves, until it was pointed out that the lead could easily be cast into bullets and the shovels rendered into pikes. Newspaper articles in rural papers ran columns about how to build weapons, and thick envelopes arriving from places like Boston and New York ensured that secret societies had the funds they needed for such enterprises. Violence against landlords also continued, and many of the landed class no longer felt safe moving about the countryside.

Neither did Britain's much-beloved queen. At the height of the uprising, she and her family had taken refuge at Osborne House, their estate on the Isle of Wight. Now back in London, she was finding the threat to her safety all too real. On a temperate evening, she took a carriage drive through the parks of Buckingham Palace. The carriage was within yards of returning home when a loud pistol shot rang out across the grounds. William Hamilton, a wiry young Irishman dressed in corduroy trousers and a flannel jacket, was quickly subdued by palace guards. Once in police custody, Hamilton calmly explained that he was a bricklayer from Limerick who had emigrated to England a year prior, buoyed by the promise of work and relief from the famine. Not surprisingly, he had found neither. The queen, he said, ought to pay. Plenty of his countrymen agreed.

At 14 Downing Street, Henry Grey railed in equal measure against the plight of vessels like the *Jeanie Johnston* and the Irish unrest. Both were evidence that his policies were flawed, if not altogether failing. Grey did not take defeat lightly. And frankly, the timing for this one couldn't be worse: 1849 was supposed to be the year for new Navigational Acts, a lynchpin in the battle for a free market. If passed, the acts would bring an end to strict restrictions on British trade and would allow foreign-flagged vessels to import goods directly into Britain. As far as Grey was concerned, passage of the acts was integral to Britain's dominance as a global power. Still, conflict continued, mostly in the colonies, who feared for their livelihood if they lost their preferential subsidies. In Canada, agitators were threatening to secede; protests against Grey in Australia were building in force; and a bloody insurrection on the Cape of Good Hope was creating what he called "difficulties and embarrassments."[4]

Ireland was likewise in rebellion. Under Grey's initial emigration scheme, it was the peasants who were supposed to vacate Ireland in favor of British North America. But instead of the poorest of the laborers, emigrant vessels were increasingly filled with people like the Reillys—successful, respectable farmers. Their absence was seen as a significant drain on any possibility for future economic well-being in Ireland. Why send some of the island's greatest capital to America? Or even worse, allow them to die on vessels like the *Londonderry*, where 72 of the 206 steerage passengers had recently suffocated to death below deck?

Instead of debate over free trade, Grey found himself mired in yet another parliamentary investigation concerning the safety of immigrant vessels.[5] It was not an investigation he welcomed. Grey made no bones about accusing his fellow parliamentarians of using this discussion as a way of deflecting attention from his new policy. He scolded them, insisting that everything about their new attention to the safety of immigrant vessels seemed "calculated to create and to keep a most mischievous agitation against" the idea of further colonization—even in North America.[6] Worst of all, much of London was now jumping on the bandwagon, staging protests in which otherwise reasonable people were appearing at state events wearing sackcloth and ashes as a sign of protest against Grey's policies.[7]

It was, Grey had to admit, an exceptionally effective campaign. In Parliament, Lord Redesdale had taken the floor, speaking at length about "dreadful cases" on immigrant ships where women were observed holding dead babies, children were killed by exposure, and emigrants huddled together in unsanitary conditions more deplorable than the world had ever seen. Redesdale was joined by the Earl of Harrowby and the Earl of Mount Cashell, who spoke passionately about similar accounts: immigrants were complaining of mistreatment; no one was protecting their interests; England had failed to curb the villainy of ship masters and owners.[8] The crusade was no less impassioned in the House of Commons, where Thomas Chisholm Anstey had effectively halted discussion on the Passenger Acts with reports from his time aboard an immigrant ship. The proceedings of the speech, published throughout London, recorded Chisholm Anstey as saying "he could assure the House that not a day passed in which the passengers were not in fear of plague, pestilence, and famine; and on looking into the law, on their arrival at port, he found they had no remedy whatever."[9]

It would take a deft hand and diplomacy to quell this latest bout of dissension, neither of which Grey possessed. He had always been considered something of a blunt instrument when it came to politicking, and the harshness with which he had treated his opposition over the past two years would clearly not be forgotten. He attempted concession: more clearly needed to be done, he admitted, to ensure the safe passage of Irish emigrants. He assured members of Parliament that he was "perfectly ready to admit that many of the suggestions which had been made were well deserving of consideration." But surely, they ought not "risk the Bill by attempting more than what it already embraced." And didn't these extra mandates serve to further infantilize the emigrants? To suggest that they were incapable of acting on their own accord? "It was his opinion that if persons who were about to emigrate would make proper inquiry of respectable ship owners, they would have no reason to complain of the accommodation afforded to them, or of the provisions with which they were supplied."[10]

Grey would have liked to believe that what occurred in Ireland was also of little consequence, but of course he knew otherwise. This new year was already bringing a whole host of problems. Private charity had all but evaporated in Ireland. Even the Quakers were ceasing aid, citing their frustration with the government's handling of Ireland as the chief cause. Charles Trevelyan lobbied hard for them to remain, even offering them cash if they would do so, but the Quakers refused. What Ireland needed, they wrote in response, was "far beyond the reach of private exertion[.] The government alone could raise the funds and carry out the measures necessary in many districts to save the lives of the people."[11]

Perhaps, they concluded, the government ought to begin by considering the new raft of evicted cottiers desperate for shelter and support.

Grey didn't so much mind that these cottiers had been forced from their land; that, after all, had been the point all along. But what he hadn't anticipated and now deeply regretted was the fierce political fallout. The Encumbered Estates Act was intended as a way to reinvigorate the Irish landscape by forcing the sale of heavily mortgaged estates on which the owners had failed to pay tax. The government hoped that wealthy English investors would buy the estates; however, in many cases these lands continued to languish or were purchased by Irish Catholics. Neither result was considered an appealing option by those back in London. William E. Gladstone, who had risen to power in the previous government, went on record declaring that the Encumbered Estates Act was motivated by "lazy, heedless, uninformed good intentions," the effects of which were "disastrous."[12] Edward Twisleton objected too and brought his concerns to Trevelyan. The assistant Treasury secretary was far from sympathetic and chastised his Poor Law commissioner. "We must not complain," he wrote to Twisleton, "of what we really want to obtain."[13]

So began the tension between two of the men most closely associated with the fate of Ireland. No longer bound by a desire to please his superior, Twisleton began making a series of increasingly pointed statements about the need for more attention to Ireland. Trevelyan shot back that Twisleton had a penchant for melodrama and was "lavish" in his handling of Irish relief. Twisleton countered that it was Trevelyan's miserliness that continued to kill so many across Ireland.[14]

Trevelyan had always been as impatient as Grey when it came to opposition, and these recent developments prompted a vitriol that surprised even those closest to him. He blanketed the desks of his subordinates with polemical arguments for greater self-sufficiency on the part of the people and laissez-faire on the part of the government. He sent copies of Adam Smith's treatise on the free market, *The Wealth of Nations*, to each officer and clerk of the Commissariat. He mailed Edmund Burke's *Thoughts on Scarcity* to each relief officer. Both, he insisted, would surely prove the dangers of reliance on governmental assistance. When that didn't work, he ordered copies made of any report that emphasized the dire state of affairs in Ireland and insisted that their study become a duty of all those who worked for him.[15]

Still, his reputation continued to suffer. The previous season, Trevelyan had announced publicly that the famine was over. That, along with his prediction that the potato would return stronger than ever in 1849, was proving patently false.[16]

Then, though it barely seemed possible, things took yet another turn for the worse. Trevelyan arrived at his office in early March to find an urgent letter from Colonel Stokes and the Tralee Board of Guardians. Lord Clements, a curmudgeonly former member of Parliament and a notorious landlord (he would later be murdered because of his draconian treatment and heartless evictions of tenants), was planning what they called "an awful attack" on Edward Twisleton, Ireland's chief Poor Law commissioner.[17] Clements, it seemed, objected to Twisleton's commitment to aid and tenant rights.

It was the last straw for the commissioner. His budget was broke, and he no longer had funds to help even the most distressed Irish unions. Trevelyan had not only been given a bonus of twice his salary from the previous year but was now also ignoring his pleas for disbursements. Just a few days after receiving a copy of Stokes's letter, Twisleton sent one of his own: a letter of resignation directed to the House of Commons. In it, he insisted not only that the destitution of the Irish was the fault of the British government, but that the government's famine relief policy had become a policy of extermination rather than salvation. Twisleton was not about to play the part of executioner.[18] In short, Britain's handling of Ireland was a "deep disgrace."[19]

But the former Poor Law commissioner didn't stop there. As a final blow, he issued a parting public statement in which he denounced the Russell government: "I wish to leave distinctly on record that, from want of sufficient food, many persons in these Unions are at present dying or wasting away; and, at the same time, it is quite possible for this country to prevent the occurrence there of any death from starvation, by the advance of a few hundred pounds."[20]

That stung, but not nearly as much as Twisleton's harshest criticism, which he directed at Trevelyan and the Treasury Office:

There are many individuals of even superior minds who now seem to me to have steeled their hearts entirely to the sufferings of the people of Ireland, and who justify it to themselves by thinking it would be going contrary to provisions of nature to give any assistance to the destitute in that country. It is said that the law of nature is that those persons should die . . . and that you should let them alone; there is thus a sort of philosophical colour given to the theory or idea, that a person who permits the destitute Irish to die from want of food is acting in conformity with the system of nature. Now my feeling is, that it is wholly the contrary; that it is part of the system of nature that we should have feelings of compassion for those people, and that it is a most narrow-minded view of the system of nature to think that those people should be left to die.[21]

John Ball, the newly appointed assistant Poor Law commissioner, agreed. Trevelyan's approach to famine relief, he insisted in a published tract against the Treasury secretary, was "the grossest infraction of justice, and the most insane defiance of common sense."[22]

It was the harshest criticism against Trevelyan yet. Nevertheless the assistant secretary remained firm. Ireland was sick, it was true, but like any good doctor, he had issued a thorough treatment. What the patient now required, he insisted, was "rest and quiet and time for the remedies which have been given to operate. Continual dosing and dependence upon physicians is not good either for the body politic or corporate."[23]

20

Clearances

1849

At least one Irish doctor thought Trevelyan's prognosis required a second opinion. As he awaited the *Jeanie*'s next voyage, Richard Blennerhassett could see firsthand that the famine was showing no signs of abating. Although farmers and landowners alike had been initially hopeful about the potato crop that year, their hopes were dashed that spring by heavy rains prompting the return of the blight.[1] Soon it was obvious that, at least in County Kerry, the potato crop would be a complete failure. Famine victims continued to flood relief sites: more than 800,000 impoverished Irish inundated outdoor aid stations alone, far exceeding the relief available to them.[2] Those turned away were dying by the thousands, and even doctors were helpless to prevent it.[3]

Life was little more secure in the Tralee workhouse. There several hundred of the one million total Irish inmates in workhouses across Ireland at that time toiled for their bread. Each week, Richard Blennerhassett's father, who was serving as medical advisor for the region, would return from the Board of Guardians meeting, looking dismayed. He brought with him stories of the conditions there: families separated first by gender and then by age; over two dozen inmates sequestered with confirmed cases of influenza and smallpox. Most distressing of all, the mortality rates that season were already exceeding those of 1847, forcing many of the workhouse's most needy inmates to flee lest they too become statistics.[4]

Those who remained were a bedraggled lot, with men, women, and children sporting shaved heads and weeping, blistered feet from the wooden shoes they were forced to wear. Their clothing—if one could call it that—was provided by Royal Navy surplus. The sight of bald young women wearing sailor's jackets and warm-weather tunics was difficult for even a seasoned physician to bear.

To pay for this bizarre costume, the Board of Guardians had proposed what both Blennerhassetts insisted was a ludicrous plan: the guardians, it seemed, were determined to install a capstan mill in the workhouse. An enormous device capable of grinding over five hundred pounds of corn an hour, the mill would be employed by teams of forty workhouse paupers at a time. Even better, the chief Poor Law inspector avowed, it would provide "great health-fulness" for the inmates, who would surely enjoy the physical challenge of pushing its immense spokes.[5] The elder Blennerhassett had a feeling that that wasn't the only physical challenge being asked of the female inmates. Some appeared to be with child. When asked how this could have occurred in a segregated building that allowed for no unsupervised contact between the sexes, all eyes turned to the workhouse master. He resigned shortly thereafter.

Conditions failed to improve. The Tralee Board of Guardians petitioned the Poor Law commissioners for permission to allow the paupers to cut turf to heat the workhouse; they were denied. They proposed that the inmates grow food; once again, they were denied. Meanwhile the workhouse—and those within it—continued to rot. Despite having made appeals to improve conditions, Henry Blennerhassett was blamed by the local press for the deteriorating situation. There was nothing, it seemed, that Henry Blennerhassett could do except endure the criticism.

Amid this censure, a fellow physician by the name of Crumpe visited both the Tralee workhouse and the jail to investigate allegations of neglect. He marveled later that, even as a seasoned doctor accustomed to misery and the stench of death, he could be as affected as he was by conditions there. Overcome by retching, Crumpe could barely make an investigation. But what he did see concerned him greatly: "In this horrid den those laboring under local disease, those ill from fever, those dying, and the dead from fever and dysentery, were promiscuously stretched together." Crumpe warned in his published report that mortality, already troubling, was about to become catastrophic: cholera had been identified throughout Europe and was marching westward. Soon the dark angel would be upon all of England and Ireland, threatening to detonate in places like immigrant ships.[6] No one had to tell Henry Blennerhassett or his son what that harbinger would bring.

Nicholas Donovan certainly would have benefited from Crumpe's prophecy, assuming the importer had even been willing to listen. In the spring of 1849, that was more doubtful than ever; as far as Donovan was concerned, the season had brought him more than enough problems to keep him occupied.

On the surface, it seemed as if things were going well for Donovan. True, he had been criticized for his decision to import New York grain, which the *Kerry Evening Post* claimed had flooded the market and dropped prices of Irish grain to uncompetitive lows. But the editor had also acknowledged, as had much of the town, that this new delivery was succeeding in establishing Tralee at last as "an independent warehousing port."[7] Donovan had also just received word that the Incorporated Merchants of Tralee Company, of which he was the head, had been granted certified registry, which made them a full corporate body. He instantly set to work creating a new marketplace capable of hosting the trade of corn, potatoes, and other bulk produce in earnest. At long last, the merchants and farmers of Tralee were a single, unified entity. And that made them a force to be reckoned with.

Still, the importer found himself plagued by difficulties. Just a few months earlier, a series of freak storms flooded Tralee's river and canal, causing what residents said was the "highest and most sudden risings ever remembered." The "foaming torrent," further exacerbated by an exceptionally high tide, rushed into the city, smashing stone archways and surging into cellars, as well as first-floor offices and homes through-out downtown. The surge was so sudden and unexpected that two young girls were swept off a town bridge they had begun to cross. That these were the only casualties was somewhat miraculous, particularly given the damage visible once the water receded.[8]

Denny Street had turned into a cesspool of mud, debris, and waste, rendering travel impossible and raising questions about the construction of the town's grand business district. Detritus from the flood littered the Donovan supply yards, and stagnant water pooled in their first-floor offices, saturating paperwork and ultimately ruining everything contained there. The impenetrable swamp created by the flood, coupled with downed telegraph lines, severed communication in the town. At the center of it all stood the County Kerry Club House, with four feet of water in its hold; pumps ran for days to extract the water.

The same storms had wreaked havoc on Ireland's agriculture that season, flattening many of the grain fields. That, along with the news of the potato's failure, was enough to dismay anyone.

But what really shook Donovan was news from the sea. The *Maria*, the first ship Donovan had leased to transport emigrants, struck an iceberg and sunk in the North Atlantic. Twenty passengers managed to make it up on deck before she slipped beneath the waves. The impact caused a torrent of icy water to enter the hold, and the vessel's twelve survivors reported that the screams coming from below deck were as deafening as they were brief. Those who jumped onto the iceberg itself were later saved by the first mate and cabin boy, who had the wherewithal to secure a lifeboat. There they floated for nearly twenty-four hours, enduring frostbite and life-threatening hypothermia until they were rescued by the barque *Roslyn Castle*. Everyone else—over a hundred people in all—perished in the icy water.[9] The disaster was a sober reminder of just how dangerous these passages could be.

For over two years, Donovan had held a monopoly on emigration from the port of Tralee. Now, propelled by Grey's commitment to market competition (not to mention their own dislike of Donovan's business dealings), the town leaders appeared resolved to end Donovan's reign as the emigrant baron of Tralee.

Earlier in the season, the American Passengers' Corporation had set up an office on Canal Street, and its staff was now hard at work recruiting and processing potential passengers. On the short walk from his office to the Pikeman for lunch, Donovan had passed five large flyers advertising the company. As if proving the people's confidence in this and other emigrant companies, the bay itself teemed with schooners, barques, and even full ships vying for mooring space. Fourteen vessels in all would depart that year, filled with the farmers and laborers Donovan had been working so hard to woo. A good number of these vessels had been pulled from Pacific routes: Henry Grey's plan to send prisoners, orphans, and peasant women of a marrying age to places like Australia had received even more criticism than his North American plan. The controversy forced the earl to abort the project and ship owners to find new routes for their vessels. This included the *Aliwal*, an Irish-owned vessel rerouted from her Cape Horn course in order to take emigrants to New York, and the *Rajah*, the massive 560-ton ship that normally ran the Bombay route out of London. American ship owners were also quick to capitalize on the opportunity, and at least four of the ships in the harbor—the *Lesmahagow*, the *New Brunswick*, the *Gypsy*, and the *Anne*—hailed from U.S. ports.

Worst of all, thought Donovan, was the enthusiasm the town was showing for these new competitors. The relief committee had already begun sending down workhouse inmates in droves. And in a move that would have no doubt made Henry Grey proud, Sir Edward Denny determined to do his part to help evicted tenants by dedicating an enormous sum of his own money—£265 by most accounts—to place homeless cottiers on ships owned by people other than Nicholas Donovan.[10]

It was a clear affront, both to his business and to his family, and Donovan was furious. All interaction with the town would stop immediately, he determined. That included his work on the planning board and Katherine's commitments to the soup kitchen. She would be upset, of course, but there would be other ways for her to dispense the Murphy fortune. So long as it did not involve Tralee officials, that would be fine with him. In the meantime, he would find a way to preserve his dominance in the emigrant industry—on his own terms.

Without preferential subsidies, London didn't seem to need Ireland's grain anymore, at least not the way it was being grown and harvested. That meant Irish farmers were no longer financially profitable to landowners. Even raising their rents would not result in the kind of profits that could be obtained through a large-scale farming enterprise. All around the island, landlords were realizing this. If the famine had taught them anything, it was that fewer people working and living on the land meant much greater financial returns. Donovan could help them on their way. There would be additional criticism, he knew. Like every other newspaper subscriber, he had read the recent editorial posted by a Dublin correspondent based in the United States. "For god's sake," the correspondent had written, "if you know any who intend coming out here, whether you care about them or not, do not advise them to come out to America without means, as there are thousands of young men in New York with wives and families who are unemployed. . . . It is really enough to make one wish to be transported to Ireland for the purpose of preventing, if possible, any more from leaving it."[11]

But Donovan was insistent. Jobs be damned, the residents of Ireland wanted to leave. Nearly 300,000 Irish men, women, and children would emigrate that year alone. Hoping to capitalize on these numbers, Donovan leased a second vessel, the brig *Eliza*, to take emigrants to Quebec. Then he announced that, instead of joining her, the *Jeanie* would sail to Baltimore, the American South's largest port and one that promised unsurpassed opportunities for immigrants. What had begun as a modest outpost for the tobacco and grain trade during the colonial era had since blossomed into a formidable city, eclipsed in size and tempo only by New York and Philadelphia.[12] That season, Baltimore was giving both a run for their money. The 1849 shipping season was already the largest on record for the port city. "Indeed," wrote the editor of the *Baltimore Sun*, "we have never known our wholesale warehouses to be filled with such extensive stocks of goods of every variety."[13] Baltimore homes had their own extensive stock, and the average home had comforts potential passengers aboard the *Jeanie Johnston* couldn't imagine: high post beds and mahogany tables, glassware and fine linens for every occasion, and of course the omnipresent sugar box, filled to capacity with newly arrived sweetener.

Yet for would-be immigrants, the opulence in Baltimore paled in comparison to what was being promised on the other side of the continent, where flakes of gold had been discovered the year before at Sutter's Saw Mill in Coloma, California. Since then, a variety of settlements had taken root with names like El Dorado, Gold Hill, and Diamond, all seeking to capitalize on the gold rush that was now taking place. Since its discovery in late 1848, California gold had, as the *New York Herald* put it, "set the public mind almost on the highway to insanity." Up and down the eastern seaboard, cottage industries had sprung up in response to the rumors of unimaginable riches to be had on the opposite coast. Dry goods stores began specializing in everything needed to outfit a prospecting forty-niner: pans and gold-testing kits, pickaxes and rubber boots, and for the most optimistic of the lot, money belts and safes.[14] Longtime citizens and newly arrived Irish immigrants alike joined in the frenzy, pawning assets and leveraging savings to join in the mad rush westward.

At St. Joseph, Missouri, alone, more than four thousand wagons had crossed the Mississippi River that season, all on their way west. They brought with them nearly 20,000 people and an estimated 300,000 animals, mostly oxen and mules. Those not interested in traveling overland thronged the docks in places like Baltimore, where masses of people crowded onto schooners and barques, headed for the treacherous Cape Horn and, eventually, the streams of California. They were wooed by what promised to be the first pure experiment in free market economies: tent cities were springing up with names that evoked the climate there: Whiskeytown and Rough and Ready. It was, at long last, proof positive that Manifest Destiny was not only an appealing idea, but also a viable policy.

News of this boom had taken all of Europe by storm. Promoting Baltimore as a stop on the road to California would allow Donovan to charge a premium on tickets and to once again distinguish himself from the other ship owners, as no other vessels from Tralee would be landing there. In preparation, he printed up additional passenger contract tickets; he ordered rice and molasses to feed his passengers. He blanketed the newspapers with ads for his fine, fast ship, noting with no small amount of irony that, while they wasted little ink in speaking out against him, these same newspapers still happily took his advertising business. Not that he really needed the ads anyway. Word had spread quickly that the *Jeanie* would sail again. The story of Nicholas Reilly, already a year old, was still fresh in the minds of many, and even though the barque had completed only one passenger voyage, the *Jeanie Johnston* was known to be a lucky ship.

21

Crossing the Bar

J AMES ATTRIDGE didn't know what to make of his cousin's decision. Had Donovan forgotten about the massive crew losses he sustained in New York? Donovan had insisted that the *Jeanie* carry ballast, not passengers, on this previous voyage, which meant that the ship's quarters had been drastically altered for the nonhuman cargo. U.S. naval law was too restrictive and the season too short to prepare the *Jeanie* to ferry passengers to America. Apparently those regulations were no longer of much concern to the importer.

They were plenty troubling to Attridge, though, who was now responsible for the retrofit needed for the *Jeanie* to pass inspection. America had new rules about the number of people on board, the size of their bunks, the amount of ventilation and provisions they would require while on board. Getting the *Jeanie* up to standards was clearly going to take some work. Who was going to do it? Once upon a time, Attridge had been famous for preserving his crewmen from voyage to voyage. This new immigrant trade seemed to have changed all that; not even the promise of uninterrupted paid work was enough to keep most of his crew on board. After returning from New York, nearly all his men left the vessel, including Gabriel Seldon, who had signed on to the barque *Glory*, a Baltic timber ship, for the winter months. Seldon knew he was welcome on board any of Attridge's ships; the captain just had to hope that his cook and steward made it back in time. Meanwhile he would depend more heavily than ever on his first mate, Thomas Campion. The rest of the crew, he supposed, could be found in Liverpool and Cork.

That left the matter of his apprentices; for at least another year the Shipping Acts required Attridge to carry them on all voyages. Daniel Collins remained on board from the previous season; he was joined in early February by Florence Sullivan, a fifteen-year-old also from Tralee. Signing on an apprentice like Sullivan was the law, but that didn't make it any less onerous a task for a captain. The 1835 amendment to the Merchant Shipping Act expanded the apprentice program specifically to accommodate boys like Sullivan, who, destitute, might otherwise be considered a strain on their local community. The thinking behind the act was that a multiyear apprentice program would provide the boys with applicable skills and employment while maintaining the strength of the merchant fleet. The Board of Guardians was empowered by the British government to bind such boys by indentures, provided they could prove to two justices of the peace that they were at least thirteen and "of sufficient health and strength." It was at the board's expense that Florence Sullivan was delivered to Attridge, along with a copy of his baptismal record and £5 for clothing and bedding, to be worked off over the duration of his apprenticeship—and beyond, if necessary.

This was far from a popular program for many ship captains, who found themselves responsible for young boys with as little sailing experience as they had vested interest in being at sea. That many resorted to rough treatment of their bound charges is apparent from the language of the 1835 revised act, which created extensive punishments for "hard or ill usage" of apprentices and reminded captains in no uncertain terms of the British statutes regarding assault and battery.

Florence Sullivan could neither read nor write when he arrived on board the *Jeanie* in February of 1849. That alone was hardly remarkable; three of the able-bodied seamen on that voyage were also illiterate, but unlike Sullivan they at least came with sail-handling experience and an understanding of what kinds of hardship the next several months would have in store. Sullivan had never before left the confines of Tralee, let alone climbed aboard a large vessel destined for North America.

Nevertheless the boy arrived on the docks at the appointed time. Fair-skinned and a little short for his age, he kept his gray eyes turned down, as if apologizing for his tenderness or already regretting the choice that had been made for him.

He arrived at a nearly deserted vessel. Attridge had not yet secured a replacement crew, and Campion was overseeing a skeleton staff that included two British seamen, John Kneen and Robert McIntyre, as well as Christian Peterson, a Danish sailor who had recently left the schooner *Bideford*, which had been making immigrant runs between southwestern England and Newfoundland. Attridge's situation began to look up when Seldon returned, and just in the nick of time. The steward quickly went to work assisting Campion with preparations for the passengers and their departure.

Attridge meanwhile struggled to locate his remaining crew. The confused ship's articles from that voyage—a sharp contrast to his normally fastidious record keeping—say much about his sense of urgency. For the first time in his career, Attridge was finding it hard to come by a crew. A week before their scheduled departure, only ten had signed on. Along with the late addition of Thomas Twyford from Limerick as second mate—apparently, none of the other men had the qualifications necessary for this position—the remaining four seaman were added in the last days leading up to the departure. It was a highly unusual state of affairs for a captain who so prided himself on organization and protocol.

A total of 135 immigrants, including five infants under the age of one year, boarded the newly refitted vessel in early March, then settled into a hold that still smelled of grain and freshly cut wood. The average age of the passengers was twenty-two; most were men who, if not single, at least were traveling without wife or family. The majority listed their occupation as laborer or artisan; there were coopers and cart wrights, smiths and shoemakers, carpenters and cattlemen. The second largest group were young women traveling alone, including Catherine Martin, a spinster from Tralee, and Mary Evans from nearby Ardfert. The remaining passengers were mostly farm families with small children, including the widow Eliza O'Leary and her three children: Mary, age thirteen; Jerry, ten; and Anne, seven. At forty, Eliza was one of the oldest passengers on board, and as a widow she had a certain status among both the single women and the young families.

The *Jeanie* left on March 14 under nearly perfect sailing conditions— a rare and beautiful gift on the North Atlantic. The good weather held for two weeks, giving the O'Learys much-needed time to get adjusted to life at sea. During their walks on deck, the children spied porpoises with faces like pigs and whales bigger than they could have imagined. They marveled at sea swallows and flying fish, which leaped from the water and seemed to glide alongside the *Jeanie*'s massive black hull. Such wonderment was a welcome relief from the cramped and shadowy conditions below deck.

As bleak as it could be on board, a tight camaraderie was forming nevertheless. Eliza O'Leary had taken Catherine Martin and Mary Evans under her wing; the two young women counted on Eliza as something between an older sister and a second mother, and they were glad for the extra care—especially when the storms came.

The worst of them arrived on the morning of April 11 and grew increasingly violent throughout the day, sending the *Jeanie* over "mountainous" waves, only to then drop the vessel into a "deep abyss." Others crashed across the deck, submerging much of the vessel before dissipating in furious foam. The passengers were certain they would all perish.[1]

Had they been privy to what was occurring above them, they would have been all the more terrified. Not long after departing from Tralee, John White and John Jenkins, two of the halest crew members on board, fell ill. Both were from Cardigan, Wales, where rumors of a resurgence in cholera were surfacing. Dr. Blennerhassett sequestered the two men at once, monitoring them closely for the telltale signs of a disease he knew well. As the storms bore down on the vessel, he knew these two men would be missed terribly by the rest of the crew. It was imperative that he get them back on their feet—and that he keep others from falling ill. Over the course of the voyage, the young doctor had far more luck with the latter than he did the former. As far as he could tell, the two men did not have cholera. Although they would remain in the barque's makeshift hospital until arriving in Baltimore, at least they would be the only two people there.

Neither White nor Jenkins saw America appear like a mirage on the horizon, but many of the passengers did. And at least some were on deck when a pilot boarded the vessel and directed them into the Chesapeake Bay. They watched with wonder as Annapolis and the Virginia coast passed by, as forest changed to farmland and eventually the growing skyline of Baltimore.

Restrictions at the port of Baltimore were as tight as any in the world. The pilot directed the *Jeanie* to the quarantine ground on the main branch of the Patapsco River. There, not far from where Francis Scott Key wrote "The Star-Spangled Banner" nearly forty years earlier, an invisible line ran between Fort McHenry and the Board of Health Hospital, marking the stopping place for any passenger-carrying vessel. Once there, Attridge ordered his men to raise a large yellow flag atop the mainmast, a warning that the *Jeanie Johnston* arrived in the United States carrying disease on board and was to be avoided at all costs.

Nearby, passengers aboard the German vessel *Johanis* were awakened at 4 A.M. on their inspection date so that there would be plenty of time for everyone to scrub and dress. Richard Blennerhassett probably insisted on similar protocol, particularly given the implications of the quarantine flag.

Once the Maryland state physician arrived, he conferred briefly with Attridge and then set about examining each of the passengers. Chief among the doctor's mandates was to check for any appearance of smallpox, which had reached epidemic levels in Baltimore in each of the previous four years.[2] Any sign of the disease would require Attridge to dock the *Jeanie* at the infectious lazaretto established on the north side of Fort McHenry, where additional purifications would take place—all at significant cost (and delay) to the captain.[3] The penalty for not doing so would be even more severe: $500 (about $13,000 today) for the initial infraction, an additional $50 for every hour the vessel remained in breach of quarantine.

For many residents of the port city, that seemed a small price to pay to prevent the return of 1847's mortality rates. But it soon proved insufficient. By the time the *Jeanie Johnston* arrived in Baltimore, Dr. Crumpe's prediction had proven all too accurate: the real killer that year was cholera, and it arrived with great ferocity. In Liverpool, more than four thousand people would die that year; in Ireland, cholera was rumored to be killing more people than starvation.[4] Mortality rates there were already topping 40 percent. By the end of the year, an estimated thirty thousand Irish would die as a direct result of the disease.

For Blennerhassett, these statistics soon hit close to home. One of the first to succumb was his cousin Annabella. Barely thirty years old and known for her kindness and her beauty, Annabella was a favorite in Tralee. Two years earlier she had witnessed both the birth of her baby daughter and the death of her husband. Since then she had struggled to raise the girl alone while dedicating herself to the service of the poor and her parish church. That she had fallen victim to the scourge seemed too much to bear for those who knew her, and, as with the so-called respectable victims of typhus, her death rattled public perception of the disease.[5] Here, once again, was disturbing proof that none of the gentry wanted to acknowledge: just like typhus, cholera made no class distinctions, attacking the most polite of the upper class with the same force as it did the indolent peasant.

Whatever was plaguing White and Jenkins, it wasn't enough to concern the state physician inspecting the vessel. He ordered the two sailors to a marine hospital operated by Washington University medical students.[6] Once they were removed, he then cleared the vessel—still reeking of the sulfur and vinegar used to disinfect it—for Baltimore proper.

22

No Irish Need Apply

THE DOCKS at the foot of Baltimore's Clinton Street were busy on May 3. There the *Jeanie Johnston* vied with seventeen other vessels for space in the crowded harbor. Traffic was congested with brigs and schooners, some arriving from other cities on the eastern seaboard. Dozens of others arrived from the Caribbean with sugar and molasses, then quickly departed again with the grain and iron needed to support the sugarcane industry.[1] Dwarfing all these ships were enormous Brazilian freighters, all loaded deep with coffee—America's favorite commodity—and destined for one of the nearly two hundred warehouses flanking the wharf.

As soon as he arrived, Attridge dashed off a letter to Nicholas Donovan assuring him that all of the passengers had arrived in good health. He promptly deposited it on the first steamer heading back across the Atlantic. Luckily for him, that steamer departed before the rash of bad news he would have been bound to report as well. The very evening the barque landed, two of his newest crew members, Christian Peterson of Denmark and William Thomas of Cork, went missing without leave. Peterson would eventually become a blacksmith in Chicago, where he died in 1917. Thomas was never heard from again.

The next day young Florence Sullivan also fled the vessel, no doubt wooed by the promise of what America had to offer. Like Peterson, he quickly moved westward but soon found that the Horatio Alger myth was harder to realize than it seemed. He eventually enlisted in the army in Albuquerque, New Mexico, where he joined recruits with names like Byrne, Kelley, and Feeney in the fight against New Mexico, Native Americans, and anyone else who did not believe in the Divine Providence of his race. Attridge would have to receive special dispensation to sail without the required number of apprentices.

But that was the least of his worries. The longer the *Jeanie* remained at the dock, the more men she lost. By May 22, Attridge was down eight crew members, leaving him with a little more than half the men necessary to sail the vessel back to Tralee. While the remaining men busied themselves tearing out the well-worn emigrant bunks and replacing them with tons of Indian corn, Attridge sat first in the Baltimore police station and then its customs house, giving depositions about the deserted sailors. He had lost others before, but not on this scale. He had plenty of time to think about this exodus as he walked the docks for a week, eventually securing six sailors for the return trip. All of them hailed from North America; there would be little chance they would desert upon arrival in Tralee.

The *Jeanie* set sail on June 6, leaving behind a stack of forms and depositions no doubt embarrassing to Attridge. She also left behind her 135 passengers, many of whom were finding their new city more than a little shocking. Baltimore may have done a fair business in coffee and molasses, but in 1849 its real commodity was human beings. Forty years earlier, the United States had prohibited the importation of captured African people, but that didn't make the country any less dependent on their enslavement. More than ever, trafficking slaves between states was big business, and Baltimore was at the very heart of it. For many in Baltimore, the appearance of a gang of slaves, handcuffed in pairs and paraded by the dozens in heavy chains, was commonplace. Not so for Eliza O'Leary, who, like the Reillys, had never seen a person of color before meeting Gabriel Seldon. On many a night, long bands of slaves were marched down her street, the dull footsteps and clank of chains rising up to her second-floor window. This was not the America she had been promised.

Eliza had found a house for rent on the edge of Baltimore's already notorious neighborhood, "Pigtown." A three-story row house made of common brick and crowded onto a dusty road, her new home was a far cry from the pastoral landscape surrounding the cottage she left behind. While her new neighborhood had little of the starvation and disease she had witnessed back in Ireland, Pigtown nevertheless took more than a little getting used to.

Though never as seedy or villainous as New York's Five Points, Eliza's new home came with a much-deserved reputation. Originally the site of the nation's first agricultural industrial complexes, the area quickly became the hub for the new B&O Railroad. Built by the rail company to house the largely immigrant population responsible for laying its tracks, Pigtown was the first of its kind in the United States: a planned neighborhood that came into existence as a direct consequence of the Industrial Revolution and its new demands for workers. Just as the workers back in England were finding new residences and making do on sweetened coffee and bread with jam—quite possibly the original fast food—so too were those in America. Industrial magnates knew that the best way to manage their employees was to keep them close. They also kept close their commodities, which is how the neighborhood earned its unfortunate name. Each day, railway cars would offload their occupants, sending hundreds of pigs into the narrow streets, where most were flushed through the neighborhood to the slaughterhouses in South Baltimore. In a single year, 150,000 pigs would pass within reach of Eliza's front door.

The muck from the pigs of Pigtown was only one of the challenges facing the O'Learys. A single pump at the end of the block was their only source of water, but because its well was only ten feet deep and covered in sand, the water it produced was little better than the puddles that settled into the manure- and trash-filled street. Even the barrels they used to collect rainwater were covered with an ashen sheen that seemed to permeate every inch of this newly industrialized city and its inhabitants. Nevertheless they had a home of their own. Jerry and Anne could both attend school, and Mary, the eldest, would stay home to help her mother.

In many ways, the living conditions in Pigtown perfectly embodied the lives of the railway workers and their families who lived there. Construction of the B&O Railroad, like the Ottawa and Erie Canals, had been both a boon and a blight for its many Irish workers. Injury and casualties were common; so too was unruly behavior fueled by camp whiskey. Fights broke out there, though it took the inflamed pen of a critical press to convert them into the "brawls" reported in the pages of Maryland's newspapers and beyond. No doubt, this reportage was part of the reason so many Irish were finding it difficult to locate the golden opportunities they had been promised. In places like Baltimore, their poverty and lack of opportunity rivaled that of African Americans.[2] Try as they might, even the women couldn't deny their Irishness. In America in 1849, there weren't many things worse than that.

The contempt for the Irish people that had begun several years earlier was growing into something far more insidious—and codified—throughout America. What had begun as privately held stereotypes was now equal to Britain's public system of racism, and no venue or medium seemed immune. "From Ireland," reported the editor of the *Baltimore Sun* just as the *Jeanie Johnston* was arriving, "we have the usual quantity of misery and crime."[3] The same ideology behind Manifest Destiny that lured Florence Sullivan west was making it hard for women like Eliza O'Leary and her fellow passengers to stay in the east. America may have been providentially chosen, but that was far from true for a good number of its inhabitants. The same racist ideology that allowed this generation of people to so easily take land from the Mexicans and Native Americans was also endowing them with the justification they needed. The Irish, a growing number of Americans maintained, were not just a different race; they were visibly inferior.[4] Throughout the country, "Irishism" described a "condition of depravity and degradation."[5] Concomitantly organizations such as the Order of the Star-Spangled Banner were springing up all over the United States, united in their distaste for all things Catholic and, more specifically, Irish. As such, they were proving themselves at least as deft as their British brethren in making a racist argument against the Irish people. John Sanderson's *Republican Landmarks*, first published in 1849, described Irish Americans as "creatures more debased than the Yahoos of Swift—creatures having only a distant and hideous resemblance to human beings."[6] Others referred to the Irish as simian or brutish. James Redfield's *Outline of a New Physiognomy*, also published in 1849, claimed,

"The Irishman walks heavily upon his heels . . . his gait being more like that of a horse on a bridge than like that of a cultivated gentleman. The slow, heavy tramp of the iron-shod 'heder and ditcher' is in keeping with the 'don't care' spirit of the lower ten thousand, be they white or black."[7]

While "Irish" and "black" were becoming synonymous when it came to social standing, some took it even further. When the legendary landscape architect Frederick Law Olmsted visited the docklands of Alabama, he was surprised to see black slaves throwing bales of cotton into the holds of ships, where they were caught by Irish workers. When asked about this distribution of labor, an overseer replied, "The niggers are worth too much to be risked here; if the Paddies are knocked overboard or get their backs broke, nobody loses anything."[8]

Small wonder, then, that Catherine Martin and Mary Evans were having difficulty finding work. Each day the ads for employment were littered with exceptions for the Irish:

> Wanted—a white woman to cook. German preferred.
>
> Laborers wanted to do farm and dairy work. No objection to Irishmen—but North Ireland preferred.
>
> Wanted: German woman who understands housework.
>
> Wanted: protestant girl.

These were the first manifestations of NINA, a multigenerational boycott of potential employees in which No Irish Need Apply. As Mary and Catherine soon discovered, those audacious enough to apply for a job would never receive a second glance.

Now penniless in addition to being homeless, the two women found refuge in Eliza O'Leary's small row house, where they could at least count on room and board and the kindness of a friend. Catherine, at least, would soon find work as a domestic servant for an Irish family who farmed just outside the city. But in the meantime, life outside Eliza O'Leary's new plaster walls was feeling awfully fragile.

23

Royal Visit

THE *JEANIE JOHNSTON* returned, laden with grain, to Cork's port town of Cobh on July 23, 1849. The shipping news made polite mention of her return, but few papers could spare more than a line or two announcing the barque's entry into customs. All of Britain was focused on what was, for the time being at least, a far more impressive vessel. The royal yacht *Victoria and Albert* would soon be arriving in Cobh as well, and on it were not only the queen and her husband but four of their children. It was Victoria's first visit to Ireland; both she and the Irish dignitaries intended it to be a memorable one.

That began with her ship. At 1,034 tons, the *Victoria and Albert* dwarfed the *Jeanie Johnston*, and everything else about the royal yacht was designed to be larger than life. Two enormous paddlewheels flanked the midship; between them an imposing smokestack rose above her 430-horsepower steam engine. Powerful, reliable, and built to succeed when the wind failed, the *Victoria and Albert* represented the future of shipping. The queen herself ensured that no money was spared when it came to appointing her state-of-the-art staterooms and salons.

But no amount of opulence could save the queen from the seasickness that plagued her as she crossed the Irish Sea in late July and arrived in Cobh on August 2. Given the timing of her arrival, it is entirely possible that the *Victoria and Albert* passed by the *Jeanie Johnston* upon entering

Cobh. An artist's rendering of the queen's arrival shows two barques the size of the *Jeanie* anchored on either side of the yacht, dwarfed by the *Victoria and Albert*'s multiple decks, not to mention the two large guns permanently fixed there.

The splendor and armaments were a powerful metaphor for the conditions that brought Victoria and her yacht to Cobh that summer. Many of her advisors had warned against such a trip; although the political agitation present earlier in the year appeared finally to be subdued as far as physical violence was concerned, the groups supporting the protests were still plenty hostile to a royal visit. It was a dangerous time to arrive, both for the queen's safety and her popularity. But Victoria was resolute: despite protestations from many in Parliament, she would make good on her promise to visit Ireland and her desire to become "personally acquainted" with the island. More important, it was an opportunity to declare the famine over once and for all. Charles Trevelyan's troubled Board of Health had been disbanded. The potato was expected to return. Henry Grey's policies heralded a new beginning for the Irish economy. The future, she insisted, looked bright for all.

Victoria had urged John Russell to join her on this mission of hope and accord, but the prime minister refused, citing a need "to remain quiet for three weeks."[1] In response, the monarch sent her regrets, along with spirited accounts of Ireland and its people. They were receiving the queen with enthusiastic and open arms—at least so it appeared. Bedecked with bunting and streamers, Cork put on its most celebratory face for the arrival of Victoria, who anchored her royal yacht there for two nights, enjoyed a tour of the town, and met with local dignitaries, including representatives of the Murphy family. Not to be outdone, town officials in Cobh petitioned Victoria to rename their city Queenstown, a request she was happy to grant. And so it would be called until 1922, when the founding of the Irish Free State necessitated a return to the original. But for now, the town leaders seemed content with their new royal associations.

Still, those watching emigration trends in Queenstown could see even then that something was amiss. Key members of the Catholic clergy were noticeably absent from receptions and lines of dignitaries welcoming the queen. Protestors chanted in the streets. Victoria, however, was carefully shielded from all of this and observed that the crowd of people who came out for her arrival was "noisy, exciteable, but a very good natured one, running and pushing about, and laughing, talking, and shrieking."[2] Ireland, she concluded, was very much a foreign place, and throughout her trip, she and Albert lectured repeatedly on the importance of loyalty—even to a seemingly foreign crown.

That this message was delivered by a stylish young mother and the husband she clearly adored, and that she also happened to be the queen of the most powerful empire in the world, was enough to engage even some of her most ardent Irish critics. The positive response to Victoria in places like Cork was undeniable. Dublin too was swept up by the queen's arrival there; having endured the worst of the summer's cholera outbreak in Ireland, the city was described by at least one nationalistic paper as "a city rose from the dead." Perhaps, conceded Victoria's advisors, the queen really had succeeded in establishing allegiances in Ireland and promoting greater affinity for the crown.[3]

However, as the queen departed for England, much of the enthusiasm seemed to depart as well. Her visit did little to end the evictions and hardships across the island, not to mention the desire of thousands to vacate as soon as possible. Coffin ships continued to leave Ireland in droves. As the royal yacht dropped anchor in the Thames, the *Jeanie Johnston* raised hers, departing once again with a full complement of passengers for North America.

The *Jeanie*'s reputation for maintaining health and order preceded her, and to no small degree. Captain Attridge made this late-season trip to Quebec, the *Jeanie*'s third as a passenger ship, in record time and, upon arriving there in late September, found an uncharacteristically easy reception from George Douglas. The captain wrote to Nicholas Donovan that the quarantine doctor "saw the passengers in such good health this voyage and the last, that he did not require to land the passengers at Grosse Ile as usual."[4] In appreciation, a group of passengers collected what meager funds they had remaining and spent them on an ad that ran in all the Quebec newspapers:

TO CAPTAIN JAMES ATTRIDGE

We, the passengers of the ship Jennie Johnston, *under your command, take leave to express our deep sense of the kindness which characterised your conduct during a voyage marked by tempestuous weather and demonstrations of your abilities as a mariner.*

Permit us to say, in fulness of our gratitude, that your affability and characteristic benevolence have not failed to win the hearts of all your passengers. And, let us add, that we will not fail to advise those of our friends and relations in Kerry, who may be disposed to emigrate to this country, to come by the ship under your command—the fast sailing Jennie Johnston. *We have a good warrant for doing so in your long experience as a navigator, as well as the good qualities of which you are the rich and happy possessor.*

This is our humble judgement, and it is the language of our hearts—the present testimony of our admiration and gratitude. Nor do we presume too much when we say that it is sanctioned by the high authority of our much esteemed medical attendant, Doctor Blennerhassett, of whom it is but justice to say, that he spared no exertions on his part that had for its object the health and comfort of the passengers. The total absence of disease amongst us during the voyage is the happy result, under God, of his long experience at sea as emigration physician.

Dear and much esteemed Sir, long and fondly will you be remembered by us. Long will your deeds of kindness be fresh in our memory. May you live long, and glide along the vale of life crowned with the best gifts of Heaven.

Signed, John Corridon. James Dunn. Francis Twiss. George B. Hare. Charles Mason. John Hallinan. John Egan. Alex Murphy. John Sullivan. John Gwinn. Patrick Sheehan. William Quinn. Philip Johnston. James Reardon. Edmund White. James Bailey. Thomas Moriarty. Bartw. Griffin. Michael Real. Maurice Stack. Patrick Horgan. John Carroll. Daniel Connell. Francis Sullivan. [5]

Donovan wasted little time ensuring that both of Tralee's major papers ran the letter. It was a welcome piece of good news for a region that had yet to see any evidence of an end to the famine and its misery, despite the pronouncement of its queen. Evictions remained rampant and appeared to be growing more atrocious by the day. On the Marquess of Lansdowne's estate, more than 150 individuals were suddenly homeless after their cottages were leveled. As a kind of peace offering, Lansdowne's manager offered the dislocated tenants their choice of destinations in North America. Long since grown distrustful of British policies, most chose New York. When they arrived, even Gotham, a city accustomed to the arrival of so many destitute Irish people, was appalled by their condition. Lansdowne responded by sending the remaining tenants to Quebec, which was cheaper, aroused significantly less bad publicity, and required fewer regulations.

In many ways, Lansdowne represented the newest—and perhaps gravest—problem to plague Ireland: powerful landlords acting out of self-interest. As the calendar turned to 1850, more than four thousand paupers continued to languish in the Tralee workhouse, 445 of them in the hospital. Try as they might, there was no way for the Board of Guardians to hide the fact that their Poor Union was failing; there was just not enough money or vision to keep it afloat. The board passed a resolution alerting the Poor Law commissioners in Dublin to what they called "the inconveniently large size" of the Tralee Poor Union and urged that it be divided, if not abolished altogether. They also elected to reduce Henry Blennerhassett's salary from £100 to £60 a year. He resigned from his post as their medical advisor. The commissioners thanked him for his work and issued an ad for his replacement. Annual salary: £52.[6]

Faced with growing pecuniary shortages, the board consented to the appointment of a visiting committee headed by Nicholas Donovan. Donovan had just won a lawsuit against a local farmer who the importer alleged had tried to claim payment twice for one load of grain. That kind of careful bookkeeping was precisely what the guardians felt they needed. It was also the kind of recognition that Donovan had always longed for. Still, his reintroduction into town politics was all but eclipsed by his latest and perhaps greatest achievement: victory at a massive land auction that arose as part of the Encumbered Estates Act. It was the first real opportunity for a Catholic—even a wealthy merchant Catholic—to own land in Ireland. More than thirteen thousand acres of John O'Connell's "very important estate" were in play in Ardfert, and they represented an opportunity, if not to buy a part of the city on a hill, then at least to own a piece of the hill of miracles. By afternoon Donovan had outbid even his father on multiple occasions. Nine parcels were his at the price of approximately £13,000 (about $1.3 million today).[7] So too was the nearly £1,000 in annual rent. Nicholas Donovan was not only a landowner now; he was also a landlord.

24

Steaming Ahead

1850

BACK IN QUEBEC, John Munn welcomed the New Year without much enthusiasm. Try as he might, he too was finding it increasingly difficult to care for those in his charge. For that matter, he was finding it increasingly difficult to care for himself.

To a casual observer, all looked well at the Munn establishment. The reconstruction of his yard had been a success: with 1,650 feet of shoreline, he now commanded the lion's share of property in St. Roch. A large brick office—it would have to be brick; no fire would again destroy all that he held dear—served as the nucleus of the yard. Brick and stone structures also housed his employees and the shops, along with the new addition of boilers for steam work. They were backed by the dramatic cliff that separates lower and upper Quebec. Looking down from that promontory, Cousin Elizabeth kept house in a grand home once owned by Montcalm, the French war hero, and even had time to tend the large gardens and orchard there.

Despite his seeming prosperity, John Munn knew what was on the horizon. In places like the shipping quarters of Quebec, the fanfare over the queen's recent Irish visit was less about royal gowns and promises and more about the mighty steamer ship that ferried her. The age of sail was coming to an end, and the new world of steam was proving unkind to Munn. Since launching his first steamship, he had struggled to remain current in the industry. Philanthropic to his very core, he had agreed to back the People's Line of Steamers, a consortium comprising mostly local grocers with more ambition than acumen. Perhaps, Munn hoped, with his yard and expertise, he could make the line a success. Instead it was proving a disaster.

The grocers, it seemed, didn't actually have the capital to buy the steamers they had contracted from Munn, and for the first time in his career, he had borrowed heavily from the Bank of North America in order to front their construction. Now he was deeply in debt, his property heavily mortgaged. His uncle James, loyal to Munn until the last, bequeathed to the wright all his assets, dispersed upon James's death that year. Still it wasn't enough. Quebec was moving into the steam age with all the speed that technology could buy. It was about to leave behind its most successful shipwright.

That same steam couldn't carry the Reillys away from Quebec fast enough. While some passengers from the *Jeanie Johnston* had opted to stay in Canada as Earl Grey and his cronies in Parliament had hoped, Daniel Reilly was committed to reaching Indiana. He and his family departed Quebec City on an emigrant train, bound for Buffalo and points west. Progress was halting at best. First, there was the long delay at the station, where crowds of Irish and German immigrants packed onto a single platform waiting to hear their names called. Then there was the rush to claim a seat—a wooden bench on which to lay a bag of straw—which dispersed some families throughout the train and left others at the station, wondering if they would ever make it to America. The Reillys were lucky: they all got on board. For days they crowded on a narrow wooden bench inside a third-class car, sandwiched between other new arrivals and their luggage. Many looked far worse for wear than the Reillys when they climbed aboard, but all would be both sooty and hungry by the time the train rolled into the Buffalo station.

Each time the railway company needed to add another freight car, it would switch the immigrant cars to a side rail, where they sat for hours.

Inside, the crowded passengers stood and stretched, hoping for relief from the wooden benches and Spartan conditions. A single bucket of water on the car's disused stove was the only hydration available; slop buckets became privies. It was like a steerage Atlantic crossing all over again.

There were differences, of course. One could at least lie down on the *Jeanie Johnston*. Not so on the emigrant railcar. Captain Attridge had made sure that rations were available to everyone every day while they were at sea; on the train, the family had to settle for the occasional visit from a vendor who climbed aboard to sell fruit, bread, and milk during a delay. On the rare occasion that the emigrant car was stalled in the vicinity of a station, those aboard could hope for a hot meal—assuming, of course, that they had enough cash. Here again the Reillys were lucky: they had enough money to eat and made it to New York and then Indiana in seven days without incident.[1] Once there, they found a town struggling to embrace the new world of steam and the supposed boons it offered.

25

Liberty?

THE TOWN OF LIBERTY was situated about halfway between Indianapolis and Cincinnati in a dense forest of walnut, hickory, and oak, the likes of which a person newly arrived from County Kerry had never seen before. Wolves still roamed the woods, and a terrifying disease called rabies preyed on dogs, raccoons, and even humans. Massive thunderstorms built in the afternoon far out on the horizon, bringing with them deeply fluctuating temperatures; the thermometer in Liberty was said to spend as many days at 100 as it did at minus 15, and regularly moved every degree between. Even more terrifying were the funnel clouds that dropped from those storms without warning, said to be strong enough to level an entire town.

Still, Liberty had made a go of it, and by 1850 it was the thriving seat of Union County. People there wore the latest in American fashion: Panama hats for the men, bloomers for the women and girls. The town boasted its own drugstore, five dry goods shops, and twenty-one mechanics. There was a courthouse and jail, a county seminary, and a Methodist and a Christian church. The town didn't have a place for Catholics to worship, but that wasn't of much consequence for a family living in a railroad shanty far from the town's center. Living in the country was certainly something with which Margaret Reilly had been familiar in Ireland; the farm she had shared with Daniel in Ballybeggan was far enough from Tralee that she rarely made the trek there with her husband. But that didn't make her new situation feel any more familiar.

Instead of a stone cottage with a thatched roof, Margaret now occupied a grimy two-story house made of plywood. The house had been built by the railroad for its employees, and neither group expected people like the Reillys to occupy it for long. Trains needed to move across states and nations; so too did their tracks and those who laid them. This kind of thinking was foreign to a young woman born and raised in one small corner of Ireland. But then again, just about everything in Liberty seemed unfamiliar, including the men also occupying her new home.

Margaret and Daniel weren't the only people from Tralee to make their way to Liberty that year, but they were two of the more financially stable—enough so, at least, that Daniel was given a lease on their flimsy house. As was the custom in places like Liberty, he had opened the tiny space to other new arrivals in need of room and board. In the spring of 1850, eight men between the ages of twenty-five and forty were living under their roof, and the Reilly family now included John, Nicholas and Robert's new baby brother. In all, thirteen people crowded into the wooden house. Margaret's busy daily routine seemed focused almost entirely on feeding everyone. A dry goods store catering to railway workers provided the staples: flour, sugar, salt, molasses, eggs, beef, pork, mackerel, tea, coffee, and whiskey, all sold in huge portions, as was the soap and starch she used to fight the unending grime accumulated by nine laborers. It was a far cry from the empty shops she had left behind in rural Kerry. So too was the imposing forest she now called home.

For Daniel's part, he didn't so much see the trees as he did the cornfields that surrounded them. This was fertile country, and farmers did well on their land, most even raising their own livestock as well as row after row of grain, all surrounded by more squash and pole beans than he had ever seen. During harvest time, he could see the teams of wagons working their way through the fields, pulling in bushel after bushel of corn. It was clean, honest work, and a far cry from the life of a railroad worker.

When passengers traveled on the railroad, Henry David Thoreau would write fifteen years later in *Walden*, they did so on the backs of Irish immigrants. Railway mania was well under way in Indiana, and over a dozen lines transected the state, all part of the growing network of midwestern rails replacing water as America's preferred venue for transportation. Over the next two years, workers like Daniel Reilly would be responsible for laying nearly 150 miles of track in Indiana alone, enough to double the state's lines.

Eastern Indiana is mostly level, but the elevation from one end of the track to the other still dropped three hundred feet, requiring grading and excavation—backbreaking work in a geography defined by limestone and shale. Those not leveling the earth itself were clearing it of boulders and virgin growth or digging ditches alongside the tracks. The men did their work with picks and shovels, grubbing their way across the landscape from dawn until dusk six days a week. Daniel and the other men in the house would leave before sunrise, walking the ever longer path to their worksite and the twelve hours of toil that awaited them there. This was not work for the faint of heart; injuries and death—from explosions and falls, from cave-ins and runaway trains—were common. So too was illness; in fact just west of Liberty in Funk's Grove, Illinois, more than fifty Irish railway workers would soon succumb to cholera, and were then buried in a mass grave.

Then there was the violence Irish workers brought upon themselves as long-held national feuds found new roots in the United States. Riots were epic battles sometimes nearly nine hundred men strong, and they included enough arms to make even a military battalion wary of interfering. On the Chesapeake and Ohio Canal, one particularly severe skirmish left fifty-six men dead and required intervention from both the local militia and the army before it was quelled—the first time federal troops were required to settle a labor dispute in America.

Daniel didn't want this kind of life any more than he wanted the violence and suffering back in Ireland. He was just a shy farmer, late to marry and more comfortable in his fields than anywhere else. Railroad work was exhausting, dangerous, and foul. The men toiled until they could no longer think straight, then drank themselves to sleep—or into a brawl—

every night. They had little individuality working the line and even less respect from their supervisors. Farming, by comparison, was work that Daniel knew and loved. More than anything, he wanted a farm where he could raise his family.

The Liberty newspaper was filled with ads for fertile farmland in nearby Michigan. Just a few decades earlier, Michigan had been the site of border wars between Britain and America. It had become a state in 1835, and since then officials there were eager to see it settled. Brochures for upland immigrants abounded, most promising the kind of pastoral life Daniel had once known in Ireland. The family had been in Indiana for just a year, but that was enough for Daniel to know it wasn't the place for them. And so, with a little American money in his pocket, he again packed their belongings, this time for what he hoped would, at last, be their promised land.

The air was crisp and cool that night, unseasonably so, even for the northern prairie. Men were glad to wear their jackets; women donned their autumn dresses. The temperate air was a welcome relief for Jim O'Brien's tenants, who, like the schoolchildren before them, had come to rue the extremes of an old and poorly insulated schoolhouse.

Nicholas Reilly was now the father of five, and his youngest, Eugene, was barely a month old. Above the Reillys lived the Finklesons and their four children. Two couples, the Champlins and Coopers, rounded out the tenantry. From their apartments, they could hear Rat Matthews working his racehorses in the morning and the clamor of John Whitaker's and Jim O'Brien's saloons at night.

Whenever Finkle Finkleson asked about O'Brien's Saloon, Nicholas quickly changed the subject. How could he explain to his new Norwegian friend that he may very well be renting his apartment from a criminal? For all he knew, Nicholas himself was on the wrong side of the law. For weeks now, official-looking men had been coming around and asking a lot of questions about Jim's extracurricular business pursuits. They seemed particularly interested in the stack of bonds in his massive safe. New taxes on whiskey were making it increasingly difficult for distillers to front their batches without auctioning off futures in the form of bonds. These bonds—at least the legitimate ones—had the same currency as a bank's savings bonds, but keeping track of them was a nightmare. Forged receipts were everywhere, despite a massive national sting a decade previously that sent 176 distillers throughout the Midwest to court, and many to prison. Nicholas had begun to wonder if a similar fate might befall his brother-in-law, who was clearly feeling the pinch of scrutiny. Not to mention the pain of debt, which was making Jim more erratic than ever. Harriet was uncharacteristically absent these days, and Nicholas couldn't help but worry about her. When Jim left to buy what he insisted was the finest racehorse to ever run in Minnesota, Nicholas was relieved. If nothing else, the horse would distract everyone from the rising tension.

Jim did everything with great fanfare, and the arrival of his new racehorse that evening was no exception. All of the schoolhouse tenants turned out to watch as the trailer arrived at Rat Matthews's and a gorgeous chestnut stallion emerged. Clearly elated, Jim played the part of ringmaster as the horse was led around for all to admire. The children cheered, and even Nicholas had to admit the horse was worth the attention.

It was well after dark when everyone returned to their apartments for the night. As they did, no one noticed the lights in the armory or the distinct smell of cigar smoke pouring out of one of the guards' weekly meetings. Nor did they notice that one of the cigars had been left to smolder—probably accidentally dropped or set down by a guard and then forgotten. Certainly John Whitaker, who was too busy preparing for last call at his tavern, didn't have the time to notice.

Several hours later, nearly everyone in town was fast asleep— including the two underemployed police officers responsible for patrolling the town's streets. Years of law-abiding behavior on the part of a hard-working citizenry had taught the officers that there was little reason to leave the quiet comfort of their office at that time of night.

But Whitaker's young servant girl was suddenly awake, though she didn't know why until she went to the window and saw the blaze: all of the armory was engulfed in flame and threatening to collapse at any second. She rushed to wake her employer. Without bothering to don his trousers, Whitaker ran from the saloon to the police station, where he roused the sleeping officers. Another neighbor raced to O'Brien's tenement building to wake the Reillys. While Cecilia gathered the children, Nicholas ran upstairs to wake the Finklesons. By then the fire was lapping at the tenement house itself. Finkle grabbed an armful of clothing and bedding, then pitched it out the bedroom window. Eliza managed to save only a beaver hat and the family Bible. Their younger son, Johnny, jumped out the second-floor window after discovering that the main stairway to their apartment was cut off by smoke and flame. The rest of the family just made it out by using a secondary staircase that led into the rooms occupied by the Reillys.

All four tenants and their families had made it safely to the street by the time the fire brigades arrived to find the biggest fire in the history of Fergus Falls awaiting them. Soon there were enough firefighters to staff twelve brigades. Their exuberance in addressing the problem caused nothing short of chaos, as warring chiefs fought over how best to contain the blaze and where to direct the stream of water from their trucks.

The town's shopkeepers, alerted to the blaze, ran to their stores and began piling their goods in the street in an effort to save inventory from the blaze. The fire meanwhile kept right on burning, collapsing the roof of the armory in a cloud of embers and debris and consuming Jim O'Brien's tenement building, before moving on to Rat Matthews's training stable and the rest of Jim's outbuildings. But before it did, someone—perhaps Jim himself—had the foresight to open the stall containing his new thoroughbred. The frightened horse bolted from the stable and wasn't seen again until the next day, when someone on the outskirts of town managed to subdue the animal long enough to get a halter around his neck.

By morning the neighborhood was in ruins. Jim O'Brien, already strapped with debt, lost $4,200 worth of property (more than $80,000 today), only half of which was insured. The Reillys, along with the other tenants, lost everything they had, save for the bedding and beaver hat salvaged by Eliza Finkleson. It was a great blow. Over a century later, Cecilia's granddaughter would recall the way she spoke about the fire—the fact that it destroyed all her wedding gifts, which she said were "the nicest things she ever owned."[1] The Finklesons, along with the Champlins and Coopers, would settle into a new home just a few blocks away; the Reillys decided they had had enough of life in Jim's frontier town.

But first they had to settle up with the insurance adjuster. They were visited the next day by A. W. Perry, special agent of the St. Paul

Fire & Marine Insurance Company, who arrived prepared to settle the loss incurred at the tenement. Upon arriving, however, the adjuster discovered that Jim O'Brien was nowhere to be found; he had taken the new horse, rechristened "Fireball," to race in nearby Stillwater, where he hoped to recoup some of his loss. Without him there to answer questions and sign the paperwork, no one would receive a dime.

While Jim bet his future on Fireball, the town of Fergus Falls opted for a more salubrious approach, dedicating itself to bolstering its fire ordinances and disaster protocols in an effort to prevent such a disaster from occurring again. As far as they were concerned, the fire would forever be known as the greatest tragedy to occur in Fergus Falls.

They were wrong.

26

The Rising Tide

1852

BY ALL ACCOUNTS, the Great Exhibition of 1851 had been a huge success. For five months people from around the world poured into London's Crystal Palace, an enormous exposition center. Made almost entirely of glass, the nineteen-acre building was a daring testament to architecture, complete with grand halls, ceilings towering over a hundred feet high, and a domed roof. It was, many said, a tribute to man's triumph over nature.

So too was much of the Great Exhibition itself, which was in large part funded by Prince Albert and Queen Victoria. Considered by many to be the first real World's Fair, the exhibition billed itself as the "The Great Exhibition of the Works of Industry of All Nations," but in truth it was Britain that took center stage. In the main hall, visitors were treated to massive installations celebrating colonial products, including sugar from the Caribbean and timber from Canada. Cotton gins spun cloth and telegraph demonstrations offered visitors their first opportunity to transmit messages across the globe.

It was, Victoria hoped, a clear sign that the modern technological era had finally arrived, supplanting the upheaval and turmoil of the previous decades of inefficiencies. So successful was the exhibition in highlighting Britain's superiority in these realms, that she was now planning a smaller triumph in Cork: Ireland's Industrial Exhibition, the first to be held on the beleaguered island and one intended not only to demonstrate Ireland's phoenix-like rise from the famine but also its full embrace of the Industrial Revolution.

But there was a problem. Violence and unrest were continuing throughout Ireland, particularly in the north, where nine landlords had been murdered since the queen's visit three years earlier. Clearly her visit and statements of loyalty and peace had not worked.

The monarch was as displeased as she was concerned. On February 3, as she opened a new Parliament with her traditional annual speech, she minced few words in her concern for Ireland's continued troubles, leaving both Houses little choice but to dedicate the lion's share of their first efforts to addressing the problem of Ireland. For many members of Parliament grown tired of failed Whig policies, it was also an opportunity to address the problem of their colonial secretary. In the House of Commons, accusations of Whig neglect and mismanagement abounded. One member accused the party of systematically driving the entire middle class from Ireland.[1] Another insisted that the Whigs had left the island in a more disturbed state than they found it.[2] But the greatest vitriol was reserved for Henry Grey himself.

To confront the continued upheaval in Ireland, Prime Minister Russell had charged Grey with the formation of a Special Commission. Their investigation, however, had been halting at best, and an official report on their findings had yet to arrive. Russell urged his fellow parliamentarians to be patient, but they were in no mood for indulgence. Amid accusations that Grey's committee had been deliberately "abortive" and the first truly "failed" commission appointed by Parliament, members demanded that something be done.[3]

The earl had never been popular, but British politesse had at least been willing to keep up appearances. No longer. Across the British Empire, Grey's reputation appeared to be in free fall. The British military was suffering mightily in the Cape of Good Hope, where it had found itself again at war with the Xhosa people. Colonists in New Zealand were clamoring for their autonomy. Grey seemed helpless to confront the problem of his colonies.

At a gala dinner hosted by the mayor of Newcastle, one of the guests, Sir John Fife, described by the *London Times* as one of Grey's most loyal "lacqueys," proposed an admittedly tepid toast to the health of the earl. His tribute was met with silence, followed by a growing din of hissing, "the expression of contempt and reprobation being the more signal and significant as emanating from such a source, and on such an occasion." That descriptions of the incident were reprinted in newspapers throughout England and Ireland only intensified the sting.[4]

Worst of all was the lack of confidence engendered in Grey's fellow parliamentarians. A committee of inquiry formed to investigate Grey's handling of Ireland returned with a damning report that concluded it was public neglect that had resulted in so much suffering there. It was the closest thing to an admission of responsibility Ireland would receive from the British government until Tony Blair made a public apology in 1997.

That statement would come far too late for many in Ireland, particularly in County Kerry, where Richard Blennerhassett was once again biding his time between voyages. From his family's estate, he saw firsthand the monstrous impact of too many years with too little food for the residents of western Ireland. Young men and women had been rendered blind, their bodies contorted and behaving as if animated by a malevolent external force. Children stumbled bowlegged and hunchbacked, their mouths permanently toothless and bleeding. Others, stricken by marasmus, a severe protein deficiency, looked ancient, their skin wrinkled and gray.

Even those people with all the corn they could eat were wasting away. Henry Blennerhassett's peers in Dublin had diagnosed the condition as pellagra, a vitamin deficiency responsible for the black tongues, painful skin lesions, and debilitating cramps that caused people to drop to the ground, even in the middle of the road. Those symptoms were upsetting enough; even worse was the fact that the entire region seemed to be suffering from a collective and inexplicable madness: otherwise peaceful individuals were, unprovoked, perpetrating inexplicable acts of violence against one another. Others were suffering from wild hallucinations and full dementia, totally unaware of who or where they were.[5] Nightmares haunted many famine survivors each night: terrifying collages of the horrors so many had witnessed. Blennerhassett's patients and friends alike awoke in a cold sweat or lay awake each night, so filled with anxiety that sleep eluded them.

So severe was this fallout from the famine that, for the first time, it became a prominent subject of study for doctors throughout England. One such physician, Daniel Donovan (of no apparent relation to the *Jeanie Johnston*'s owner), conducted an extensive survey of those still going hungry in Ireland. In his subsequent report, he documented the experience of a famine victim, beginning with an acute pain that was soon replaced by weakness, insatiable thirst, and an inability to get warm.

> In a short time the face and limbs become frightfully emaciated; the eyes acquire a most peculiar stare; the skin exhaled a peculiar and offensive foetor, and was covered with a brownish, filthy-looking coating, almost as indelible as varnish. This I was at first inclined to regard as incrusted filth, but further experience has convinced me that it is a secretion poured out from the exhalants on the surface of the body. . . . Want of food produced a very different effect on the young and infant population: the same cause that paralysed the faculties of the adult served to sharpen the instinct of the child: babies scarcely able to speak became expert beggars. . . . Another symptom of starvation and one that accounts for the horrible scenes that famine usually exhibits is the total insensibility of the suffered to every other feeling except that of supplying their own wants. I have seen mothers snatch food from the hands of their starving children; known a son to engage in a fatal struggle with a father for a potato; and have seen parents look on the putrid bodies of their offspring without evincing a symptom of sorrow.[6]

It would take much longer for some of the other effects to become known. In the meantime, people seemed to be giving up. Not only had Tralee town leaders ceased to take action, but now the famine sufferers themselves seemed to be doing whatever they could to accelerate the process. On more than a few cabins still standing, hand-painted signs advertised hard cider and "strong water"—a euphemism for pure grain alcohol, though distilled from what Blennerhassett could not imagine, given this ravaged landscape. He could see the effects of the drink as it destroyed what little stamina still remained in these people.

The same could not be said for the new landlords who oversaw this suffering multitude. And no small amount of that criticism was reserved for Nicholas Donovan. As far as he was concerned, his new land was still encumbered—not by taxes but by the hundreds of people who, despite their enfeebled condition, continued to try to make a life as a cottier there. Sir Edward Denny had successfully financed the emigration of similar people on famine ships. Why couldn't he?

His was a controversial plan: It bucked the town's official policy concerning the handling of immigrants and risked the appearance of impropriety. Evicting or even persuading his new tenants to leave would cast him in the same unpopular light as people like Lansdowne. And there was no clear explanation as to how Donovan would finance any such voyage, a problem that undoubtedly raised further questions. Nevertheless, Donovan approached Denny with his plan and found the baronet surprisingly receptive. Together they would ensure the exodus of some of Kerry's remaining peasant farmers. News of their project soon spread, and few in town doubted that Denny and Donovan were looking for anything other than their own personal gain. Even fewer in town responded with nothing short of disapproval or spite. Shortly after making the announcement concerning this new assisted-immigration project, Denny awoke one morning to find protestors had lopped off the manes and tails not only of all of his horses and cattle but of those of his more established tenants as well.[7] Donovan meanwhile was facing censure of a more codified variety as newspaper editorials began to wonder aloud what was afoot.

This criticism came to a head at the second monthly meeting of the Board of Guardians. Its membership had convened that afternoon for what was supposed to be a routine discussion of the state of paupers in the Union. It soon proved anything but routine, when one member suggested that Donovan had been using the guardians' offer to subsidize emigrant passage to his own advantage. A representative of the board was dispatched at once to retrieve Donovan, who was surprised to find the man at his Denny Street office. He quickly donned his coat and arrived at the board meeting out of breath and no doubt on the defensive. But if Donovan had learned anything during his twenty years in business, it was the importance of placating anyone who appeared ruffled. So he stood silently as several of his peers observed aloud that the parties being sent from his Turbid property to North America were not in fact paupers, but rather, small tenant farmers who had agreed to surrender their land to Donovan in exchange for free passage. That accusation alone would have been enough to raise an eyebrow among those who remembered Lord Lansdowne's treatment of his tenants. Even worse was the suspicion that Donovan had sought to exploit the troubled Board of Guardians. Donovan, it seemed, had arranged entry into the already overcrowded and underfunded workhouse for twenty-five of his tenants, knowing perfectly well that the Board of Guardians subsidized emigration from there. What made this action particularly egregious was the suggestion that these individuals were far from destitute—that Donovan had simply made them appear penniless and desperate so that they would be given fare on the *Jeanie Johnston*.

For this, said the board, Donovan had no right whatsoever. Clearly he had overstepped his bounds. There was a process in place to select paupers from the workhouse for emigration, yet Donovan was preempting this process and for his own benefit. Donovan tried to explain, emphasizing that he and Lord Denny were working together to assist Kerry's suffering poor. His explanation halted further scrutiny, but the damage had already been done. His perfect record was tarnished. So too was his short-lived alliance with Denny, who immediately distanced himself from Donovan, objecting publicly to what he called Donovan's "high hand" and "very free use" of his name.[8]

If asked, Donovan would no doubt have responded that he had little choice. In the aftermath of the famine, the face of emigration was changing. So too was the business of exporting emigrants. And it was very much a business: the increased ship traffic had been good for town revenues and had prompted expansions at every level, including a new lighthouse, the illumination of which would hopefully attract even more ships. The Board of Guardians desperately needed that to be so. Another year of heavy expenses was sure to break them if they could not reduce the number of inmates for which they had to provide care. Guardians in surrounding towns had also begun seeking bids from ship owners to convey paupers from their workhouses to North America.

Donovan's bids were repeatedly undercut by the Kennellys, a rival importing firm that had chartered newer, larger, and faster ships to carry the famine sufferers. Their *Toronto*, bragged the local papers, made an "unprecedented quick passage of 17 days" from Quebec to New York, landing all of her passengers well and in record time. Their flagship vessel, the *Lady Russell*, was capable of carrying five hundred passengers, well over double the legal limit of the *Jeanie Johnston*. The *Jeanie*, it seemed, was poised to lose her status as Tralee's most beloved ship.

By February 1852, the *Jeanie Johnston* had made eight successful voyages to North America, seven of them with passengers. Nearly a thousand passengers had safely ridden below her deck, and the sterling survival rate—her reputation for keeping every soul alive—continued to be the greatest in all of Britain. But that didn't seem to matter quite as much anymore. Newer, faster ships offered greater convenience and comfort. Who would want to spend twice as long at sea—and in a leaking wooden hull that was beginning to show its age—if a more dependable alternative existed? Ticket sales for the upcoming voyage had been sparse, and as the departure date neared, Donovan was clearly dismayed by the number of bunks still available for purchase.

The *Jeanie* and her crew, meanwhile, were on their way back from Cardiff, where the barque had spent the winter. James Attridge, who had enjoyed a much-needed respite in Cork, was back at the helm, joined again by Thomas Campion. But Campion was the last of Attridge's original men. Gabriel Seldon, the captain's longtime steward, decided he had had enough of the drama inherent in emigrant transport and stepped off the vessel in favor of shorter cargo runs. The captain would be hard-pressed to find anyone to replace him. He had other concerns as well. By the time she was unloaded, there would be less than a full month to prepare the *Jeanie* for emigrant transport, including the careful insertion of additional ballast that would keep the vessel level in the water. The crew, especially Campion, would have to work hard to meet the deadline.

It was a deadline that Richard Blennerhassett was none too excited about either. Despite having formed friendships with both Attridge and Campion, the ship's doctor appeared, for the first time in his career, reluctant to climb aboard. Once again there were reports of a resurgence of cholera cases in the United States, and in Quebec the *Georgiana* and all three hundred of her passengers had been indefinitely detained after several on board were found to be suffering from typhus. The outbreak had prompted George Douglas to once again increase his staff at Grosse Île, where everyone expected a resurgence in a death toll that had only recently fallen.[9]

There were other, more personal considerations for Blennerhassett to make as well. Criticism of ship surgeons was on the rise. Blame had to fall somewhere, and the people most directly responsible for passenger health seemed as good a place as any. The toll on the doctors was pronounced. Just recently one of Blennerhassett's peers, a twenty-nine-year-old surgeon named Nathaniel English, had returned from a stint as doctor on the *Wellington*, whose captain had been relieved of his post in Australia on charges of drunkenness. When these charges were expanded to include English himself, the young doctor became distraught and was seen moving about London looking for someone to take down a narrative about his sober character. Finding none, he returned to his room, ordered a glass of soda water, and extracted a razor from his bag. The first cut to the throat was deep enough to send him rolling off his hotel bed but did not kill him. The second, which was deep enough to nick his spine, did. He was found the next morning lying in a pool of blood.[10]

English's suicide only intensified the scrutiny now awaiting Blennerhassett and the other doctors who rode aboard coffin ships. Admittedly, many were grossly underqualified and appointed only to satisfy British regulations. But others, like English, were victims of circumstances far beyond their control and responsible for maintaining health in conditions that were still worse than the slave ships that sailed fifty years earlier.

Blennerhassett had never balked at his calling. His family's motto, "Fortune favors the brave," had always guided his work. Still, he was beginning to think that his tenure on the *Jeanie Johnston* had come to an end. His mother was gravely ill; she would die within the year, in fact. His brothers Townsend and Aremberg had left the family estate near Dingle, and his youngest brother, Edward, would soon be departing for medical school. For the first time in a life marked by wanderlust and a sense of public duty, Richard Blennerhassett wanted to stay home. No doubt he felt a great sense of obligation to his mother; perhaps he had reached a breaking point concerning Donovan's management of the vessel and his growing demands regarding its use. We'll never know for sure.

But we do know he decided that the upcoming spring run to Quebec would be his last. The *Jeanie*, with 188 passengers, twenty fewer than she was allowed to carry, sailed from Tralee on April 14, 1852. Her departure was all but completely overshadowed by the departure of the Kennelly vessels, which garnered the bulk of the press that month. Maybe that was a good thing, for the *Jeanie's* trip did not begin well.

A few days after departing Tralee, Attridge noticed something was amiss: the vessel, never smooth-sailing or responsive, became even more unmanageable and began to list to one side. The concerned captain dispatched one of his crew below. He returned with confirmation of Attridge's fears: the thousands of pounds of lead ballast that lay above the *Jeanie's* keel had shifted. Without ballast, even the most stable hull is likely to tip, but loose ballast can be an even bigger problem, particularly for a ship the size and shape of the *Jeanie*. The motion created by a single wave could easily send the immense lead careening from one side of the hull to the other. Its force could capsize the vessel in seconds. Even worse, it could break like a cannonball through her wooden hull, sending the vessel and her occupants spiraling to the ocean floor.

Attridge wouldn't take that chance. He ordered Campion and his men to tack the vessel, turning her around and heading to Queenstown, where proper repairs could be made. It was an unfortunate delay; they arrived in Queenstown on May 1, over two weeks after departing from Tralee, and would remain in the port town for another twenty days before again heading for North America. Not only would the *Jeanie Johnston* fail to meet the new speed records set by the Kennellys, but she'd be hard-pressed to match even her slowest previous journey.

While anchored in Queenstown, Blennerhassett cared single-handedly for his 188 charges, who were growing restless in the busy harbor.

It was a courtesy they would not soon forget. The *Jeanie Johnston* did not arrive in Quebec until the end of June, but when she did, all of her passengers were healthy.

Blennerhassett and his captain looked forward to the efficiency they had come to expect from George Douglas upon arriving at Grosse Île. The man who boarded their vessel, however, bore little resemblance to the curt doctor who processed patients with a stern professionalism. Douglas was stoop-shouldered and ashen, and Blennerhassett soon understood why. Less than a month earlier, Douglas's beloved wife, Charlotte, had succumbed to complications from the delivery of her seventh child. Douglas had attended the birth, which had been difficult and prolonged. It weakened Charlotte terribly, and, try as he might, Douglas could not save her. He was stricken with grief and overwhelmed by the prospect of raising seven children, all under the age of twelve, alone.

Death, Blennerhassett knew, was a part of his profession. But that didn't make it any easier to bear, particularly when it claimed the life of a loved one. He could only imagine what Douglas was experiencing. Just forty days aboard a vessel was enough for the young doctor to feel forever invested in the health of his charges. In return, they felt forever connected to him. After arriving in Quebec later that month, a group of these passengers wrote an impassioned letter to James Attridge, published first in the *Quebec Mercury* and then reprinted in the Irish papers:

Sir—We feel that we would appear ungrateful did we leave your ship without returning you our sincere and heartful thanks for your unremitting kindness and attention to us during the voyage.

The character you have long since won for yourself has been well preserved since our meeting with you, and we trust that any of our friends, who wish to follow us, may be fortunate enough to meet with one possessed of as much skill and humanity. This, we have no doubt, is also the wish of our respected Medical Officer, Dr. Blennerhassett, whose unceasing attention to us shall not soon be forgotten.

It must be a source of much gratification to you, as indeed it is to us, that neither death nor sickness have made their appearance among us, owing, we consider, under God, to the wise regulations that have been observed on board.

Long may you continue to enjoy the high reputation you possess, and long may you live to receive the thanks and blessings of your truly grateful and obliged passengers.[11]

If George Douglas read that letter, perhaps he found some solace in the notion that a fellow doctor's good work had allowed others to live. There is no doubt that John Munn read the letter, and he must have been heartened to know that the vessel he had built with such care was being run with similar attention. Certainly Nicholas Donovan enjoyed the accolades of the passengers for their doctor. Probably Attridge and Blennerhassett himself did as well. It was proof positive of their hard work, and an unexpectedly grand gesture, extravagant even, particularly for artisans who had just spent their life savings on the passage to North America. But it wasn't enough to dissuade the doctor from leaving the *Jeanie Johnston* for good. He must have made his intentions known, at least to Campion. The two men had become close during their time at sea, and though we have no record of their conversations, it appears that Blennerhassett did tell Campion that although he was leaving the *Jeanie Johnston*, he had no intention of leaving his role as ship's doctor. For when the vessel returned to Ireland, he was presented with a gift even more extravagant than the *Quebec Mercury* letter: a collapsible marine surgical saw made of brass and ivory and engraved "From the crew of the *Jeanie Johnston*."

27

Departures

1853

QUEEN VICTORIA returned for an unparalleled second visit to Ireland in September 1853. Bolstered by the success of the 1852 Cork Exhibition, Prince Albert and his supporters had helped to organize an even grander display in Dublin. Rumors of a new war in Turkey along with a sudden outbreak of the measles in the royal house delayed the visit by a month; however, Victoria and Albert were determined to participate in the event that would mark the dawn of a new technological era for Ireland. To commemorate the event, the royal couple, along with their two oldest sons, traveled again by royal yacht and were seen waving from the deck as they entered the mouth of the River Liffey.

Victoria and her family spent three days at the exhibition, which invited innovators from around the world to participate. Colt and Singer both made the long trip from America; the former sold a disappointing forty pistols (and all to the Irish prison system) during the entirety of the one-month exhibition; the sewing machine company fared even worse. The Irish people simply had no money to attend the gala event, let alone purchase the merchandise. Those Irish firms participating did their best to impress the queen, who was particularly taken by the displays of Irish linen and whiskey.[1]

The exhibition aside, the timing of her visit couldn't have been more poignant. Just as the royal yacht was docking in Kingstown, census officials were releasing their official tallies from the 1851 count. Ireland's population had not risen to nine million, as predicted, nor had it maintained its 1841 count of eight million. Instead the famine had reduced the population of the island to 6.5 million. It was the first conclusive and irrefutable evidence of just how catastrophic losses from the Great Hunger had been. At least half a million people had staked their future to the hold of a coffin ship; another million died before they had the opportunity to leave.

The significance of these new figures could scarcely be ignored. Nevertheless the queen was determined to remain positive during her visit. She reported that Ireland looked "greatly improved" since her previous visit.[2] Although the famine and its aftermath had reduced many to the depths of despair, illness, and poverty, she was certain the exhibition "had raised the feelings of enterprise among the people, showing them that if they try, they can succeed." The year 1853, she predicted, would be a watershed for Irish industry.

It would be one for emigration as well. More landlords were capitalizing on estate acts and changing public perception concerning the relocation of tenants. By the end of the year, a whopping 10,448 emigrants would depart from Tralee alone. The Kennellys took advantage of the opportunity, taking out bigger and bigger ships and subsidizing the cost not only of conveying the emigrants but also of getting them to the docks. Twice that summer they sent out vessels capable of carrying more than three hundred ticketed passengers, including the 1,600-ton flagship *Lady Russell*, which the *Kerry Evening Post* described as "one of the finest ships ever brought into this port for immigration purposes." She was about to depart again with 450 passengers and a new physician: Richard Blennerhassett. She and three other ships left in early August, hoping to make North America before the worst of the hurricane season. The Kennellys' *Telegraph* left on August 20—already late in the season—and was assumed by many to be the last vessel to depart from Tralee that year. But Nicholas Donovan had other plans.

These plans no doubt troubled James Attridge. Sailors are a superstitious lot, and even an optimist had to admit it looked as if the *Jeanie*'s luck was changing. On the first of her two North American runs that year, Attridge encountered his first and only casualty aboard the vessel. Samuel Nichols, a new cook hired from Hamburg, became visibly agitated and unruly during the voyage. After repeated reprimands, Attridge had no choice but to sequester him in the vessel's jail. Shortly thereafter he died.

There is no record of Nichols's cause of death, but we do know that the British customs official in Quebec signed off on the disposal of his body and the mustering of a replacement without any suspicion or alarm. That suggests that Nichols died of what at least appeared to be natural causes. Without Blennerhassett on board, Attridge would have been hard-pressed to say for sure.

News of Nichols's demise quickly spread across Quebec's busy waterfront, and whether it was suspicion that his death had been caused by ill treatment or just standard superstition about filling a dead man's shoes, no one seemed willing to take the cook's place. Four times that month Attridge hired a cook, and each time he waited in vain for the man to arrive. These would-be deserters included a sailor named Henry Roberts, who at fifty-two would have been the oldest crew member ever to sail on the *Jeanie*. Perhaps his decades at sea had been enough to make him change his mind.

Attridge had other concerns too, such as the absence of his now-legendary right-hand man, Richard Blennerhassett, and his equally essential first mate. He and Campion had made nearly twenty voyages together. Why Campion, who would never go on to serve as captain aboard a vessel, left his post with Attridge is a mystery, but contemporary historians have two theories: that Campion grew increasingly distrustful of Donovan's decisions regarding the maintenance and management of the *Jeanie Johnston*, and that Campion's life had become so entwined with Blennerhassett's that he simply could not imagine sailing without him.

Attridge's primary concern, however, was preserving the *Jeanie*'s safety record in the face of all challenges and speculation. To replace Campion, the captain chose a young sailor from the United States who boasted a résumé of multiple transatlantic crossings but was still very much an unknown entity. That was not a good attribute for the second in command on a large vessel.

Attridge was likely alarmed by the increasingly suspect demands being placed on him by his cousin Nicholas Donovan. In the face of the Kennellys' success, Donovan had reduced his ticket prices and encouraged all those with the funds to climb aboard. He had also contracted with the Earl of Kenmare, who was more than happy to pay the reduced fare for sixty of his tenants. When Attridge arrived at his cousin's office to collect the passenger manifests for their upcoming voyage, he was dismayed by what he saw: despite a clearly stated occupancy of two hundred passengers, Donovan had sold 230 tickets for the journey. It didn't matter that the earl had sworn he would take care of all clothes and provisions his tenants would need at sea. Donovan's decision was testing Attridge's unparalleled reputation for strict adherence to naval law. Attridge knew that even the legal limit of individuals taxed the crude berths in the *Jeanie*'s hold. An additional thirty would mean more overcrowding—six or even eight people to a single bunk in some cases, not to mention the extra ton of food he would need.

September was already well upon them. There was a chill in the air and frost in the mountains. The shipping season had all but closed, and for good reason. Any departure that late in the year would send a vessel and her occupants directly into the epicenter of the North Atlantic's storm season. Each autumn, massive storm cells, some more than a thousand miles wide, often spun off from tropical hurricanes as they collected energy from the cold waters of the North Atlantic. The result could easily include hurricane-force winds, dangerous thunderstorms, and even blizzard-like conditions. Square-riggers like the *Jeanie Johnston* were not built to hold a steady course close against these types of winds. The only chart point Attridge could fetch would be the one dictated by the winds. That meant, at best, long delays in their trip. At worst, they would never reach their destination.

As Attridge prepared for this late launch, the season's first real storm pushed in hard from the Atlantic, funneling wind into the unprotected bay. It halted construction on the new lighthouse for days and delayed the arrival of packet schooners from the north and west. But that didn't matter to Donovan, who watched as a stream of small cargo boats battled their way to the *Jeanie*, carrying the bulky construction equipment

Attridge and his crew would need to build extra bunks and storage. The voyage could still come off without a hitch—of that Donovan felt certain.

But the North Atlantic had other plans. Autumn's infamous storms soon began to burgeon, traveling miles from the Caribbean and picking up force as they did. The first major storm occurred a thousand nautical miles off the coast of Ireland and soon grew to hurricane strength. It broke masts and capsized vessels. Ships still within reach put back into various ports in Britain, where their captains hoped to save both vessels and lives.

The *Jeanie Johnston* departed Tralee on Saturday, September 17, with 248 souls aboard. As Attridge steered his northern course, he could see evidence around him of the vessels that had failed to reach safety during the most recent storm; spars and splintered masts floated by, as did beacons and lifeboats. There were sheared sections of bows and crushed wheelhouses. Timber, casks of wine, and other cargo bobbed among them, silent testimony to the vessels that once carried them and now lay somewhere deep below on the ocean floor. As he pushed through the debris, the seas became heavy, rolling upon a northwestern gale. Reports of casualties began to grow: the *Annie Jane*, an emigrant vessel, was lost completely; the name board of the *Mary & Elizabeth* was found, with no trace of the rest of the ship or its passengers. Then there were those anonymous casualties for which it was known only that a vessel had foundered: three nearly submerged here, four bottom up there.

But there were also survivors. The Kennellys received word that the *Sophia Elizabeth*, a Dutch barque on her way from New York, had made contact with their immigrant vessel the *Lesmahagow* and that all was well. John Munn was delighted to hear that the *England* pushed through the brunt of the storm and arrived, somewhat miraculously, at the same docks from which she and the *Jeanie* were sold. But on both sides of the Atlantic, people searched in vain for news of the *Jeanie Johnston*. Would her great luck hold?

It would be months before Donovan would hear word. In the meantime, Attridge was battling for the life of everyone on board.

28

Storm Season

ATTRIDGE AND his crew managed to steer the *Jeanie Johnston* through the dregs of the deadly hurricane that claimed so many vessels that season. But on the other side of the massive cell, the captain confronted a series of gales just off the coast of North America. The first tore across the Maritimes on September 29, wrecking vessels across Halifax's harbor before pushing out to sea. Along the way, it prompted casualties as strange as they were tragic: all the horses aboard the *Eudocia* had perished in the storm; a cook and his cookhouse from another vessel were washed to sea, while the rest of the ship, and those aboard, remained unharmed.

That same storm met up with the *Jeanie Johnston* less than a week later, having lost little of its punch along the way. The storm bore down hard, heralded by a dramatic front line and followed by ominous clouds and a wind-chopped sea. Within an hour, the winds had collected and were hammering the *Jeanie* against angry black waves that had grown to twice the height of a man. To save his vessel from sinking, Attridge was forced to stall it directly into the wind, where she would continue to be rocked by waves but at least would remain stable.

Once the seas began to calm, Attridge wasted little time in ordering the sails raised and the *Jeanie* back on course. Nothing stayed tranquil for long on the North Atlantic at that time of year, and he would need to clear Newfoundland before the next storm if they were to make it to Quebec without incident.

Somehow the weather held. The *Jeanie* made her way past Labrador and approached the Gulf of the St. Lawrence. Cape Breton was visible from the top of the observation deck, but so too were the rolling clouds of the next frontal system. The winds began to mount, more severely this time. By nightfall they had reached hurricane proportion and would remain that intense for the next fifteen hours—enough time to wreck seven vessels within striking distance of the *Jeanie*. Visibility had been so reduced that Attridge could not see those vessels or the detritus they left. All that existed, it seemed, was the unrelenting face of those leaden waves. Attridge and his crew tried repeatedly to beat the *Jeanie* to windward, listening as the strain of the wind threatened to tear their shrouds and rigging from the deck. The waves continued to pound hard against the deck, forcing apart her seams and sending sprays of icy water onto the terrified passengers below. Still the storm showed no sign of relenting. If anything, it seemed to build as Attridge tried to force the *Jeanie* into the St. Lawrence. There the wind and waves were funneled by the surrounding land, concentrating the punch of the storm directly onto his vessel.

Attridge doubted the ship could withstand the strain much longer. Pushing forward would mean enduring even greater force. It was too great a risk. He called in the *Jeanie*'s mighty sails and allowed the gale to blow him back out to sea.

No doubt his decision saved the lives of many if not all of those on board. But it also meant that they would again have to attempt the dangerous rounding into the St. Lawrence. It was now the end of October, and the Gulf's stormiest month was about to arrive. Still, the crew agreed with their captain's decision. It was a testament to Attridge's leadership that they were willing to try again. Not far from the *Jeanie*, the crew of the *Eliza* mutinied when their captain suggested they do the same.

In the early days of November, another erratic and volatile storm approached, sending barometers and weatherglasses spinning into chaos. Sailors and the weather-wise were utterly baffled by the unsettled conditions—but not for long. Soon the storm regulated itself into a single, persistent fury greater than even the oldest residents of New Brunswick had ever witnessed. Again Attridge attempted to knuckle through it. Again he was beaten back amid the wreckage of dozens of less fortunate vessels.

By now the *Jeanie's* passengers had been aboard the vessel for two solid months. They had been jostled, sickened, and bruised. They had spent days in a dark and stifling hold. They were terrified. Above deck, Attridge assessed the situation. The storms had torn through two entire sets of sails. Delays and repairs meant that most of the food and water supply had been consumed. Even if they made it back into the Gulf, there was no assurance they would arrive in Quebec; this late in the season, Canadian ports iced over, sending all traffic to ports along the Maine coast. The *Jeanie* would never make it that far.

For the first time since taking command of the *Jeanie Johnston*, Attridge was forced to admit defeat. He limped his vessel around the thumb of Nova Scotia, taking refuge in the protected Bay of Fundy. A day later, he laid anchor at St. Andrews, New Brunswick, a small coastal town just across the Maine border. There Thomas Jones, the town's resident customs official, received them. He was visibly incredulous—and more than a little relieved—to see that everyone aboard this strange vessel was safe. What to do with these late-season arrivals, however, was a conundrum. Even if Attridge had been able to procure the food and repairs needed to make another attempt at Quebec, the onset of winter had long since made reaching the port by sea an impossibility. He couldn't take the emigrants back to Tralee; legally he was bound to deliver them to the destination printed on their ticket, so long as that was where they desired to go. Jones could help arrange steamer passage to Portland, Maine, where they could then catch a train for Quebec. All but fifty-seven of the passengers chose this option. For the rest, the prospect of yet another voyage—and one so soon after their terrifying experience—was more than they could bear. What, Attridge asked, would become of them? Jones didn't know. But he did know that St. Andrews already had a large Irish population and that many of them worked on the railroad. Railroad officials were delighted at the prospect of more labor and hired the men on the *Jeanie Johnston* who wished to remain in St. Andrews.

Attridge, now content that all of his passengers were provided for, made his slow way back across an icy ocean.

John Gaynor was one of the *Jeanie*'s passengers enticed by the railroad's offer to stay in St. Andrews. He had married late in life and found himself widowed after the birth of his second son. Now forty-seven and with two young children, he was more committed than ever to providing them with a stable life. Everything the railroad offered seemed directed at just that: regular work that, though dangerous and taxing, would nevertheless keep food on the table and provide a house in which to live and a chance for the boys to become part of a community.

But life in the St. Andrews railroad shanty soon proved anything but stable. The house he was given was as hastily constructed as any other in the railroad districts across North America. The cold Canadian wind whipped through the clapboards. Heat, Gaynor soon learned, was not included in his room and board; neither was bedding nor food and clothing for the kids. Work too was in short supply.

The brutal winter that year made progress on the railroad difficult. Further complicating matters was a lawsuit over where the tracks would run. With a surfeit of employees, the railroad company had no qualms about establishing restrictions for those who wanted to earn a paycheck. Immigrants who did not speak English were too much bother. Those who were aging or sick were ineffective. A single father was a liability: What did Gaynor intend to do if one of his sons needed him? Drop everything and race home? Each time he reported for work, Gaynor found that he wasn't needed that day. Neither, it seemed, was anyone else who had sailed with him aboard the *Jeanie Johnston*.

Christmas came and went. Gaynor began skipping meals so that his sons could eat. He grew gaunt and weak. The lack of heat continued to take its toll on his children. The winter refused to relent. By February the situation had become life-threatening.

As a blizzard squalled through the region, the Gaynors, along with the other *Jeanie* passengers, convened for an emergency meeting. They would die if they remained in the railroad camp. The only person they knew who could help was Thomas Jones, the customs official who had helped them to secure the jobs in the first place. St. Andrews was twenty miles away and the snowstorm was growing more fierce by the minute. Even so, thirty of the passengers donned every article of clothing they owned and set out.

They arrived at Jones's home well after midnight. Later he would admit he thought their desperate knocking was a loose shutter rapping in the storm; surely no human would be out in such weather. But the pounding continued, and so, donning his robe, Jones went to investigate. He opened his front door to a blast of cold air and over two dozen "wretchedly-clad" Irish immigrants, all starving and suffering from exposure.[1]

Jones was a British civil servant well-schooled in Whig policies, and assisting immigrants was clearly not one of those policies. He resisted the pleas of those wet and hungry refugees for as long as he could, but then humanity interceded, and he allowed them inside.

They were a miserable group. A man named Doyle had made the walk with a serious injury sustained on the railroad; Jones could not fathom how he had managed to survive the trek. The same was true for a man named Sullivan, whose hypothermia now appeared life-threatening. They were both sent immediately to a hospital. So too were John Gaynor's sons, both of whom were gravely ill and suffering from severe frostbite—so severe, in fact, that Jones doubted whether their feet could be saved. Somehow they survived—and even kept their feet.

But despite Jones's pleas and grave assessment of the situation, his supervisor in St. John's refused to lend assistance. The railroad contractors, who Jones saw as the real culprits, could not be bothered either. And so Thomas Jones learned the same truth Daniel Reilly had learned in Liberty. "The constructing of this railroad," he wrote, "will never benefit the Irish immigrant." It seemed there was nothing he could do.[2]

While John Gaynor remained to watch over his sons and the other immigrants who went to the hospital, those well enough to continue on determined to do just that. Penniless and without proper clothing, they left St. Andrews that February on foot, following the Maine coast for 250 miles before arriving in Portland. They were exhausted, cold, and very, very hungry. But they were alive.

—w—

Detective Mike Hoy knew a lot about dogged patience. Born in Philipstown, Ireland, he and his family survived the famine not much the worse for wear. It was a decade later, in 1858, that his family emigrated to the United States. They landed in New York, where Hoy quickly found a job working as a stonecutter, an apt occupation for what would be a lifetime of Sisyphean toil. Breaking stone took him to Louisiana, where he worked on the levee for days that never seemed to end. It then took him to Minnesota, where he laid the foundation for the State University and then for the East Side Irish Catholic Church. He might have made a life of this kind of back-breaking labor had the Civil War not erupted, compelling Hoy to enlist. He rose in the ranks during the Sibley expedition against the Sioux in the Great Plains, and by the Battle of Nashville he had been named the commander of his own company. During the fighting there, he was shot, the bullet entering just above the wrist, severing arteries, shredding tendons, and rendering his arm all but useless.

That's why it was easy to pick out Mike Hoy in a crowd. Even a heavy overcoat couldn't mask the fact that the detective's arm, which had all but atrophied in the years since the war, hung limply at his side. He shook hands with his left and had devised his own left-handed system for jotting notes on a pad of paper and navigating doorways and equipment. In everything he did, he applied the dogged persistence of a stonecutter and relied on his mind's incredible clarity.

He was now one of Minnesota's most celebrated detectives. The Hennepin County's jail was known affectionately as "Hoy's little brown jug." Officials bragged that more than a few criminals moved their operations elsewhere rather than risk Hoy's inevitable discovery.[1]

When the mayor of Minneapolis realized that he and the Great Northern Railroad had been swindled out of tens of thousands of dollars by a man posing as an English lord, he sent Hoy to Winnipeg to fetch the suspect. Hoy managed to capture the man and travel a fair distance back toward Minneapolis before he was detained by Canadian officials in what quickly became an international debate over extradition. It was months before Hoy was allowed to return to Minnesota, which he did with the same measured calm for which he had become known.

It was that measured calm that Mayor Brackett was banking on when he called Hoy into his office once again. Brackett had received a visit from a pair of private detectives from Chicago who meant business. And their business was tracking down James K. O'Brien.

Hoy already knew O'Brien. He had served him papers for debts, and he had detained him for petty assault—hardly noteworthy offenses for an officer charged with overseeing law enforcement for an entire county. But now it seemed that O'Brien had gone too far, attempting to deposit $10,000 in the National Union Bank. The bankers got nervous and called in the private detectives, who knew enough to enlist Hoy.

Hoy slipped unseen through Minneapolis's Bridge Square, where the streets were clogged with construction workers, trolleys, and dozens of carriages. But when he stepped into Nicholas Reilly's Bar just before closing time, everyone noticed. Hoy was no stranger to Reilly: he walked the beat surrounding the bar when Nicholas first purchased it a few years prior. And even though Hoy was no longer a street cop, he knew Bridge Square was already becoming a little scruffy around the edges. There were plenty of reasons for an investigating officer to make an appearance in these parts and to wonder if a witness or suspect might be stopping for a pint. That particular afternoon, Nicholas Reilly had few doubts as to the nature of Hoy's visit. He was looking for Jim O'Brien, who had disappeared—this time maybe for good.

Nicholas wasn't all that surprised that Jim had left, but he was disappointed. Mostly, of course, because of Harriet and her six kids, who were now staying in the Reillys' small home across town. Harriet spent her days with Cecilia and confided in her sister that she was convinced Jim had gone out west to make his fortune; she even had letters he had sent along the way. They all promised the same thing: that he loved her and would soon send for her. But even with the letters, Nicholas was skeptical. And he was worried. Jim was deeper in debt than ever; not even he, with all his smooth talk, could explain why he was walking around with $10,000 in bank checks from the biggest bank in Fergus Falls—not a penny of which he left with his wife before departing.

Then the rumors started. It was said that Jim had been seen leaving in the company of a woman. Harriet went from assured to distraught, and Cecilia slid right down with her. It wasn't long after that Mike Hoy stopped wandering into the bar, and regulars remarked they hadn't seen the usually omnipresent detective in days. There were rumors he wasn't even in Minneapolis any longer. That could mean only one thing: Hoy was in pursuit. If Nicholas noticed the sudden absence of Mike Hoy, he didn't say as much. Nevertheless, it was indisputable and surely not a coincidence that Hoy's departure from town aligned nearly perfectly with Jim's. But until newspapers across the country carried the story, most people in Minneapolis would not learn of the pursuit that ensued. The truth, it soon appeared, was much stranger—and more fantastic—than even Nicholas thought possible.

The thing was, Jim never had any intention of going west, particularly not when the influence of Chicago could be felt there. He was in trouble in that city, and there were far too many creditors looking for him. So instead he went north, to Toronto, where he staked his fortune on a thoroughbred horse. Little did he know that he was being followed by a team of detectives, some hired by the Chicago whiskey bonders, others by bank presidents who got nervous when they considered just how much money they had agreed to lend to the smooth-talking Irishman. Hoy knew his subject well enough to know he was an easy mark for easy money, so he sent out the same two Chicago detectives, disguised as wealthy men about town, to woo Jim with the promise of opportunity. Meanwhile Hoy obtained a bench warrant from the chief justice of Ontario, authorizing Jim's arrest and imprisonment.

Something about their plan raised Jim's suspicions enough to force him back south, across the border, this time to Buffalo, New York. There, under a variety of assumed names, he worked feverishly to sell his fake bonds, moving from hotel to hotel, barely staying a night before skulking on to his next destination. But no matter how many names he employed, his handwriting was always the same, and a daily roundup of hotel registers was all it took to confirm where he had been and who he had said he was.

Jim must have been nervous the day he returned to one of the banks to collect his bond proceeds—nervous or just plain short-sighted. He never noticed the dogged way Will Watts, a junior detective from Buffalo, followed him from his hotel to a saloon. He certainly didn't notice that Watts and another detective watched with interest as he won $35 throwing dice. Maybe it was the easy winning that made Jim careless, made him oblivious walking to the bank, never realizing that the two men for whom he held open the door matched his every step as he approached the teller. He certainly didn't notice the third man, dressed in a wool suit, who stood with one arm dangling useless at his side. But Hoy noticed Jim. And he waited until Watts, who by then was nonchalantly leaning against the teller's counter, asked the man with the fake bonds if his name was O'Brien.

Hoy couldn't help but smile when Jim responded, "Yes, sir." He paused. "I mean, no sir." And then it was all over.

Hoy stepped forward, placing his one good hand on Jim's shoulder. "How are you, Jim?"

Jim's face turned ashen. "Great God! Are you in this part of the country?"[2]

In all his arrogant desperation, it had never occurred to Jim that he had been tailed all the way from Minnesota. He gave himself up easily to Hoy, who, in an act of compassion, made it known to all of the papers back home that Jim O'Brien had traveled alone and was faithful to Harriet. Hoy would later say that Jim wanted to do the right thing—he just needed to be given a chance.

Out on bail and as full of brazen indignation as ever, Jim returned to Minnesota. He promptly took up residence above Nicholas's saloon

Minneapolis, Minnesota, December 1886

at 253 Hennepin Street. He thanked the local papers for their kind interest in his business proceedings and their anxious concern about his well-being. He reminded the readers that he had been a loyal and law-abiding citizen of Minnesota for twenty-one years. It didn't matter that neither was true, nor was it the case that, as he insisted, he "had always paid 100 cents on the dollar." He was floundering and trying hard to save face. And Nicholas took pity, hoping he could save Jim from himself.

29

That Deadly Angel

1854

CHOLERA WAS AGAIN sweeping across the globe. For the better part of the summer, it seemed as if the disease's mortality rates would mirror those of 1849. Then, suddenly and without warning, contagion rates skyrocketed. By August it was clear that this epidemic would be even deadlier. British health officials were visibly concerned: this iteration of the disease was plotting a wide course across the globe.

Hospitals in the United States were reporting mortality rates as high as 54 percent, particularly in immigrant towns like Pittsburgh. From there, the disease followed the railroad to Indiana, where it killed an entire family living just yards from the tracks. By the end of the summer, the state had reported sixty cases, twenty-two of which had ended in death.

Out on Grosse Île, George Douglas and his employees were inundated with more immigrant ships than the island had ever seen at one time. Still grieving the loss of Charlotte, Douglas had been taking longer and longer trips to England with the children whenever his schedule allowed. No doubt concerned about the fortitude of their chief quarantine doctor, officials in Quebec appointed a second physician. Dr. Anthony Von Iffland was given the title of assistant medical chief, but it seemed clear to everyone that he had been summoned at least in part to keep an eye on Douglas. With expertise in cholera and other infectious diseases, Von Iffland seemed just the man to keep Grosse Île under control.

But even Von Iffland was soon bested by the disease. As it took hold of Grosse Île, the island degenerated into chaos. The volume of waste excreted by the victims was almost inconceivable. Laundresses worked throughout the day and night in an effort to manage the mountains of soiled bedding. Douglas ordered that large wooden cages be constructed at the low-tide line. There, as the tide rose and fell, the women could fill them with wheelbarrows full of sheets and mattresses and allow the river to rinse away much of the waste before they boiled the bedding. It never occurred to anyone that they were flushing the microorganism into a habitat where it could grow and spread.

On the other side of the island, Douglas and Von Iffland struggled to maintain protocols among the thousands of passengers arriving there. On June 13, the German vessel *Glenmanna*, an enormous ship with three decks and 674 passengers, arrived at the island and promptly raised its contagion flag. During its Atlantic voyage, the *Glenmanna* had lost forty-five of its passengers to the disease, and although everyone still on board appeared healthy, Douglas wasn't about to take any chances. He ordered the entire lot of them to a sick bay quarantine. Somehow, however, Douglas's orders were never received. Once on Grosse Île, passengers from the *Glenmanna* were allowed to mingle and share space with a group of immigrants cleared for steamer transport to Quebec City. Within days of arriving, nine of them died of a severe onset of cholera—but not before they had spread the disease throughout the city. By August, 724 people would die there. Despite their best efforts, the staff at Grosse Île had failed. They were not alone.

This sort of predicament occurred in communities across the globe, and it created terror. The epidemic stormed through neighborhoods, pushing mortality rates over 50 percent in England, twice that of the deadly 1847 typhus outbreak, and taking entire families in a matter of hours. Black flags flew at street corners, alerting passersby to the scourge's presence on those blocks. Streets were thick with lime and flanked by hearses and mourning coaches, which shuttled to and from the dead-house from morning to night.[1]

Meanwhile baffled officials continued to search for reasons behind the uncontrollable spread of the disease. At this point, they were open to just about anything. An unnamed man appeared before the Board of Health and then the Fraternity of Millers, insisting that he had traced the root of the disease to stale grain. His discovery, he explained, came after a bout of diarrhea that occurred shortly after he consumed outdated flour. Upon further investigation, he discovered that disease was more rampant around rivers and bodies of water—no doubt, he surmised, because of the grain vessels there. It was enough to encourage the disposal of huge loads of grain thought to be stale—a bitter pill to swallow for those still famished in Ireland.[2]

Then the rains came, pelting all of Britain and forming the kind of deadly pools in which cholera, a water-borne illness, loves to live. In Tralee, streets overflowed to a height not seen since the 1849 deluge. Outside Donovan & Sons, the center of town had become a swamp, which slowly drained toward the post office, leaving behind "pestiferous odors" and questions concerning the safety of the town's infrastructure.[3]

John Snowe's discovery of the cause of the spread of cholera would come too late to help many in Tralee. The graveyard adjoining the work-house had seen an addition of almost two thousand bodies since 1850, and groundsmen there had begun the grisly practice of exhuming older graves to make room for more. Not surprisingly, hungry dogs returned in a scene familiar to those who had survived 1847. Soon rumors began to spread that the bodies of babies were in plain sight and packs of animals were feeding on them. When the Poor Commission was criticized pub-licly over the exhumations, Thomas Hurly, chairman of the commission, shot back, saying that only one infant had been exhumed, that the body was still in its coffin (albeit in plain sight), and that all but the bones had already decomposed. As for the charges that wild dogs were once again scavenging among the dead, Hurly assured townspeople that that too would be coming to an end: he had hired a local man to shoot "those famishing dogs as they attempted to crimson their mouths with the gore of human beings."[4]

That still left the problem of what to do with the bodies of additional victims. In light of the brewing cholera epidemic, even Hurly had to admit there would be hundreds of them. In response, the Tralee Board of Guardians agreed to rent an acre of land for future pauper burials. They also formed a special cholera committee, headed by none other than Nicholas Donovan. Their mandates soon graced placards throughout town: manure was to be carried away from homes and town, all gutters and drains were to be cleaned, and fever sheds were to be cleared for quarantine. They promised legal proceedings against anyone who refused to comply.

Drafts of lead, injections of scalded milk mixed with egg, and poultices of hot sand were again proving ineffective against the disease. So too were the tinctures of opium and other remedies attempted by baffled doctors. The only thing to do for cholera sufferers, it seemed, was pray.

The irony, of course, is that, unlike typhus, cholera is one of the most easily treatable diseases; merely keeping the patient hydrated while the microorganism runs its course is often enough to save the person. Water, though, was considered inadvisable for a patient suffering from such severe diarrhea, particularly when that patient was languishing below the deck of a seagoing vessel with no obvious way to clear the waste. That's what happened aboard the 2,000-ton *Guiding Star*, which left Liverpool that fall with 550 passengers on board. Not long after, she encountered a gale that sheered away her main topmast and yard, along with several key spars and sails. Disabled, she limped toward Belfast, hoping to seek refuge in the Irish port. But once she arrived, officials there could see that the storm damage was the least of the ship's problems: during the storm and subsequent attempt to reach the north of Ireland, six passengers had died. The sailors on board tried to pass off the deaths as simple diarrhea, but officials in Belfast could see that the ship was carrying yet another outbreak of cholera. Eleven people lay collapsed on deck; many others were suffering down below. Emigrant officers worked with the city's guardians to secure space for the emigrants in the workhouse hospital, while the dead, now numbering thirteen, were buried in the pauper cemetery nearby.

The *Guiding Star* brought with it an urgent warning for port towns everywhere: cholera was on the move and eager to make landfall. The

question to be asked was no longer if it would arrive at Ireland's docklands, but when and what to do once it did. When an emigrant vessel,
also disabled by the gale, sought refuge in the newly named port of
Queenstown, customs officials there were forced to admit that they had
no facilities for them. Town officials worried aloud what they would have
done if the vessel had contained anyone stricken with the disease. The
"consequence," they said, would "have been dreadful."[5]

No one needed to wait long to see the truth in their prediction. On
July 11, the full-rigged ship *Dirigo*, chartered by the Colonial Land and
Emigration Commission, arrived in Cork Harbor, having left Liverpool
a week earlier with just over four hundred passengers. Prior to departure, two children had died. The cause of death of the first was not clear
to the ship's doctors; the second, a girl of thirteen, was believed to have
succumbed to a fever, and so the captain, believing that nothing was
amiss, dropped his anchor lines and began the vessel's long journey to
Melbourne, Australia. Less than twenty-four hours later, an infant died.
Not long after that, the thirteen-year-old girl's father perished as well. A
four-year-old boy soon followed. The ship's surgeon observed that some
passengers had "assumed an altered aspect." A few hours later, the cause
was obvious. As night wore on, several other passengers began showing
the characteristic signs of acute cholera. The onset of the disease was so
rapid and so utterly destructive to those who contracted it that the ship's
doctor beseeched the captain to put in at Cork. He agreed, believing that
a marine hospital or other such accommodation was available there or in
nearby Queenstown. Summoning a tug steamer, he allowed his vessel to
be towed into the harbor, where he reported the condition of his ship and
passengers. Almost immediately he was visited by emigration and medical officials, who later said they were shocked by the conditions on board:
three women lay dead and dozens upon dozens were incapacitated by
"premonitory diarrhea."[6] The officials called for a muster of passengers
and then ordered a steamship to tow the *Dirigo* back to Liverpool, saying
that they simply did not have the capacity to tend to its ill passengers.

No one could deny the warning brought by the *Dirigo*: without proper
medical facilities, Queenstown could soon become the new epicenter of
a pandemic.

In Liverpool, tensions were also rising. Philip Finch Curry, the city's coroner, was at the breaking point. Born prematurely and with a severe case of epilepsy, Curry had never been strong. This latest cholera outbreak had sent him to the edge of exhaustion. As coroner, he was part doctor, part magistrate, responsible not only for declaring the cause of death of the bodies he examined, but also, if need be, deciding who should be held responsible. As far as he was concerned, blame for this rash of deaths and the turmoil they were creating rested squarely on the immigrant vessels moored at the city's Mersey wharves.

Those same docks were playing temporary home to the *Ben Nevis*, a ship destined for Galveston, Texas, with 446 German immigrants, a crew of forty-four, and two physicians. One of those doctors already had enough experience with cholera to last a lifetime. But not even his time aboard the *Bussorah Merchant* could prepare Richard Blennerhassett for what was coming. On September 17, 1854, a confirmed case of cholera elsewhere on the emigrant docks forced the immediate evacuation of all vessels there, including the *Ben Nevis*. Six days later, after the ship was cleaned and purified, the captain was allowed to reload his now visibly shaken passengers and crew. On September 26, two children, one twelve years old and the other several years younger, were found dead in their berths. Not long after, Regina Lehatta, the mother of one of the children, died as well, apparently so overcome by grief that her brain swelled. Blennerhassett and his fellow physician, Dr. Hankay, were sent for.

The two doctors debated the cause of the girls' deaths for some time and failed to agree; later reports would indicate that one of them maintained the children had died of cholera, and the other contended it was fever. History has lost track of Hankay's medical training and experience with cholera, but given Blennerhassett's commitment to studying the disease and his time on the *Bussorah Merchant*, it seems unlikely that he would miss the telltale symptoms.

The mere fact that the two physicians disagreed was enough to alert an already vigilant medical staff back on Liverpool's wharves. The death certificates for the two children, which stated that the physicians were in conflict regarding the cause of death, aroused the suspicions of Chief Emigrant Officer Major Greig, who ordered further inquiry into the case. He contacted Curry, who ordered the doctors to send another certificate, this one with a single cause of death. When the paperwork failed to arrive by 10 A.M., Curry, who by now was more than impatient, ordered a full inquiry into the vessel. But he was too late: the *Ben Nevis* had left the port, bound for Texas.

Curry had enough suspicion that something was amiss to order further investigation. The bodies of the three victims remained in repose at the Liverpool deadhouse, and the coroner ordered a full autopsy of each. He was shocked by the results: the two children, it appeared, had died of neither fever nor cholera, but starvation. Regina Lehatta, Curry later testified, had been similarly misdiagnosed; as far as Curry could tell, the woman died of inflammation of the lungs, not effusion on the brain.

Appearing before the Coroner's Court, Curry presented his findings. His revelation that Blennerhassett and Hankay had misdiagnosed not one but three patients prompted an audible gasp from the jurors, followed by disruptive murmuring. It was all the encouragement the coroner needed. "I am told," he informed the court, "there is a class of men who go and represent themselves to be surgeons, and who are not surgeons at all." This statement produced an even greater disturbance in the courtroom, and it was several minutes before order could be restored. Curry went on to tell the court that he had evidence that mere chemists and, in one particularly egregious case, a hospital doorman had stepped aboard vessels purporting to be medical doctors. Richard Blennerhassett signed his name "M.D.," Curry conceded, but there was no proof of what that entailed or whether it even meant "medical doctor" at all. Perhaps the abbreviation would be more aptly rendered as "most damned" or some other construction.[7]

This was all the jury needed to hear. Too many people had died in Liverpool, and no one had yet been held accountable. The jury foreman rose, saying he had been sailing out of Liverpool for eighteen years and had never seen an appropriately trained doctor on board. Ask them for medicine, he said, and they'll swear nothing's wrong with you. It wasn't uncommon, he claimed, for fifteen bodies to be tossed overboard as a result of negligence. Clearly the *Ben Nevis* was proof of this. By the time the *Ben Nevis* made an emergency stop at Queenstown on September 29, it had become known as the vessel that sailed, to quote *The Nation*, "unprovided with competent medical officers."[8]

Those aboard might have taken the time to disagree, had they not been so overwhelmed with the tragedy that had since overtaken the vessel. On the first day out, eight passengers fell ill. Later the captain of the vessel would say their illness "was conceived as sea-sickness," though whether this was his diagnosis or the doctors' or even true at all is not known. The next day, an additional four passengers died. By September 29, twenty were confirmed ill and seven had died. Once the vessel anchored in Queenstown, officials there were quickly dispatched. They confirmed what all on board already knew to be true: the *Ben Nevis* had been wracked by cholera. The official diagnosis, though, would come too late for Richard Blennerhassett.

It's unclear when the young doctor felt the first symptoms. Probably he was distracted enough by the condition of his patients that he could have ignored the nausea and abdominal cramps—but not for long. Cholera attacks as quickly as it does virulently, and in no time he would have been unable to stand and would have been taken to his berth. At that point, he would have known better than anyone on board that it would be only hours before he died. First, he would become rapidly and violently dehydrated. That would make him confused and disoriented, perhaps forgetting that he was on a ship or even who he was. His eyes would sink into his skull and become unfocused. He would cry out in agonizing thirst before finally dropping into a stupor. His blood pressure would plummet; his heart rate would become irregular. Not long afterward, it would stop altogether.

Richard Blennerhassett, the doctor who had saved so many, succumbed to cholera on the *Ben Nevis*. His body and those of the thirteen others who had died were piled in carts on the dock and taken up a steep and winding hill to the Old Church Cemetery. Richard's father, reading the news, barely arrived in time to see his son buried along with the other victims in a mass grave. There they remain in an unmarked plot, now flanked by trees and wild grasses but still showing dimensions large enough to hold them. Theirs would be the largest mass grave in the yard until 193 of the 1,100 victims from the sinking of the *Lusitania* were buried there in 1915.

While Henry Blennerhassett laid his son to rest, customs officials worked tirelessly to remove fifty of the *Ben Nevis*'s healthy patients to the retired hulk of the HMS *Inconstant*. There they were visited daily by local physicians and given enough provisions to last until the *Ben Nevis* could be properly quarantined, disinfected, and released for Galveston.

That would be more than enough time for Curry to intensify his assault against the ship's doctors with an editorial in the Liverpool newspapers. But his smear campaign would not go unchallenged. Curry soon met with fierce opposition from Henry Blennerhassett, who responded to Curry's public assault with one of his own. The elder Blennerhassett lambasted Curry's "prosy and rambling" editorial as well as the official's own medical acumen. He reviewed every action taken by his son, beginning with the case of Regina Lehatta. Everyone in the medical field, he insisted, ought to know that inflammation of the lungs and effusion on the brain often coexist in a patient. Surely, he added, any competent doctor who attended her would be best suited to diagnose of what she actually died.

Lest there be any question concerning his son's competency, Blennerhassett also went to great pains reviewing his son's qualifications: a doctor of medicine from Edinburgh, his surgical qualifications from there, qualifications for midwifery in Dublin. He wrote of Richard's experience on the *Bussorah Merchant* and included letters from ship's doctors and owners, including one from Nicholas Donovan.

If the owner of the *Jeanie Johnston* was still smarting over Blennerhassett's resignation, it did not show in the published commemoration of his one-time employee. "We can testify," Donovan wrote,

> that nothing could exceed his care and attention to the emigrants under his charge, and his popularity amongst the people in this district, and his reputation for skill and humanity were so great, that one of the first questions asked before taking a berth by an emi-

grant, was "does Doctor Richard Blennerhassett sail in the ship this voyage?" Previous to sailing on our ship in 1848, Dr. Blennerhassett bore the reputation in his own neighborhood of being a well informed and clever medical man, and was generally liked and respected. We believe that few British ships taking emigrants to North America were ever supplied with a more efficient or careful medical officer.[9]

APRIL 1900

—⁓—

A new century. It was hard not to be excited by the prospect. Irish leaders were calling for a revolt against British rule. Queen Victoria— as beloved as ever among her own people—responded by forming the Irish Guards, a branch of the Royal Army. In America, Manifest Destiny had reached all the way to Hawaii, where the residents were now demanding representation. Electric buses were running in New York. Electric lights were illuminating much of Chicago.

Daniel and Margaret Reilly had taken up residence in the latter city with their daughter Annie and her husband, John, a streetcar driver. Chicago at the dawn of a new century couldn't have seemed more different from the Ireland where Daniel had been born eighty years earlier. The Industrial Revolution had been a success, and the world was moving faster than ever. For his part, Daniel was content to let it pass by. He had long since retired from the farm. His legs hurt; his heart hurt. And so he lay down.

That had been over a month ago, and in the ensuing days, he didn't notice the dark spot that formed on his foot. By the time it grew up his leg, there was little the doctors could do: senile gangrene moves quietly through an elderly body, killing the extremities before shutting down the circulatory system entirely. Daniel Reilly lived to see his son Nicholas's fifty-third birthday and then died days later.

Had he traveled to Minneapolis in his final days, Daniel would no doubt have been proud of his son, who had moved to one of the city's first suburbs. The area around the saloon on Hennepin Avenue was falling into disrepair, becoming a skid row that would be demolished within the decade. Still, Reilly's Bar was as pristine as ever, with its elaborate white molding and columns, its mirrored walls and gleaming taps. The granite bar top was polished to such a state that patrons

202

could see their reflection. Nicholas himself tended bar, a squat man in a pristine white shirt, neatly buttoned and topped with a small black bow tie. His hair was white and thinning, but his face was still round and ruddy. These days, he was often joined by his son Robert. Thirteen years old, he was the fourth of Nicholas's six children, and everyone agreed that the resemblance between the two was striking. Robert had a natural aptitude for the work; more important, he seemed to like it. Nicholas couldn't help but be pleased.

In fact Nicholas couldn't complain about anything, not even the knowledge that his brother-in-law, Jim O'Brien, up to his old tricks, had returned to Minnesota after escaping a string of bad business deals. Nicholas had a wife he loved, six beautiful children, a successful business, and a house in the suburbs. That, it seemed, was more than enough to keep him busy.

30

Down with the Ship

1856

AT SIXTY-EIGHT, John Munn had neither the stamina nor the will to muster the kind of dramatic showing needed to pull his yard out of financial ruin. He transferred the title of his house to his cousin Elizabeth, hoping to protect her from the debt that would plague him even after a death he knew was soon in coming. Each day he continued to visit the massive complex of buildings and timber yards a lifetime of shipbuilding had created, and he continued to follow the daily reports in the shipping news of his beloved vessels.

The world was a very different place from when he sat down to craft the *Jeanie Johnston* and her three sibling vessels a decade earlier. Henry Grey, tired of the criticism over his policies, had resigned and now kept busy writing book after book defending them. Charles Trevelyan was casting his sights eastward, to a plum position serving as governor of Madras in India. The British Army was preparing to vacate its garrison on Grosse Île. And perhaps most dramatically, Irish immigration rates had fallen to pre-famine numbers. Those who arrived now did so largely by steamship, making the barque all but obsolete for human transport. Some of Munn's barques had been commissioned as naval ships in the Crimea, where the world's first truly modern war was in its last months. Others were serving their original function as cargo vessels on the North

Atlantic. Even the *Jeanie Johnston*, after twelve successful runs that safely deposited more than two thousand immigrants on North American shores, had been retired as an immigrant ship. There just wasn't enough money in it for Nicholas Donovan to continue, and so he sold the vessel to an importer in the north of England. Better, he decided, to do what he did best: move goods to and from Ireland.

The *Blake*, the vessel Munn launched just days before the *Jeanie*, had also returned to a career as a cargo vessel, and it was a load of timber she was carrying when she set sail from Ship Island, Mississippi, on February 8, 1856, destined for Cork. Despite her winter departure, all seemed well during the *Blake*'s first month at sea. But on March 5, the waves became heavy and the wind began to blow a gale. The barque labored heavily through the storm and began taking on a dangerous amount of water. Her captain, a longtime veteran of the seas named Edward Rudolf, ordered his crew to begin pumping. But their actions soon proved futile. As the winds continued to squall, the hold filled with water—thirteen feet by March 12. Meanwhile the southwesterly winds became northerly, bringing with them dangerously cold temperatures, freezing rain, and pelting snow. Rudolf's men were exhausted. Had they been better rested, they might have stood a chance when a punch of wind knocked the vessel hard into the waves. As it was, they were helpless to do anything other than watch as the ocean swept away the vessel's lifeboats and water casks, along with her helmsman.

Now completely waterlogged, the *Blake* could no longer be righted and lay breeched in the roiling sea. The remaining crew clung to the rigging, hoping to escape the fate of their fellow sailor. Few would be so lucky. The winds had now reached hurricane strength and were pelting the men with driving hale and freezing waves. A particularly large wave caused the ship again to capsize, this time carrying away seven men before slowly, laboriously righting. Rudolf ordered the men to tie themselves to the rigging. The waves continued to break over them—for days—as the storm showed no sign of abating. At least one crew member died from hypothermia. The others grew dangerously thin, having had no food for over a week, save for a drowned rat the captain eviscerated and shared with his remaining men. "A delicious morsel," he would later recall. As the storm began to weaken, the men, now frantic with hunger, spied two ships, but neither ship saw the beleaguered vessel.[1]

Conditions continued to deteriorate. So much so, in fact, that when a tenth crew member died, Rudolf and his men chose not to throw his body overboard but, instead, strung it up above the deck and ate it with the same steely resolve that had seen them through the previous twenty days. "I did not see how we ever lived, not having a dry place to lay and the sea constantly washing over us, and as some of us would drop off in our dosing dreams, dreaming of feasting at some friendly table; in a few minutes we would be awakened by the wash of a sea, then see our situation and also the dead body swinging in the pale moonlight."[2] The men's moans of discomfort and hunger subsided, until the ship was as quiet as a coffin. Rudolf admitted that even he had given up and was merely waiting for death to relieve him. That was when the schooner *Pigeon* appeared. Assisted by the crew of the *Mercury*, which arrived soon afterward, the men of the *Pigeon* managed, with great difficulty, to remove the survivors of the *Blake*, their clothes disintegrating with the slightest touch and leaving the emaciated men with the added problem of being naked. Between the crews of the *Pigeon* and the *Mercury*, a hodgepodge of shirts and trousers were amassed, and Rudolf's men looked like ghostly children playing dress-up.

Hundreds of miles north of them, James Attridge was encountering his own difficulties. After leaving the *Jeanie* in 1855, Attridge had found work as master of the *Wilson Kennedy*, that grand ship built just a few steps away from the *Jeanie* back in 1847. The *Wilson Kennedy* had enjoyed a career almost as dazzling as the *Jeanie*'s, having first served as an immigrant ship to Australia and then forming part of the fleet supporting the Light Brigade as it charged through the Crimean War. Now she too had been converted back into a cargo vessel. She was the biggest ship Attridge would ever captain. Laden with salt and sailing from St. John's, New Brunswick, the ship foundered in the Bay of Fundy and began taking on a dangerous amount of water. Attridge flew the distress flag and began to prepare his crew for the worst. But then, almost out of nowhere, the schooner *Sultan* appeared and rescued all those on board. They were delivered to Boston, where they soon scattered, many of the crew taking work on other vessels. But James Attridge, now fifty-one, had had enough. He returned to his quayside home in Cork and eventually settled in nearby Passage, on the west bank of the Cork harbor, where he served the remainder of his days as deputy harbormaster, ensuring the safety of thousands of passengers and crew. He died an old and much celebrated man.

Nicholas Donovan, whose success continued in the years after he sold the *Jeanie Johnston*, died on November 9, 1877, one of Tralee's wealthiest men and a landlord several times over. And, to what must have been his great satisfaction, he also died a town leader. His death was enough to halt, at least temporarily, trade in the busy city. The Chamber of Commerce turned out in force for his funeral, marching as a body, wearing mourning crepes and scarves, to a place more than a mile from town, where they paid their respects at the enormous pink tomb that had been erected in Donovan's honor.

Katherine Donovan's health declined sharply with the death of her husband, and in her final days she developed a nearly pathological fear of death. Revising her will, she left a large sum so that two doctors could check her body for at least eight days after she had been declared dead, lest the original proclamation be made in error. Her coffin, she said, was to be kept open during that time until it was determined that she "was *really dead*." Afterward masses were to be said weekly for her "poor soul" and those of the other Donovan family members.[3] Well into the twentieth century, they were.

31

The Final Test

1858

THE *JEANIE JOHNSTON* was a testament to one of the greatest
nautical feats of all time and the very embodiment of the
New World Order. But that alone could not save her from
the deadly gale of 1858. Overloaded with timber from the Ottawa River
Valley, the three-masted barque lurched through the water that October,
hampered by the shifting weight in her hold. Despite this, the *Jeanie* and
her crew managed to travel nearly a thousand nautical miles—almost half
the journey from Quebec City to northern England—before the storm
overtook her.

Just after midnight, the winds increased to an easterly gale. As it began
to squall, the crew turned in all standing, retiring only briefly to their
bunks, fully dressed and drenched in spray, but at the ready whenever
needed. Meanwhile the ship heeled dangerously from side to side, pitching the stacks of timber against her hull. The men knew they would have
to disarm the storm's punch as best they could before she capsized. Captain Johnston ordered the crew to lie to, turning the vessel into the wind
so that she would yield to rather than fight the growing storm.[1] That
also meant shortening all fourteen of the *Jeanie's* square sails, which were
capturing the wind's blast and threatening to overturn her. Those men
standing evening watch climbed high into the ship's spars, trying unsuc-

cessfully to furl the heavy canvas. Again and again the winds pushed them back onto the deck. After a dozen attempts, they finally secured the shortened sails, only to discover that their efforts did little to abate the power of the storm.

The seas continued to grow. Down below, Johnston's wife and two-year-old son were bracing themselves in the officers' quarters. It was customary for wives and young children to travel with a captain, and indeed Johnston's wife had made many a voyage with her husband. Even still, she was far from prepared for the rush of seawater that soon burst through the hull. Above her, the captain ordered all hands to man the pumps as he cursed this late-season run and the extra load of timber, both of which now threatened to bring down his tired ship. As the storm continued to grow, he knew the crew had but one option remaining: they'd have to disable the barque and hope for the best. Johnston ordered all men on deck and sent the main watch back up into the rigging, this time to bring in all but the main topsail, which he hoped would at least stabilize his imperiled vessel.

Weary and dangerously chilled, the crew nevertheless labored throughout the night, furling the remaining sails. But their efforts weren't enough. By 9 P.M., the storm had reached hurricane proportions. Waves now topped twenty-five feet; they slammed against and over the *Jeanie*, shearing away lifeboats and the massive crane, and crushed the wheelhouse and galley, sucking the cookstove and navigation table into the roiling ocean.

The storm continued throughout the day and showed no signs of abating. At 9 P.M., a rogue wave described by the captain as "a monstrous sea" struck the ship with such force that it crushed the main cabin, sending a torrent of water deep into the hold. It would be only minutes before the entire ship was swamped, and the crew would have to act fast if they hoped to survive. They grabbed what little food they could and then climbed the hundred-foot masts. Meanwhile Johnston hurried to his own quarters, where he found his wife and son crouching in terror. There was no time for either of them to change out of their nightclothes before they too made the climb up into the topmasts of the sinking ship. There Johnston and his family and crew tied themselves to shrouds with the ship's tattered sails. They hung there in the dark and the pelting rain, not knowing how much time remained before the ship, already submerged up to her splintered deck, would sink. Throughout the night, the crew was certain the masts would snap off in the violent winds, sending them all to their deaths. More than one was surprised to see the next morning dawn.

As the sun rose somewhere behind the raging storm, Captain Johnston raised his distress flag. During the course of the next several days, at least two large ships sailed within a mile of the beleaguered vessel, but she sat too low in the water for them to see her. The *Jeanie's* crew remained tied high up in her masts for over a week, eating only the hardtack and bacon grabbed before the galley was consumed by the storm and sucking water from the saturated sail canvas. When their thirst became too great, they chewed on pellets of lead, believing this might lessen their discomfort. Their skin blistered and split from the sun. Their hands and feet swelled painfully from the pressure of the shrouds and lack of water.

Miraculously, on the ninth day the Dutch barque *Sophia Elizabeth*, the very same vessel that had spied the Kennellys' *Lesmahagow* in the storm of 1853, spotted the sinking ship. Her captain was certain no one had survived. Still, he commanded his crew to launch the auxiliary boats and sail over to the *Jeanie Johnston*. Once there, they were amazed by what they saw: fifteen people, severely sunburned and dehydrated, dangling in the ship's rigging seventy-five feet above the deck. The *Sophia's* men had to carry down the *Jeanie's* captain, family, and entire crew, so weak were they from dehydration and edema. They had arrived not a moment too soon. As the *Sophia's* crew loaded their new passengers and prepared to sail for New York City, the *Jeanie Johnston* shuddered and then slipped below the waves.[2] She took with her an unparalleled safety record: save for Samuel Nichols, each of the more than one hundred men who sailed as crew lived to tell their story. So too did the fathers and mothers, the weavers and farmers, the spinsters and children who huddled below her deck. For the rest of their lives, they would say proudly that they came to America aboard the world's luckiest ship.

The day was cold enough to snap the axles on several streetcars. By afternoon the thermometer had yet to climb above zero. Most of the Midwest was still snowed in after an unexpected January blizzard dumped feet of snow from Illinois to New York and everywhere in between. Snowplows worked around the clock to clear streets and rails, though few people ventured outside.

Three weeks earlier, Nicholas Reilly had been walking to work when his heel caught a patch of ice and sent him tumbling to the ground, breaking a hip. He had been bedridden ever since. On this day, Cecilia went to their bedroom to check on him late in the afternoon. Nicholas seemed as cheerful as ever and asked her to fetch him a cigar from his dresser. When she turned back around to give it to him, he was dead.

Two weeks later, she would win a settlement against the city of Minneapolis for improper care of their sidewalks. In the suit, she presented his death certificate, showing that he had died of cardiac paralysis. But that didn't interest the city clerk nearly as much as Nicholas J. J. Reilly's place of birth. In letters cramped to fit on the slender line provided, that place was listed as the Atlantic Ocean.

EPILOGUE

⌘

Fergus Falls, Minnesota
June 22, 1919

After nearly six months of negotiation, the Paris Peace Conference was in its final days. Woodrow Wilson, the first U.S. president to visit Europe while in office, had been holed up for what felt like ages, waiting to see if Germany, defeated after a world war, would accept the Treaty of Versailles. Wilson promoted an ideal first generated in the era of Manifest Destiny: that America had a mission to defend democracy around the world. This ideal, though, was meeting with plenty of resistance at the conference. France, still dealing with horrific casualties and a war-bruised landscape, remained bellicose in the face of concessions for Germany. Britain was balking at the idea that both Canada and Ireland had become independent during the fighting. Both, albeit for divergent reasons, objected to Wilson's commitment to self-determination and a true end to colonial powers. Neither had much patience for his Presbyterianism, which seemed to smack of the previous generation's Providentialism. What resulted were days upon days of debate between Wilson, Prime Minister Georges Clemenceau of France, and Lloyd George, prime minister of Britain. When asked, upon returning home to London, how he had fared in Paris, George would famously reply, "Not badly, considering I was seated between Jesus Christ and Napoleon."[1]

But that was still days away. In the meantime, America was waiting to see what would become of a world torn apart by the war to end all wars.

212

Soldiers, many irreparably scarred, were returning to a nation changed in their absence. Those who never left struggled to receive them.

At the Rathskeller Café on Marquette Street, Robert E. Reilly stood behind the bar, preparing for the afternoon. The weather was oppressively humid that day, and the air both outside and in pressed down on Minneapolis with the weight of water. With a stout build like his father's, Robert toiled in the humidity, wiping the sweat from his round face and pushing back the sleeves of his starched shirt. A few blocks away, his mother was helping her youngest daughter, also named Cecilia, prepare Sunday dinner in the house she rented with her husband, Florenz. Since Nicholas's death, his wife had moved between her children's homes, and when President Wilson reintroduced the draft in 1917, Robert listed her support as one of his major responsibilities. Doing so was probably what kept him out of battle and, instead, pouring drinks at the Rathskeller, just as his father had done for years.

If Robert didn't begin his shift at the Rathskeller thinking about Nicholas's tenure behind the bar at places like the Grand Hotel in Fergus Falls, he certainly finished his day doing so. Just as he set about replenishing his icebox and counting his till, the sky became an ominous black as a supercell thunderstorm gathered strength on the state's western border, focusing its power on Otter Tail County.

In Fergus Falls, the rumbling began just after 4 P.M. Elsie Rathbun, who was waiting for a train at the Great Northern Station, had never heard such a noise, "like a dozen factories all full of buzzsaws running at once," she would later say. When the deluge began a few minutes later, Elsie and the other people seeking cover at the railway station thought that would be the end of the storm. When hailstones the size of marbles began to fall, they knew things were about to get much worse. The three tornados—black, massive, and twisting ominously—dropped out of the sky shortly thereafter, gaining in strength and size until the largest of them was nearly four hundred yards wide. That's when pandemonium hit. The noise, Elsie said, was deafening. Part of that was the sheer force of the wind alone—wind so strong that it blew straw and slender weeds through six-inch boards, embedded clover in living-room plaster, and sucked checks out of bank drawers, depositing them intact sixty miles away. The storm produced other oddities as well, stripping a flock of thirty chickens clean of their feathers, relocating a chest of clothes from one attic to a neighbor's, demolishing a house but leaving its piano without a scratch. But the real damage—not to mention the cause of the deafening roar—was more tragic. The force of the storm lifted the passenger cars of the Great Northern Oriental Limited and the rails underneath—the very train Elsie Rathbun was awaiting—and would have thrown them into the river, were it not for the fact that it also wrapped the baggage car around the rails, saving the train's passengers from death by drowning.

Not everyone was so lucky. John Kreidler's four children were blown from their cottage into nearby Lake Alice, where all four drowned. More than fifty people were found dead in the days that followed, thirty-five in the Grand Hotel, which was leveled by the storm. For two days rescue workers picked through the rubble of the hotel, most of which had been julienned into strips of debris the size of yardsticks. There were a few survival stories: the night clerk of the hotel was pulled alive from the wreckage with two broken legs; little Agnes Palmer was sucked from her father's lap and set down two yards away, just before the house collapsed, killing the rest of her family.

More than 150 people were taken to a makeshift hospital established at the town's insane asylum. The entire business district had been leveled—the nexus of some forty-four blocks destroyed by the storm. One hundred eighteen houses were totally demolished by the storm; another 110 were damaged beyond repair. Washed-out bridges and downed telephone lines cut off most contact to the rest of the world.

The next day, Fergus Falls began to bury its dead, beginning with four-year-old Sissenine June Slettede, who was crushed when her family home collapsed. Governor J. A. A. Burnquist declared martial law and dispatched Adjutant General Rhinow to oversee relief efforts. Chief among Rhinow's concerns was finding food for the town's seven thousand residents, who were already complaining of hunger. The irony of his solution would hardly have been lost on the Grand Hotel's one-time bartender: to feed Fergus Falls, Adjutant General Rhinow requisitioned a freight train filled with potatoes.[2]

NOTES

❧

1. The Gathering Storm

1. Christine Kinealy, *A Death-Dealing Famine: The Great Hunger in Ireland* (London: Pluto Press, 1997).
2. Neil E. Stevens, "Phytopathology: The Dark Ages in Plant Pathology in America, 1830–1870," *Journal of the Washington Academy of Sciences* 23 (Sept. 15, 1933): 435–48.
3. L. Rawtorne, *The Cause of the Potato disease ascertained by proofs; and the prevention proved by practice* (London: British Library, Historical Print Editions, 1847), 4.
4. Asenath Nicholson, *Annals of the Famine in Ireland*, edited by Maureen Murphy (Dublin: Lilliput Press, 1998).
5. IFC 1072: 1–64; Cathal Póirtéir, *Famine Echoes* (Dublin: Gill & Macmillan, 1995).
6. Shelley Barber, ed., *The Prendergast Letters* (Amherst: University of Massachusetts Press, 2006), 98.
7. Thomas Campbell Foster, *Letters on the Condition of the People of Ireland* (London: Chapman and Hall, 1846).

2. A Great Hunger

1. Evan D. G. Fraser, "Food System Vulnerability," *Ecological Complexity* 3 (2006): 328–35.
2. *London Times*, Nov. 3, 1845.
3. Robert James Scully, *End of Hidden Ireland* (New York: Oxford University Press, 1996).

3. Ships, Colonies, and Commerce

1. Henry George Grey, *The Colonial Policy of Lord John Russell's Administration* (London: R. Bentley, 1853).
2. *Hansard Parliamentary Debates* 84 (3d series) (1846), 1343–419.
3. Kinealy, *A Death-Dealing Famine*, 77.
4. Colm Tóibín and Diarmaid Ferriter, *The Irish Famine: A Documentary* (New York: Thomas Dunne Books, 2001).
5. Charles Trevelyan, *The Irish Crisis* (London: Longman, Brown, Green, and Longmans, 1848), 85.

6. John O'Rourke, *The History of the Great Irish Famine of 1847* (Dublin: James Duffy, 1902).
7. *Hansard*, 84, 1343–419.
8. *London Times*, Dec. 19, 1845.
9. Gerald Moran, *Sending Out Ireland's Poor* (Portland, OR: Four Courts Press, 2004).
10. *Information Published by His Majesty's Chief Agent and for the Superintendence of Settlers and Emigrants in Upper and Lower Canada: For the Use of Emigrants* (Quebec City: Thomas Cary, 1832).

4. Dominion

1. Eileen Reid Marcil, *The Charley-Man: A History of Wooden Shipbuilding at Quebec 1763–1893* (Quebec City: Quarry Press, 1995), 44.
2. *Kerry Evening Post*, Aug. 10, 1850.
3. Marianna O'Gallagher, *Grosse Île: Gateway to Canada* (Ste-Foy, Québec: Carraig Books, 1984).

5. Phoenix Rising

1. *Le Fantasque* (Quebec City), Dec. 10, 1840.
2. Reid Marcil, *The Charley-Man*, 66.

6. Ship's Fever

1. *Quebec Mercury*, Apr. 20, 1847.
2. André Charbonneau and André Sévigny, *1847: Grosse Île: A Record of Daily Events* (Ottawa: Parks Canada, 1997).
3. "Lecture of Public Health, Addressed to the Students of the Theological Department of the Kings College," *Medical Times*, Sept. 6, 1851, 243.
4. Anne Hardy, *The Epidemic Streets: Infectious Disease and the Rise of Preventive Medicine* (Oxford: Clarendon Press, 1993), 191.
5. W. O. Henderson, *Industrial Revolution on the Continent: Germany, France, and Russia 1800–1914* (London: F. Cass, 1961), 24.
6. Robert J. Carlisle, ed., *An Account of Bellevue Hospital with a Catalogue of the Medical and Surgical Staff from 1736 to 1894* (New York: Society for the Alumni of Bellevue Hospital, 1893).
7. E. Harold Hindman, "History of Typhus Fever in Louisiana," *American Journal of Public Health* 26 (Nov. 1936): 1117–24.
8. Charles Lee, ed., *The New York Journal of Medicine*, vol. 9 (New York: J. & H. G. Langley, 1847).
9. *Southern Patriot* (Charleston, South Carolina), June 11, 1847.
10. *Public Ledger* (Philadelphia), June 2, 1847.
11. Homer Folks, *The Care of Destitute, Neglected, and Delinquent Children* (New York: Macmillan, 1902).
12. *Daily National Intelligencer* (Washington, D.C.), May 31, 1847, 13. *Trenton (New Jersey) State Gazette*, June 14, 1847.

7. Discord on Downing Street

1. Dispatch from Earl Grey to the Earl of Elgin, Dec. 31, 1846, in *Emigration: Papers Relative to Emigration to the British Provinces in North America, presented to the Houses of Parliament, by Command of Her Majesty, February, 1847* (London: Printed by W. Clowes for HMSO, 1847).
2. *Hansard Parliamentary Debates* 89 (3d series) (1847), 355–423.
3. James S. Donnelly Jr., *The Great Irish Potato Famine* (Phoenix Mill, UK: Sutton Publishing, 2002), 57.
4. Barber, *The Prendergast Letters*.
5. Twisleton to Trevelyan, Feb. 27, 1848, Treasury Papers, T.64 369 B/1, UK National Archives, Kew, England.
6. *Hansard* 90, 3–19.
7. Quoted in J. A. Jordan, *The Grosse Île Tragedy and the Monument to Irish Fever Victims* (Quebec City: Telegraph Printing Co., 1909).

8. Visitations from a Vengeful God

1. O'Gallagher, *Gateway to Canada*, 52.
2. John Francis Maguire, *The Irish in America* (New York: D. & G. Sadlier, 1868).
3. Bill Trent, "Grosse Île: Island of the Dead," *Canadian Medical Association Journal* 131 (Oct. 15, 1984), 960–68.
4. Charbonneau and Sévigny, *1847: Grosse Île.*
5. Robert Whyte and James J. Mangan, *Robert Whyte's 1847 famine ship diary: The journey of an Irish coffin ship* (Cork, Ireland: Mercier Press, 1994), 29.
6. Ibid., 35.
7. Charbonneau and Sévigny, *1847: Grosse Île*, 87.
8. J. M. O'Leary quoted in Jordan, *The Grosse Île Tragedy*, 41.
9. Father Taschereau, May 1847 letter to the bishop, quoted in Marianna O'Gallagher, "Children of the Famine," *Beaver* 88.1 (2008): 50.
10. O'Gallagher, *Gateway to Canada*, 147.
11. Ibid., 150.
12. Anonymous eyewitness account published in *Journal de Quebec*, June 17, 1847, and reprinted in Charbonneau and Sévigny, *1847: Grosse Île.*
13. Charbonneau and Sévigny, *1847: Grosse Île*, 90.
14. Gary Thomson, "Island of Sorrows," *Beaver* 71.1 (1991): 35.
15. Charbonneau and Sévigny, *1847: Grosse Île*, 23.
16. O'Gallagher, *Gateway to Canada*, 51.

9. A Course for Disaster

1. *Quebec Mercury*, May 15, June 5, 1847.
2. Report from P. O'Neil, passenger aboard the *Birman*, reprinted in Charbonneau and Sévigny, *1847: Grosse Île.*
3. Edward Laxton, *The Famine Ships: The Irish Exodus to America* (New York: Henry Holt, 1997), 125.
4. Ibid.

5. Herman Melville, *Redburn* (New York: Harper & Brothers, 1849).
6. Nathaniel Hawthorne, *The English Notebooks* (New York: Russell & Russell, 1962), entries dated Aug. 20, 25, 1853.
7. Eileen Reid Marcil, "John Munn," *Dictionary of Canadian Biography*, http://www.biographi.ca/009004-119.01-e.php?BioId=39301 (accessed July 27, 2010).
8. *London Times*, Sept. 17, 1847.
9. *Mersey Reporter*, http://www.merseyreporter.com/history/historic/irish-immigration.shtml (accessed March 12, 2011).
10. *Hansard Parliamentary Debates* 94 (12 July 1847), 180–82.
11. *Illustrated London News*, June 12, 1847.
12. Letter from Grey to Dr. Andrew Combe, printed in *London Times*, Sept. 10, 1847.
13. Jordan, *The Grosse Île Tragedy*, 53.

10. Pestilence and Plague

1. *Kerry Evening Post*, July 21, 1847.
2. *Tralee Chronicle*, Mar. 27, 1847.
3. Quoted in Tóibín and Ferriter, *The Irish Famine*, 40.
4. Tyler Anbinder, "From Famine to Five Points: Lord Lansdowne's Irish Tenants Encounter North America's Most Notorious Slum," *American Historical Review* 107.2 (2002): 351–87.
5. *Tralee Chronicle*, Mar. 27, 1847.
6. *Kerry Evening Post*, Jan. 16, Nov. 6, 1847.

11. An Audacious Plan

1. *Tralee Chronicle*, Feb. 6, 1847.
2. Cormac O'Gráda, *Black '47 and Beyond: The Great Irish Famine in History, Economy, and Memory* (Princeton, NJ: Princeton University Press, 1999), 146.
3. *Tralee Chronicle*, Dec. 19, 1846.
4. *Tralee Chronicle*, Feb. 23, 1848.
5. *Kerry Evening Post*, Oct. 24, 1847.

12. Signing On

1. Charbonneau and Sévigny, *1847: Grosse Île*, 21.
2. *The Jeanie Johnston Project*, a decade-long initiative to re-create this historic ship, was begun in 1994 and employed historians, naval architects, and shipbuilders from around the world. The new vessel undertook a historic transatlantic voyage in 2002 and is, at the time of this writing, a floating museum in Dublin.
3. Les Archives Judiciaries, Fond 1845, Bibliothèque et Archives Nationales Quebec.
4. Richard Henry Dana Jr., *Two Years before the Mast* (New York: Signet Classics, 2009).

13. The People's Physician

1. "Riots in London," *Kerry Evening Post*, Mar. 10, 1848.
2. *Kerry Evening Post*, Apr. 18, 1848.
3. *Kerry Evening Post*, Mar. 25, 1848.
4. *Kerry Examiner*, Mar. 25, 1848.
5. Originally printed in *Liverpool Mercury*, Aug. 28, 1847.
6. Andrew Combe, letter, Sept. 10, 1847, reprinted in *London Times*, Aug. 9, 1847.
7. Ibid.
8. *Kerry Evening Post*, Feb. 20, 1861.
9. *The Jeanie Johnston Project: A Dream Rebuilt* (Tralee, Ireland: Jeanie Johnston Project, 1999).
10. *Medical Times: A Journal of English and Foreign Medicine* 2 (1840).
11. William Cullen, *First Lines of the Practice of Physic* (Edinburgh: Reid & Scott, 1802); Robert Thomas, *The Modern Practice of Physic* (London: John Murray, 1809).
12. O'Gráda, *Black '47*, 95.
13. *Kerry Evening Post*, Nov. 27, 1848.

14. Fare Thee Well

1. *Kerry Evening Post*, Mar. 28, 1848.
2. *Kerry Examiner*, Apr. 26, 1848.
3. *New York Star*, quoted in *Quebec Mercury*, May 1, 1848.
4. Laxton, *Famine Ships*, 239.
5. Dorothy Denneen Volo and James M. Volo, *Daily Life in the Age of Sail* (Westport, CT: Greenwood Press, 2002), 95.
6. *Tralee Chronicle*, Apr. 29, 1848.

15. At Sea

1. Alan Villiers, *The War with Cape Horn* (New York: Scribner, 1971).
2. Bryan Barrass and D. R. Derrett, *Ship Stability for Masters and Mates* (Burlington, MA: Elsevier, 2006).
3. Personal interview, Dec. 12, 2010.
4. Laxton, *Famine Ships*, 13.
5. Laxton, *Famine Ships*, 26.
6. Volo and Volo, *Daily Life in the Age of Sail*, 95.
7. M. F. Maury, *Explanations and Sailing Directions to Accompany the Wind and Current Charts*, 3rd ed. (Washington, D.C.: C. Alexander, Printer, 1851).
8. Ibid., 304.
9. Alan Villiers, *Cruise of the Conrad* (New York: Scribner, 1937), 268.
10. Volo and Volo, *Daily Life in the Age of Sail*, 95.
11. The Jeanie Johnston Company, *The Jeanie Johnston: The Story of a Proud Irish Emigrant Ship*, pamphlet (Tralee, 2002).
12. Volo and Volo, *Daily Life in the Age of Sail*, 99.
13. Ibid., 94.
14. Dana, *Two Years before the Mast*, 11.

16. Dead Reckoning

1. *Lloyd's List and Shipping Gazette*, May 9, 1848.
2. This re-creation of the crew's experience is based on conversations with Nicole Gardiner and other crew aboard the re-created *Jeanie Johnston*, July 2009.
3. *Lloyd's List and Shipping Gazette*, May 11, 1848.
4. *Kerry Evening Post*, June 7, 1848.
5. "Extract of the First Letter from Capt. John Richards, of the Bark Astoria, and Not Yet Published," *Quebec Mercury*, June 3, 1848.
6. *Lloyd's List and Shipping Gazette*, May 25, 1848.
7. Ibid.

17. Quarantine

1. Jordan, *The Grosse Île Tragedy*.
2. *Report from British North America, Letter from LNC Murdoch dated 3 June 1848*, National Archives (Britain), CO 386/83.
3. Ibid.
4. Quoted in Maguire, *The Irish in America*.
5. *Quebec Mercury*, June 9, 1848.

18. Passing Customs

1. *Quebec Mercury*, June 9, 1848.
2. Thomson, "Island of the Sorrows," 35.
3. Merna M. Foster, "Quarantine at Grosse Île," *Canadian Family Physician* 41 (May 1995): 841–48.

19. Adrift

1. Bibliothèque et Archives Nationales Quebec, Fond 23081845.
2. Bibliothèque et Archives Nationales Quebec, Fonds TL31, S1, SS1, 1960–01–357/147.
3. *American Review* 1 (1845): 61.
4. Henry Grey, *The Colonial Policy of Lord John Russell's Administration* (London: R. Bentley, 1853), 31.
5. J. Matthew Gallman, *Receiving Erin's Children* (Chapel Hill: University of North Carolina Press, 2000), 29.
6. Letter, Grey to Smith, Dec. 10, 1851, Papers of Henry George, 3rd Earl Grey, Durham University Library, Archives and Special Collections, GB-0033-GRE-B.
7. J. Holland Rose et al., *Cambridge History of the British Empire* (Cambridge, England: University Press, 1929),372.
8. *Hansard Parliamentary Debates* 114 (3d series) (1851), 1312.
9. *Hansard* 119 (1852), 475–76.
10. *Hansard* 114 (1851), 1163–66.
11. Jonathan Pim to Trevelyan, June 5, 1849, *Transactions of the Society of Friends* (Dublin), 1852, 452–54.

12. *Introduction to Irish Encumbered Estate Papers,* Public Record Office of Northern Ireland, Belfast, 2007.
13. Trevelyan to Twisleton, quoted in Kinealy, *A Death-Dealing Famine,* 148.
14. Ibid., 136.
15. Peter Gray, *Famine, Land, and Politics* (Portland, OR: Irish Academic Press, 1999), 232.
16. Trevelyan to Clarendon, July 15, 1849, Trevelyan Letterbooks, Bodleian Library, Oxford, microfilm.
17. Robin Haines, *Charles Trevelyan and the Great Irish Famine* (Dublin: Four Courts Press, 2004), 519.
18. Clarendon to Russell, Mar. 10, 12, 1849, Domestic Records of the Public Record Office, Volume 30, Letterbox 4, UK National Archives, Kew, England.
19. "Evidence of Edward Twisleton," *Select Committee on the Irish Poor Law,* 1849 (London: J. Ollivier, 1849), 699–714.
20. Ibid.
21. *Fourth Report from the Select Committee on Poor Laws* (Ireland), p. 1849 (148), XV, 329–33 (Cambridge, England: National Government Reports [House of Commons], 1849).
22. John Ball, *What Is to Be Done for Ireland?* (London: J. Ridgway, 1849).
23. Trevelyan to Wood, Sept. 16, Oct. 20, 1849, Hickleton Papers, A4/59/2, York University, Borthwick Institute for Archives, York, England.

20. Clearances

1. Christine Kinealy, *This Great Calamity* (Dublin: Gill & Macmillan, 1995), 232.
2. Ibid.
3. Anbinder, "From Famine to Five Points," 351–87.
4. Kinealy, *This Great Calamity,* 136.
5. *Tralee Chronicle,* Jan. 27, 1849.
6. Dr. Crumpe, "Report upon the Recent Epidemic Fever in Ireland," *Dublin Quarterly Journal of Medical Science* 7 (1849): 86–87.
7. *Kerry Evening Post,* Dec. 9, 1848.
8. *Kerry Evening Post,* Aug. 16, 1848.
9. "Total Loss of the 'Maria' Passenger Ship from Limerick to Quebec," *Kerry Evening Post,* June 16, 1849.
10. Liam Kelly et al., *Blennerville: Gateway to Tralee's Past* (Dublin: Foras Aiseanna Saothair, 1989), 134.
11. *Kerry Evening Post,* Mar. 17, 1852.
12. John F. Stover, *History of the Baltimore and Ohio Railroad* (West Lafayette, IN: Purdue Research Foundation, 1987), 4.
13. *Baltimore Sun,* Mar. 31, 1849.
14. *New York Herald,* Jan. 11, 1849.

21. Crossing the Bar

1. The account of this storm comes from the unpublished immigration diary of Michael Friedrich Radke, 1848, http://www.ingenweb.org/infranklin/pages/

tier2/radke1848.html (accessed Oct. 23, 2011). Radke's vessel, the *Johanis,* left Germany on March 5, 1848, putting them on an almost identical track and schedule as the *Jeanie Johnston.*

2. Eugene Fauntleroy Cordell, *The Medical Annals of Maryland 1799–1899* (Baltimore: Williams & Wilkins, 1903).

3. "Notice—The Attention of Pilots, Masters of Vessels," *Baltimore Sun,* May 1, 1849.

4. O'Gráda, *Black '47,* 51.

5. *Kerry Evening Post,* May 26, 1849.

6. Volo and Volo, *Daily Life in the Age of Sail,* 118.

22. No Irish Need Apply

1. *Kerry Evening Post,* May 26, 1849.

2. Kevin Kenny, *The American Irish* (New York: Pearson, 2000), 61.

3. *Baltimore Sun,* May 7, 1849.

4. Dale T. Knobel, *Paddy and the Republic: Ethnicity and Nationality in Antebellum America* (Middletown, CT: Wesleyan University Press, 1988), 98.

5. Ibid., 14.

6. John Sanderson, *Republican Landmarks: The Views and Opinions of American Statesmen on Foreign Immigration* (Philadelphia: J. B. Lippincott, 1856).

7. James Redfield, *Outline of a New Physiognomy* (Boston: Redding, 1849).

8. Frederick Law Olmsted, *A Journey in the Seaboard Slave States in the Years 1853–1854, with Remarks on Their Economy* (New York: G. P. Putnam's Sons, 1904), 550–51.

23. Royal Visit

1. Queen Victoria to Lord John Russell, July 19, 1849, in *The Letters of Queen Victoria* (New York: Longmans, Green, 1907).

2. Queen Victoria and Arthur Helps, *Leaves from the Journal of Our Life in the Highlands* (New York: BiblioBazaar, 2010).

3. Richard J. Kelly, "Queen Victoria and the Post-Famine Irish Context: A Royal Visit," http://www.vssj.jp/journal/7/kelly.pdf, accessed Apr. 13, 2012.

4. *Kerry Evening Post,* Oct. 24, 1849.

5. Kelly et al., *Blennerville.*

6. *Kerry Evening Post,* Sept. 7, 1850.

7. These figures are derived using the model proposed by Tyler Anbinder, who writes, "My calculation of the current value of Holland's savings is based on the multiplier suggested by the U.S. Department of Labor's *Handbook of Labor Statistics* . . . which suggests a multiplier of 21.34 to convert 1850 dollars into 2001 dollars. According to the Department of Labor's statistics, a dollar in 1860 was worth about the same amount in real terms as a dollar in 1850, due to the deflationary effects of the panics of 1854 and 1857. The department's figures are borne out by John J. McCusker, 'How Much Is That in Real Money?,' *Proceedings of the American Antiquarian Society* 101 (1991): 327–32, which suggests a multiplier of 16 to convert dollar amounts from the 1850s into 1991 dollars.

Adjusting McCusker's figure to take into account inflation since 1991 ... brings virtually the identical result. All subsequent estimates of the current value of nineteenth-century monetary figures are based on the Department of Labor's conversion program. It is, I admit, *very* difficult to know whether or not to trust these conversion systems. They do not produce consistently satisfactory results. Nonetheless, I feel it is important to offer estimates, because without them, the monetary figures from the nineteenth century are meaningless to most modern readers. These estimates of the modern value of the Emigrant Savings Bank account balances are different from (and should be used in place of) those appearing in my book *Five Points* (New York, 2001). At the time *Five Points* went to press, I did not fully appreciate the impact of 1990s inflation on the Emigrant Savings Bank account information."

24. Steaming Ahead

1. Kevin L. Cook, "Rolling West on Emigrant Trains," *Wild West* 13:2 (2000): 30.

Fergus Falls, Minnesota, August 26, 1885

1. Interview with Paul Roberts and Florence Keating, Aug. 12, 2011.

26. The Rising Tide

1. Mr. Grattan, *Hansard Parliamentary Debates* 119 (Feb. 3, 1852), 61–158.
2. Mr. Whiteside in ibid.
3. Ibid.
4. *Kerry Evening Post*, Aug. 11, 1849.
5. L. A. Clarkson and E. Margaret Crawford, *Feast and Famine: A History of Food and Nutrition in Ireland 1500–1920* (New York: Oxford University Press, 2001), 151.
6. Daniel Donovan, "Observations on the Peculiar Diseases to Which the Famine of Last Year Gave Origin," *Dublin Medical Press* 19 (1848): 67.
7. *Kerry Evening Post*, May 17, 1851.
8. *Tralee Chronicle*, May 1, 1852.
9. *Quebec Mercury*, Sept. 30, 1852.
10. "Frightful Suicide of an Emigrant Surgeon," *Tralee Chronicle*, July 16, 1852.
11. *Tralee Chronicle*, July 23, 1852.

27. Departures

1. Richard J. Kelly, "Queen Victoria and the Irish Industrial Exhibition of 1853," http://www.vssj.jp/journal/8/kelly.pdf, accessed Apr. 13, 2012.
2. Queen Victoria's Journal, Sept. 1, 1853, Royal Archives (Britain), http://www.queenvictoriasjournals.org/home.do.

28. Storm Season

1. "Report of the Emigration Agent in St. Andrew's, New Brunswick, 1853," Provincial Archives of New Brunswick, RS23.
2. Ibid.

Minneapolis, Minnesota, December 1886

1. Proceedings of the City Council of the City of Minneapolis, vol. 4, p. 94, Minneapolis City Archives.
2. *St. Paul Daily Globe*, Dec. 28, 1885.

29. That Deadly Angel

1. "Cholera in London," *Kerry Evening Post*, Sept. 13, 1854.
2. *Tralee Chronicle*, Sept. 22, 1854.
3. *Tralee Chronicle*, May 12, 1854.
4. *Tralee Chronicle*, Oct. 14, 1853.
5. *Cork Examiner*, reprinted in *Kerry Post*, Nov. 11, 1853.
6. *Kerry Evening Post*, July 12, 1854.
7. *Tralee Chronicle*, Nov. 17, 1854.
8. *The Nation*, Sept. 30, 1854.
9. *Tralee Chronicle*, Nov. 17, 1854.

30. Down with the Ship

1. Frank Galgay, *Rocks Ahead: Wrecks, Rescues, and a Coffin Ship* (St. John's, Newfoundland: Flanker Press, 2010).
2. Ibid.
3. Katherine Donovan, Last Will and Testament, Public Records Office of Ireland (Dublin).

31. The Final Test

1. Villiers, *Cruise of the Conrad*, 345.
2. "Captains Account," *New York Herald*, Dec. 1, 1858.

Epilogue

1. "International Relations," *The New Encyclopaedia Britannica* (Chicago: Encyclopaedia Britannica, 2002).
2. *Daily Northwestern* (Oshkosh, Wisconsin), June 24, 1919; *Evening State Journal* and *Lincoln Daily News* (Lincoln, Nebraska), June 23, 1919; *Eau Claire (Wisconsin) Leader*, June 25, 1919; "Tornado at Fergus Falls, Minn., June 22, 1919," *Monthly Weather Review* 47:6 (1919).

ACKNOWLEDGMENTS

THIS BOOK WAS WRITTEN on the shoulders of giants. Two of the tallest are Eileen Reid Marcil and Helen O'Carroll: it is because of their painstaking research that I have a story to tell. Eileen provided invaluable insights into the world of North American shipbuilding and maritime culture during the nineteenth century which she shared generously (along with bowls of beef stew and sterling conversation). Helen served as the official historian for the Jeanie Johnston Project, and no one knows more about the original owner and crew than she. Her investment in the vessel and the people associated with it is astounding, as is her selflessness in sharing that expertise with others. Thank you also to Dorothy Titera and Christine McKay, who provided essential genealogical information concerning the Reilly family. Fred Walker, the naval architect for the re-creation of the *Jeanie Johnston*, graciously advised on technical aspects concerning the vessel; Todd French and Dennis Gallant, two first-rate Maine boatbuilders, answered innumerable questions concerning hull shapes, rigging, and boat speeds. Melanie Dobbs contributed hugely to my understanding of 1850s Indiana, and Andy Bielenberg was instrumental in my education concerning Irish famine economics; his publications on the subject are the finest I have read, and he always made sure I was well fed while in Cork. Thanks also to Paul Roberts and Florence Keating, who very graciously shared stories about their remarkable family.

When it comes to Herculean efforts, no one deserves more credit than the world's librarians and archivists, who toil too often without recognition and without whom books would not exist. Be sure to hug one of these amazing people the next time you have the opportunity—particularly if you are so fortunate as to cross paths with the magicians at the Otter Tail County Historical Society, Unity College's Quimby Library, the Belfast (Maine) Free Library, the National Library of Ireland, the Tralee branch of the Kerry Library, and the talented staffs at the national archives of the United Kingdom, Canada, and the United States.

A very special note of appreciation to the brilliant minds and eyes that helped to craft these pages, including Murray Carpenter and Andrew Lawler, two writers whose work I admire and whose friendship I cherish. Chip Blake, editor-in-chief at *Orion*, was with me when this book was born and has remained an invaluable advisor and friend. Hannah Kreitzer, my indomitable research assistant, always found the answer to even my most esoteric questions concerning mustache styles and the weather forecast for *fin de siècle* Minneapolis. Thank you also to Wendy Strothman and Lauren MacLeod of the Strothman Agency—by far the best in the business—along with Hilary Redmon, Leah Miller, Edith Lewis, and Judith Hoover, my editors at Free Press, who took an idea and turned it into a narrative. It's a real honor to work with you all.

Finally, thank you to all of my friends and family who supported me in so many ways during this wonderful journey, particularly Colin Gowland, who did more to shuttle along this manuscript than he will ever know.

INDEX

About the Author

Kathryn Miles is professor of environmental writing at Unity College and editor-in-chief of *Hawk & Handsaw: The Journal of Creative Sustainability*. Her work has appeared in dozens of publications, including *Alimentum, Best American Essays, Ecotone, Meatpaper,* and *Terrain*. She lives in Belfast, Maine.